Hands-On Image Generation with TensorFlow

A practical guide to generating images and videos using deep learning

Soon Yau Cheong

BIRMINGHAM—MUMBAI

Hands-On Image Generation with TensorFlow

Group Product Manager: Kunal Parikh
Publishing Product Manager: Devika Battike
Senior Editor: Roshan Kumar
Content Development Editor: Tazeen Shaikh
Technical Editor: Manikandan Kurup
Copy Editor: Safis Editing
Project Coordinator: Aishwarya Mohan
Proofreader: Safis Editing
Indexer: Rekha Nair
Production Designer: Joshua Misquitta

First published: December 2020
Production reference: 1231220

Published by Packt Publishing Ltd.
Livery Place
35 Livery Street
Birmingham
B3 2PB, UK.

ISBN 978-1-83882-678-9

`www.packt.com`

To my beautiful wife, Siew Tok, for her unconditional love and devotion to our family.

To my sons, Zenpo and Zenson. They are the reason why I wrote this book: to share and pass on knowledge for the benefit of mankind.

– Husband and daddy, Soon Yau Cheong

Packt.com

Subscribe to our online digital library for full access to over 7,000 books and videos, as well as industry leading tools to help you plan your personal development and advance your career. For more information, please visit our website.

Why subscribe?

- Spend less time learning and more time coding with practical eBooks and Videos from over 4,000 industry professionals

- Improve your learning with Skill Plans built especially for you

- Get a free eBook or video every month

- Fully searchable for easy access to vital information

- Copy and paste, print, and bookmark content

Did you know that Packt offers eBook versions of every book published, with PDF and ePub files available? You can upgrade to the eBook version at packt.com and as a print book customer, you are entitled to a discount on the eBook copy. Get in touch with us at customercare@packtpub.com for more details.

At www.packt.com, you can also read a collection of free technical articles, sign up for a range of free newsletters, and receive exclusive discounts and offers on Packt books and eBooks.

Contributors

About the author

Soon Yau Cheong is an AI consultant and the founder of Sooner.ai Ltd. With a history of being associated with industry giants such as NVIDIA and Qualcomm, he provides consultation in the various domains of AI, such as deep learning, computer vision, natural language processing, and big data analytics. He was awarded a full scholarship to study for his PhD at the University of Bristol while working as a teaching assistant. He is also a mentor for AI courses with Udacity.

I would like to thank Marco Marchesi for not only reviewing this book but also helping me to kickstart my consulting business. Writing a book is hard: I would like to thank my editors, including Tazeen Shaikh and Roshan Kumar, for making the book more readable. Although I do not know Jun-Yan Zhu personally, I would like to thank him for his pioneering work in GANs for image generation; we owe many of the models in this book to him.

About the reviewers

Matthew Rever received his PhD. in electrical engineering from the University of Michigan, Ann Arbor. His career revolves around image processing, computer vision, and machine learning for scientific research applications. He started programming in C++, a language he still uses today, over 20 years ago, and has also used Matlab and most heavily Python in the past few years, using OpenCV, SciPy, scikit-learn, TensorFlow, and PyTorch. He believes it is important to stay up to date on the latest tools to be as productive as possible. Dr. Rever is the author of Packt's *Computer Vision Projects with Python 3* and *Advanced Computer Vision Projects*.

Marco Marchesi is a researcher, engineer, and media creator with 20 years of experience across machine learning, computer vision, human computer interfaces, and mixed reality. With a PhD from the University of Bologna and a period spent at Apple in California working with the Siri team, he joined Happy Finish in 2016, where is currently Chief Technology Officer. The work done for the "Perfect Mum" campaign in 2017 led to the first megapixel GAN image ever generated and introduced the "truncation trick," a hyperparameter that since then has been used in all major photorealistic GAN approaches. Recently Marco and his team ran the first live performance in augmented reality over 5G network.

Packt is searching for authors like you

If you're interested in becoming an author for Packt, please visit `authors.packtpub.com` and apply today. We have worked with thousands of developers and tech professionals, just like you, to help them share their insight with the global tech community. You can make a general application, apply for a specific hot topic that we are recruiting an author for, or submit your own idea.

Table of Contents

3
Generative Adversarial Network

Section 2: Applications of Deep Generative Models

4
Image-to-Image Translation

8

Self-Attention for Image Generation

9

Video Synthesis

10

Road Ahead

Preface

Any sufficiently advanced technology is indistinguishable from magic.

– Arthur C. Clarke

This phrase best describes image generation using **artificial intelligence** (**AI**). The field of deep learning—a subset of artificial intelligence—has been developing rapidly in the last decade. Now we can generate artificial but faces that are indistinguishable from real people's faces, and to generate realistic paintings from simple brush strokes. Most of these abilities are owed to a type of deep neural network known as a **generative adversarial network** (**GAN**). With this hands-on book, you'll not only develop image generation skills but also gain a solid understanding of the underlying principles.

The book starts with an introduction to the fundamentals of image generation using TensorFlow covering variational autoencoders and GANs. As you progress through the chapters, you'll learn to build models for different applications for performing face swaps using deep fakes, neural style transfer, image-to-image translation, turning simple images into photorealistic images, and much more. You'll also understand how and why to construct state-of-the-art deep neural networks using advanced techniques such as spectral normalization and self-attention layer before working with advanced models for face generation and editing. You'll also be introduced to photo restoration, text-to-image synthesis, video retargeting, and neural rendering. Throughout the book, you'll learn to implement models from scratch in TensorFlow 2.x, including PixelCNN, VAE, DCGAN, WGAN, pix2pix, CycleGAN, StyleGAN, GauGAN, and BigGAN.

By the end of this book, you'll be well-versed in TensorFlow and image generative technologies.

Who this book is for

This book is for deep learning engineers, practitioners, and researchers who have basic knowledge of convolutional neural networks and want to use it to learn various image generation techniques using TensorFlow 2.x. You'll also find this book useful if you are an image processing professional or computer vision engineer looking to explore state-of-the-art architectures to improve and enhance images and videos. Knowledge of Python and TensorFlow is required to get the best out of the book.

How to use this book

There are many online tutorials available teaching the basics of GANs. However, the models tend to be rather simple and suitable only for toy datasets. At the other end of the spectrum, there are also free codes available for state-of-the-art models to generate realistic images. Nevertheless, the code tends to be complex, and the lack of explanation makes it difficult for beginners to understand. Many of the "Git cloners" who downloaded the codes had no clue how to tweak the models to make them work for their applications. This book aims to bridge that gap.

We will start with learning the basic principles and immediately implement the code to put them to the test. You'll be able to see the result of your work instantly. All the necessary code to build a model is laid bare in a single Jupyter notebook. This is to make it easier for you to go through the flow of the code and to modify and test the code in an interactive manner. I believe writing from scratch is the best way to learn and master deep learning. There are between one to three models in each chapter, and we will write all of them from scratch. When you finish this book, not only will you be familiar with image generation but you will also be an expert in TensorFlow 2.

The chapters are arranged in roughly chronological order of the history of GANs, where the chapters may build upon knowledge from previous chapters. Therefore, it is best to read the chapters in order, especially the first three chapters, which cover the fundamentals. After that, you may jump to chapters that interest you more. Should you feel confused by the acronyms during the reading, you can refer to the summary of GAN techniques listed in the last chapter.

What this book covers

Chapter 1, Getting Started with Image Generation Using TensorFlow, walks through the basics of pixel probability and uses it to build our first model to generate handwritten digits.

Chapter 2, Variational Autoencoder, explains how to build a **variational autoencoder** (**VAE**) and use it to generate and edit faces.

Chapter 3, Generative Adversarial Network, introduces the fundamentals of GANs and builds a DCGAN to generate photorealistic images. We'll then learn about new adversarial loss to stabilize the training.

Chapter 4, Image-to-Image Translation, covers a lot of models and interesting applications. We will first implement pix2pix to convert sketches to photorealistic photos. Then we'll use CycleGAN to transform a horse to a zebra. Lastly, we will use BicycleGAN to generate a variety of shoes.

Chapter 5, Style Transfer, explains how to extract the style from a painting and transfer it into a photo. We'll also learn advanced techniques to make neural style transfer run faster in runtime, and to use it in state-of-the-art GANs.

Chapter 6, AI Painter, goes through the underlying principles of image editing and transformation using **interactive GAN (iGAN)** as an example. Then we will build a GauGAN to create photorealistic building facades from a simple segmentation map.

Chapter 7, High Fidelity Face Generation, shows how to build a StyleGAN using techniques from style transfer. However, before that, we will learn to grow the network layer progressively using a Progressive GAN.

Chapter 8, Self-Attention for Image Generation, shows how to build self-attention into a **Self-Attention GAN (SAGAN)** and a BigGAN for conditional image generation.

Chapter 9, Video Synthesis, demonstrates how to use autoencoders to create a deepfake video. Along the way, we'll learn how to use OpenCV and dlib for face processing.

Chapter 10, Road Ahead, reviews and summarizes the generative techniques we have learned. Then we will look at how they are used as the basis of up-and-coming applications, including text-to-image-synthesis, video compression, and video retargeting.

To get the most out of this book

Readers should have basic knowledge of deep learning training pipelines, such as training convolutional neural networks for image classification. This book will mainly use high-level Keras APIs in TensorFlow 2, which is easy to learn. Should you need to refresh or learn TensorFlow 2, there are many free tutorials available online, such as the one on the official TensorFlow website, `https://www.tensorflow.org/tutorials/keras/classification`.

Software/Hardware covered in the book	OS Requirements
TensorFlow 2.2	Windows, Mac OS X, and Linux (Any)
GPU with minimum 4 GB memory	

Training deep neural networks is computationally intensive. You can train the first few simple models using the CPU only. However, as we progress to more complex models and datasets in later chapters, the model training could take a few days before you start to see satisfactory results. To get the most out of this book, you should have access to the GPU to accelerate the model training time. There are also free cloud services, such as Google's Colab, that provide GPUs on which you can upload and run the code.

If you are using the digital version of this book, we advise you to type the code yourself or access the code via the GitHub repository (link available in the next section). Doing so will help you avoid any potential errors related to the copying and pasting of code.

Download the example code files

You can download the example code files for this book from GitHub at `https://github.com/PacktPublishing/Hands-On-Image-Generation-with-TensorFlow-2.0`. In case there's an update to the code, it will be updated on the existing GitHub repository.

We also have other code bundles from our rich catalog of books and videos available at `https://github.com/PacktPublishing/`. Check them out!

Download the color images

We also provide a PDF file that has color images of the screenshots/diagrams used in this book. You can download it here: `https://static.packt-cdn.com/downloads/9781838826789_ColorImages.pdf`.

Conventions used

There are a number of text conventions used throughout this book.

`Code in text`: Indicates code words in text, database table names, folder names, filenames, file extensions, pathnames, dummy URLs, user input, and Twitter handles. Here is an example: "This is done using `tf.gather(self.beta, labels)`, which is conceptually equivalent to `beta = self.beta[labels]`, as follows."

A block of code is set as follows:

```
attn = tf.matmul(theta, phi, transpose_b=True)
attn = tf.nn.softmax(attn)
```

When we wish to draw your attention to a particular part of a code block, the relevant lines or items are set in bold:

```
self.conv_theta = Conv2D(c//8, 1, padding='same',
                kernel_constraint=SpectralNorm(),
                name='Conv_Theta')
```

Any command-line input or output is written as follows:

```
$ mkdir css
$ cd css
```

Bold: Indicates a new term, an important word, or words that you see onscreen. For example, words in menus or dialog boxes appear in the text like this. Here is an example: "From the preceding architecture diagram, we can see that **G1**'s encoder output concatenates with **G1**'s features and feeds into the decoder part of **G2** to generate high-resolution images."

> **Tips or important notes**
> Appear like this.

Get in touch

Feedback from our readers is always welcome.

General feedback: If you have questions about any aspect of this book, mention the book title in the subject of your message and email us at `customercare@packtpub.com`.

Errata: Although we have taken every care to ensure the accuracy of our content, mistakes do happen. If you have found a mistake in this book, we would be grateful if you would report this to us. Please visit www.packtpub.com/support/errata, selecting your book, clicking on the Errata Submission Form link, and entering the details.

Piracy: If you come across any illegal copies of our works in any form on the Internet, we would be grateful if you would provide us with the location address or website name. Please contact us at `copyright@packt.com` with a link to the material.

If you are interested in becoming an author: If there is a topic that you have expertise in and you are interested in either writing or contributing to a book, please visit authors. packtpub.com.

Reviews

Please leave a review. Once you have read and used this book, why not leave a review on the site that you purchased it from? Potential readers can then see and use your unbiased opinion to make purchase decisions, we at Packt can understand what you think about our products, and our authors can see your feedback on their book. Thank you!

For more information about Packt, please visit packt.com.

Section 1: Fundamentals of Image Generation with TensorFlow

This section will introduce you to the fundamentals of image generation using TensorFlow, including probabilistic models, autoencoders, and GANs. By the end of this section, you will have a solid understanding of the principles of image generation using deep neural networks.

This section comprises the following chapters:

- *Chapter 1, Getting Started with Image Generation Using TensorFlow*
- *Chapter 2, Variational Autoencoder*
- *Chapter 3, Generative Adversarial Network*

1

Getting Started with Image Generation Using TensorFlow

This book focuses on generating images and videos using unsupervised learning with TensorFlow 2. We assume that you have prior experience in using modern machine learning frameworks, such as TensorFlow 1, to build image classifiers with **Convolutional Neural Networks (CNNs)**. Therefore, we will not be covering the basics of deep learning and CNNs. In this book, we will mainly use high level Keras APIs in TensorFlow 2, which is easy to learn. Nevertheless, we assume that you have no prior knowledge of image generation, and we will go through all that is needed to help you get started with it. The first aspect that you need to know about is **probability distribution**.

Probability distribution is fundamental in machine learning and it is especially important in generative models. Don't worry, I assure you that there aren't any complex mathematical equations in this chapter. We will first learn what probability is and how to use it to generate faces without using any neural networks or complex algorithms.

That's right: with the help of only basic math and NumPy code, you'll learn how to create a probabilistic generative model. Following that, you will learn how to use TensorFlow 2 to build a **PixelCNN** model in order to generate handwritten digits. This chapter is packed with useful information; you will need to read this chapter before jumping to any other chapters.

In this chapter, we are going to cover the following main topics:

- Understanding probabilities
- Generating faces with a probabilistic model
- Building a PixelCNN model from scratch

Technical requirements

The code can be found here: `https://github.com/PacktPublishing/Hands-On-Image-Generation-with-TensorFlow-2.0/tree/master/Chapter01`.

Understanding probabilities

You can't escape the term *probability* in any machine learning literature, and it can be confusing as it can have different meanings in different contexts. Probability is often denoted as *p* in mathematical equations, and you see it everywhere in academic papers, tutorials, and blogs. Although it is a concept that is seemingly easy to understand, it can be quite confusing. This is because there are multiple different definitions and interpretations depending on the context. We will use some examples to clarify things. In this section, we will go over the use of probability in the following contexts:

- Distribution
- Belief

Probability distribution

Say we want to train a neural network to classify images of cats and dogs and that we found a dataset that contains 600 images of dogs and 400 images of cats. As you may be aware, the data will need to be shuffled before being fed into the neural network. Otherwise, if it sees only images of the same label in a minibatch, the network will get lazy and say all images have the same label without taking the effort to look hard and differentiate between them. If we sampled the dataset randomly, the probabilities could be written as follows:

pdata(dog) = 0.6

pdata(cat) = 0.4

The probabilities here refer to the **data distribution**. In this example, this refers to the ratio of the number of cat and dog images to the total number of images in the dataset. The probability here is static and will not change for a given dataset.

When training a deep neural network, the dataset is usually too big to fit into one batch, and we need to break it into multiple minibatches for one epoch. If the dataset is well shuffled, then the **sampling distribution** of the minibatches will resemble that of the data distribution. If the dataset is unbalanced, where some classes have a lot more images from one label than another, then the neural network may be biased toward predicting the images it sees more. This is a form of **overfitting**. We can therefore sample the data differently to give more weight to the less-represented classes. If we want to balance the classes in sampling, then the sampling probability becomes as follows:

psample(dog) = 0.5

psample(cat) = 0.5

> **Note**
>
> **Probability distribution p(x)** is the probability of the occurrence of a data point *x*. There are two common distributions that are used in machine learning. **Uniform distribution** is where every data point has the same chances of occurrence; this is what people normally imply when they say random sampling without specifying the distribution type. **Gaussian distribution** is another commonly used distribution. It is so common that people also call it **normal distribution**. The probabilities peak at the center (mean) and slowly decay on each side. Gaussian distribution also has nice mathematical properties that make it a favorite of mathematicians. We will see more of that in the next chapter.

Prediction confidence

After several hundred iterations, the model has finally finished training, and I can't wait to test the new model with an image. The model outputs the following probabilities:

p(dog) = 0.6

p(cat) = 0.4

Wait, is the AI telling me that this animal is a mixed-breed with 60% dog genes and 40% cat inheritance? Of course not!

Here, the probabilities no longer refer to distributions; instead, they tell us how confident we can be about the predictions, or in other words, how strongly we can believe in the output. Now, this is no longer something you quantify by counting occurrences. If you are absolutely sure that something is a dog, you can put *p(dog) = 1.0* and *p(cat) = 0.0*. This is known as **Bayesian probability**.

> **Note**
>
> The traditional statistics approach sees probability as the chances of the occurrence of an event, for example, the chances of a baby being a certain sex. There has been great debate in the wider statistical field on whether the frequentist or Bayesian method is better, which is beyond the scope of this book. However, the Bayesian method is probably more important in deep learning and engineering. It has been used to develop many important algorithms, including **Kalman filtering** to track rocket trajectory. When calculating the projection of a rocket's trajectory, the Kalman filter uses information from both the **global positioning system (GPS)** and **speed sensor**. Both sets of data are noisy, but GPS data is less reliable initially (meaning less confidence), and hence this data is given less weight in the calculation. We don't need to learn the Bayesian theorem in this book; it's enough to understand that probability can be viewed as a confidence score rather than as frequency. Bayesian probability has also recently been used in searching for hyperparameters for deep neural networks.

We have now clarified two main types of probabilities commonly used in general machine learning – distribution and confidence. From now on, we will assume that probability means probability distribution rather than confidence. Next, we will look at a distribution that plays an exceptionally important role in image generation – **pixel distribution**.

The joint probability of pixels

Take a look at the following pictures – can you tell whether they are of dogs or cats? How do you think the classifier will produce the confidence score?

p(dog) = ?
p(cat) = ?

Figure 1.1 – Pictures of a cat and a dog

Are either of these pictures of dogs or cats? Well, the answer is pretty obvious, but at the same time it's not important to what we are going to talk about. When you looked at the pictures, you probably thought in your mind that the first picture was of a cat and the second picture was of a dog. We see the picture as a whole, but that is not what the computer sees. The computer sees **pixels**.

> **Note**
>
> A pixel is the smallest spatial unit in digital image, and it represents a single color. You cannot have a pixel where half is black and the other half is white. The most commonly used color scheme is 8-bit RGB, where a pixel is made up of three channels named R (red), G (green), and B (blue). Their values range from 0 to 255 (255 being the highest intensity). For example, a black pixel has a value of [0, 0, 0], while a white pixel is [255, 255, 255].

The simplest way to describe the **pixel distribution** of an image is by counting the number of pixels that have different intensity levels from 0 to 255; you can visualize this by plotting a histogram. It is a common tool in digital photography to look at a histogram of separate R, G, and B channels to understand the color balance. Although this can provide some information to us – for example, an image of sky is likely to have many blue pixels, so a histogram may reliably tell us something about that – histograms do not tell us how pixels relate to each other. In other words, a histogram does not contain spatial information, that is, how far a blue pixel is from another blue pixel. We will need a better measure for this kind of thing.

Instead of saying $p(x)$, where x is a whole image, we can define x as $x_1, x_2, x_3, \ldots x_n$. Now, $p(x)$ can be defined as the **joint probability** of pixels $p(x_1, x_2, x_3, \ldots x_n)$, where n is the number of pixels and each pixel is separated by a comma.

We will use the following images to illustrate what we mean by joint probability. The following are three images with 2 x 2 pixels that contain binary values, where 0 is black and 1 is white. We will call the top-left pixel x_1, the top-right pixel x_2, the bottom-left pixel x_3, and the bottom-right pixel x_4:

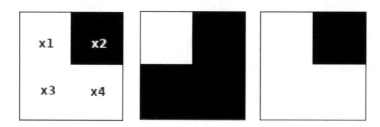

Figure 1.2 – Images with 2 x 2 pixels

We first calculate $p(x1 = white)$ by counting the number of white x_1 and dividing it by the total number of the image. Then, we do the same for x_2, as follows:

$p(x_1 = white) = 2 / 3$

$p(x_2 = white) = 0 / 3$

Now we say that $p(x1)$ and $p(x2)$ are independent of each other because we calculated them separately. If we calculate the joint probability where both $x1$ and $x2$ are black, we get the following:

$p(x_1 = black, x_2 = black) = 0 / 3$

We can then calculate the complete joint probability of these two pixels as follows:

$p(x_1 = black, x_2 = white) = 0 / 3$

$p(x_1 = white, x_2 = black) = 3 / 3$

$p(x_1 = white, x_2 = white) = 0 / 3$

We'll need to do the same steps 16 times to calculate the complete joint probability of $p(x_1, x_2, x_3, x_4)$. Now, we could fully describe the pixel distribution and use that to calculate the marginal distribution, as in $p(x_1, x_2, x_3)$ or $p(x_1)$. However, the calculations required for the joint distribution increase exponentially for RGB values where each pixel has 256 x 256 x 256 = 16,777,216 possibilities. This is where deep neural networks come to the rescue. A neural network can be trained to learn a pixel data distribution P_{data}. Hence, a neural network is our probability model P_{model}.

> **Important Note**
>
> The notations we will use in this book are as follows: *capital X* for the dataset, *lowercase x* for image sampled from the dataset, and *lowercase with subscript x_i* for the pixel.
>
> The purpose of image generation is to generate an image that has a pixel distribution $p(x)$ that resembles $p(X)$. For example, an image dataset of oranges will have a high probability of lots of occurrences of orange pixels that are distributed close to each other in a circle. Therefore, before generating image, we will first build a probability model $p_{model}(x)$ from real data $p_{data}(X)$. After that, we generate images by drawing a sample from $p_{model}(x)$.

Generating faces with a probabilistic model

Alright, enough mathematics. It is now time to get your hands dirty and generate your first image. In this section, we will learn how to generate images by sampling from a probabilistic model without even using a neural network.

Mean faces

We will be using the large-scale CelebFaces Attributes (CelebA) dataset created by The Chinese University of Hong Kong (http://mmlab.ie.cuhk.edu.hk/projects/CelebA.html). This can be downloaded directly with Python's tensorflow_datasets module within the ch1_generate_first_image.ipynb Jupyter notebook, as shown in the following code:

```python
import tensorflow_datasets as tfds
import matplotlib.pyplot as plt
import numpy as np
ds_train, ds_info = tfds.load('celeb_a', split='test',
                              shuffle_files=False,
                              with_info=True)
fig = tfds.show_examples(ds_info, ds_train)
```

The TensorFlow dataset allows us to preview some examples of images by using the `tfds.show_examples()` API. The following are some samples of male and female celebrities' faces:

Figure 1.3 – Sample images from the CelebA dataset

As you can see in the figure, there is a celebrity face in every image. Every picture is unique, with a variety of genders, poses, expressions, and hairstyles; some wear glasses and some don't. Let's see how to exploit the probability distribution of the images to help us create a new face. We'll use one of the simplest statistical methods – the mean, which means taking an average of the pixels from the images. To be more specific, we are averaging the x_i of every image to calculate the x_i of a new image. To speed up the processing, we'll use only 2,000 samples from the dataset for this task, as follows:

```python
sample_size = 2000
ds_train = ds_train.batch(sample_size)
features = next(iter(ds_train.take(1)))
sample_images = features['image']
new_image = np.mean(sample_images, axis=0)
plt.imshow(new_image.astype(np.uint8))
```

Ta-dah! That is your first generated image, and it looks pretty amazing! I initially thought it would look a bit like one of Picasso's paintings, but it turns out that the mean image is quite coherent:

Figure 1.4 – The mean face

Conditional probability

The best thing about the CelebA dataset is that each image is labeled with facial attributes as follows:

5_o_Clock_Shadow	Blurry	Male	Sideburns
Arched_Eyebrows	Brown_Hair	Mouth_Slightly_Open	Smiling
Attractive	Bushy_Eyebrows	Mustache	Straight_Hair
Bags_Under_Eyes	Chubby	Narrow_Eyes	Wavy_Hair
Bald	Double_Chin	No_Beard	Wearing_Earrings
Bangs	Eyeglasses	Oval_Face	Wearing_Hat
Big_Lips	Goatee	Pale_Skin	Wearing_Lipstick
Big_Nose	Gray_Hair	Pointy_Nose	Wearing_Necklace
Black_Hair	Heavy_Makeup	Receding_Hairline	Wearing_Necktie
Blond_Hair	High_Cheekbones	Rosy_Cheeks	Young

Figure 1.5 – 40 attributes in the CelebA dataset in alphabetical order

We are going to use these attributes to generate a new image. Let's say we want to generate a male image. How do we do that? Instead of calculating the probability of every image, we use only images that have the `Male` attribute set to `true`. We can put it in this way:

$p(x \mid y)$

We call this the probability of *x* conditioned on *y*, or more informally the probability of *x* given *y*. This is called **conditional probability**. In our example, *y* is the facial attributes. When we condition on the `Male` attribute, this variable is no longer a random probability; every sample will have the `Male` attribute and we can be certain that every face belongs to a man. The following figure shows new mean faces generated using other attributes as well as `Male`, such as *Male + Eyeglasses* and *Male + Eyeglasses + Mustache + Smiling*. Notice that as the conditions increase, the number of samples reduces and the mean image also becomes noisier:

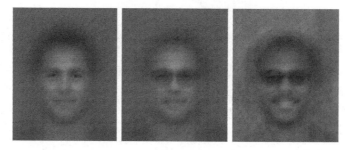

Figure 1.6 – Adding attributes from left to right. (a) Male (b) Male + Eyeglasses (c) Male + Eyeglasses + Mustache + Smiling

You could use the Jupyter notebook to generate a new face by using different attributes, but not every combination produces satisfactory results. The following are some female faces generated with different attributes. The rightmost image is an interesting one. I used attributes of `Female`, `Smiling`, `Eyeglasses`, and `Pointy_Nose`, but it turns out that people with these attributes tend to also have wavy hair, which is an attribute that was excluded in this sample. Visualization can be a useful tool to provide insights into your dataset:

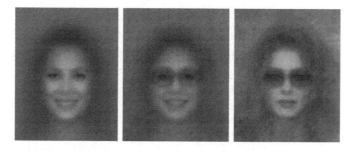

Figure 1.7 – Female faces with different attributes

> **Tips**
>
> Instead of using the mean when generating images, you can try to using the median as well, which may produce a sharper image. Simply replace `np.mean()` with `np.median()`.

Probabilistic generative models

There are three main goals that we wish to achieve with image-generation algorithms:

1. Generate images that look like ones in the given dataset.

2. Generate a variety of images.

3. Control the images being generated.

By simply taking the mean of the pixels in an image, we have demonstrated how to achieve goals *1* and *3*. However, one limitation is that we could only generate one image per condition. That really isn't very effective for an algorithm, generating only one image from hundreds or thousands of training images.

The following chart shows the distribution of one color channel of an arbitrary pixel in the dataset. The *x* mark on the chart is the median value. When we use the mean or median of data, we are always sampling the same point, and therefore there is no variation in the outcome. Is there a way to generate multiple different faces? Yes, we can try to increase the generated image variation by sampling from the entire pixel distribution:

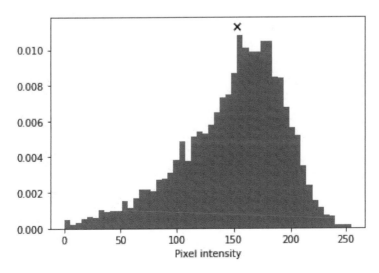

Figure 1.8 – The distribution of a pixel's color channel

A machine learning textbook will probably ask you to first create a probabilistic model, pmodel, by calculating the joint probability of every single pixel. But as the sample space is huge (remember, one RGB pixel can have 16,777,216 different values), it is computationally expensive to implement. Also, because this is a hands-on book, we will draw pixel samples directly from datasets. To create an x_0 pixel in a new image, we randomly sample from an x_0 pixel of all images in the dataset by running the following code:

```
new_image = np.zeros(sample_images.shape[1:], dtype=np.uint8)
for i in range(h):
    for j in range(w):
        rand_int = np.random.randint(0, sample_images.shape[0])
        new_image[i,j] = sample_images[rand_int,i,j]
```

Images were generated using random sampling. Disappointingly, although there is some variation between the images, they are not that different from each other, and one of our objectives is to be able to generate a variety of faces. Also, the images are noticeably noisier than when using the mean. The reason for this is that the pixel distribution is independent of each other.

For example, for a given pixel in the lips, we can reasonably expect the color to be pink or red, and the same goes for the adjacent pixels. Nevertheless, because we are sampling independently from images where faces appear in different locations and poses, this results in color discontinuities between pixels, ultimately giving this noisy result:

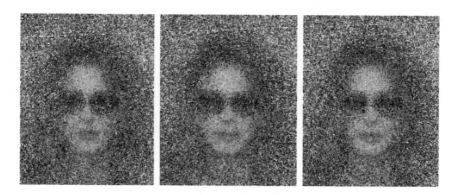

Figure 1.9 – Images generated by random sampling

> **Tips**
>
> You may be wondering why the mean face looks smoother than with random sampling. Firstly, it is because the distance of the mean between pixels is smaller. Imagine a random sampling scenario where one pixel sampled is close to 0 and the next one is close to 255. The mean of these pixels would likely lie somewhere in the middle, and therefore the difference between them would be smaller. On the other hand, pixels in the backgrounds of pictures tend to have a uniform distribution; for example, they could all be part of a blue sky, a white wall, green leaves, and so on. As they are distributed rather evenly across the color spectrum, the mean value is around [127, 127, 127], which happens to be gray.

Parametric modeling

What we just did was use a pixel histogram as our `pmodel`, but there are a few shortcomings here. Firstly, due to the large sample space, not every possible color exists in our sample distribution. As a result, the generated image will never contain any colors that are not present in the dataset. For instance, we want to be able to generate the full spectrum of skin tones rather than only one very specific shade of brown that exists in the dataset. If you did try to generate faces using conditions, you will have found that not every combination of conditions is possible. For example, for *Mustache + Sideburns + Heavy_Makeup + Wavy_Hair*, there simply wasn't a sample that met those conditions!

Secondly, the sample spaces increase as we increase the size of the dataset or the image resolution. This can be solved by having a parameterized model. The vertical bar chart in the following figure shows a histogram of 1,000 randomly generated numbers:

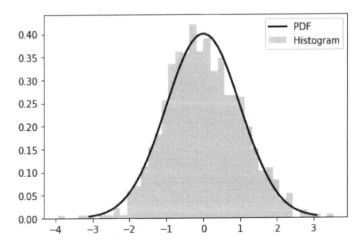

Figure 1.10 – Gaussian histogram and model

We can see that there are some bars that don't have any value. We can fit a Gaussian model on the data in which the **Probability Density Function** (**PDF**) is plotted as a black line. The PDF equation for a Gaussian distribution is as follows:

$$f(x) = \frac{1}{\sigma\sqrt{2\pi}} e^{-\frac{1}{2}(\frac{x-\mu}{\sigma})^2}$$

Here, μ is the mean and σ is the standard deviation.

We can see that the PDF covers the histogram gap, which means we can generate a probability for the missing numbers. This Gaussian model has only two parameters – the mean and the standard variation.

The 1,000 numbers can now be condensed to just two parameters, and we can use this model to draw as many samples as we wish; we are no longer limited to the data we fit the model with. Of course, natural images are complex and could not be described by simple models such as a Gaussian model, or in fact any mathematical models. This is where neural networks come into play. Now we will use a neural network as a parameterized image-generation model where the parameters are the network's weights and biases.

Building a PixelCNN model from scratch

There are three main categories of deep neural network generative algorithms:

- **Generative Adversarial Networks (GANs)**
- **Variational Autoencoders (VAEs)**
- **Autoregressive models**

VAEs will be introduced in the next chapter, and we will use them in some of our models. The GAN is the main algorithm we will be using in this book, and there are a lot more details about it to come in later chapters. We will introduce the lesser-known **autoregressive model** family here and focus on VAEs and GANs later in the book. Although it is not so common in image generation, autoregression is still an active area of research, with DeepMind's WaveNet using it to generate realistic audio. In this section, we will introduce autoregressive models and build a **PixelCNN** model from scratch.

Autoregressive models

Auto here means *self*, and *regress* in machine learning terminology means *predict new values*. Putting them together, autoregressive means we use a model to predict new data points based on the model's past data points.

Let's recall the probability distribution of an image is $p(x)$ is joint pixel probability $p(x_1, x_2, ... x_n)$ which is difficult to model due to the high dimensionality. Here, we make an assumption that the value of a pixel depends only on that of the pixel before it. In other words, a pixel is conditioned only on the pixel before it, that is, $p(x_i) = p(x_i | x_{i-1}) p(x_{i-1})$. Without going into the mathematical details, we can approximate the joint probability to be the product of conditional probabilities:

$$p(x) = p(x_n, x_{n-1}, ..., x_2, x_1)$$

$$p(x) = p(x_n | x_{n-1}) ... p(x_3 | x_2) p(x_2 | x_1) p(x_1)$$

To give a concrete example, let's say we have images that contain only a red apple in roughly the center of the image, and that the apple is surrounded by green leaves. In other words, only two colors are possible: red and green. x_1 is the top-left pixel, so $p(x_1)$ is the probability of whether the top-left pixel is green or red. If x_1 is green, then the pixel to its right $p(x_2)$ is likely to be green too, as it's likely to be more leaves. However, it could be red, despite the smaller probability.

As we go on, we will eventually hit a red pixel (hooray! We have found our apple!). From that pixel onward, it is likely that the next few pixels are more likely to be red too. We can now see that this is a lot simpler than having to consider all of the pixels together.

PixelRNN

PixelRNN was invented by the Google-acquired DeepMind back in 2016. As the name **RNN (Recurrent Neural Network)** suggests, this model uses a type of RNN called **Long Short-Term Memory (LSTM)** to learn an image's distribution. It reads the image one row at a time in a step in the LSTM and processes it with a 1D convolution layer, then feeds the activations into subsequent layers to predict pixels for that row.

As LSTM is slow to run, it takes a long time to train and generate samples. As a result, it fell out of fashion and there has not been much improvement made to it since its inception. Thus, we will not dwell on it for long and will instead move our attention to a variant, PixelCNN, which was also unveiled in the same paper.

Building a PixelCNN model with TensorFlow 2

PixelCNN is made up only of convolutional layers, making it a lot faster than PixelRNN. Here, we will implement a simple PixelCNN model for MNIST. The code can be found in `ch1_pixelcnn.ipynb`.

Input and label

MNIST consists of 28 x 28 x 1 grayscale images of handwritten digits. It only has one channel, with 256 levels to depict the shade of gray:

Figure 1.11 – MNIST digit examples

In this experiment, we simplify the problem by casting images into binary format with only two possible values: 0 represents black and 1 represents white. The code for this is as follows:

```
def binarize(image, label):
    image = tf.cast(image, tf.float32)
    image = tf.math.round(image/255.)
    return image, tf.cast(image, tf.int32)
```

The function expects two inputs – an image and a label. The first two lines of the function cast the image into binary `float32` format, in other words `0.0` or `1.0`. In this tutorial, we will not use the label information; instead, we cast the binary image into an integer and return it. We don't have to cast it to an integer, but let's just do it to stick to the convention of using an integer for labels. To recap, both the input and the label are binary MNIST images of 28 x 28 x 1; they differ only in data type.

Masking

Unlike PixelRNN, which reads row by row, PixelCNN slides a convolutional kernel across the image from left to right and from top to bottom. When performing convolution to predict the current pixel, a conventional convolution kernel is able to see the current input pixel together with the pixels surrounding it, including future pixels, and this breaks our conditional probability assumptions.

To avoid that, we need to make sure that the CNN doesn't cheat to look at the pixel it is predicting. In other words, we need to make sure that the CNN doesn't see the input pixel x_i while it is predicting the output pixel x_i.

This is by using a masked convolution, where a mask is applied to the convolutional kernel weights before performing convolution. The following diagram shows a mask for a 7 x 7 kernel, where the weight from the center onward is 0. This blocks the CNN from seeing the pixel it is predicting (the center of the kernel) and all future pixels. This is known as a **type A mask** and is applied only to the input layer. As the center pixel is blocked in the first layer, we don't need to hide the center feature anymore in later layers. In fact, we will need to set the kernel center to 1 to enable it to read the features from previous layers. This is known as type B Mask:

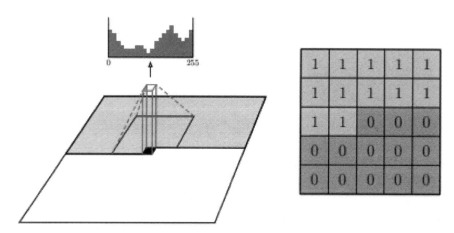

Figure 1.12 – A 7 x 7 kernel mask

(Source: Aäron van den Oord et al., 2016, Conditional Image Generation with PixelCNN Decoders, https://arxiv.org/abs/1606.05328)

Next, we will learn how to create a custom layer.

Implementing a custom layer

We will now create a custom layer for the masked convolution. We can create a custom layer in TensorFlow using model subclassing inherited from the base class, tf.keras.layers.Layer, as shown in the following code. We will be able to use it just like other Keras layers. The following is the basic structure of the custom layer class:

```
class MaskedConv2D(tf.keras.layers.Layer):
    def __init__(self):
        ...
    def build(self, input_shape):
        ...
    def call(self, inputs):
```

```
    . . .
        return output
```

`build()` takes the input tensor's shape as an argument, and we will use this information to create variables of the correct shapes. This function runs only once, when the layer is built. We can create a mask by declaring it either as a non-trainable variable or as a constant to let TensorFlow know it does not need to have gradients to backpropagate:

```python
def build(self, input_shape):
    self.w = self.add_weight(shape=[self.kernel,
                                     self.kernel,
                                     input_shape[-1],
                                     self.filters],
                             initializer='glorot_normal',
                             trainable=True)
    self.b = self.add_weight(shape=(self.filters,),
                             initializer='zeros',
                             trainable=True)
    mask = np.ones(self.kernel**2, dtype=np.float32)
    center = len(mask)//2
    mask[center+1:] = 0
    if self.mask_type == 'A':
        mask[center] = 0
    mask = mask.reshape((self.kernel, self.kernel, 1, 1))
    self.mask = tf.constant(mask, dtype='float32')
```

`call()` is the forward pass that performs the computation. In this masked convolutional layer, we multiply the weight by the mask to zero the lower half before performing convolution using the low-level `tf.nn` API:

```python
def call(self, inputs):
    masked_w = tf.math.multiply(self.w, self.mask)
    output = tf.nn.conv2d(inputs, masked_w, 1, "SAME") +
            self.b
    return output
```

> **Tips**
>
> `tf.keras.layers` is a high-level API that is easy to use without you needing to know under-the-hood details. However, sometimes we will need to create custom functions using the low-level `tf.nn` API, which requires us to first specify or create the tensors to be used.

Network layers

The PixelCNN architecture is quite straightforward. After the first 7 x 7 `conv2d` layer with mask A, there are several layers of residual blocks (see the following table) with mask B. To keep the same feature map size of 28 x 28, there is no downsampling; for example, the max pooling and padding in these layers is set to `SAME`. The top features are then fed into two layers of 1 x 1 convolution layers before the output is produced, as seen in the following screenshot:

```
Model: "PixelCnn"
Layer (type)                    Output Shape         Param #
=================================================================
input_1 (InputLayer)            [(None, 28, 28, 1)]  0

masked_conv2d (MaskedConv2D)    (None, 28, 28, 128)  6400

residual_block (ResidualBloc    (None, 28, 28, 128)  53504

residual_block_1 (ResidualBl    (None, 28, 28, 128)  53504

residual_block_2 (ResidualBl    (None, 28, 28, 128)  53504

residual_block_3 (ResidualBl    (None, 28, 28, 128)  53504

residual_block_4 (ResidualBl    (None, 28, 28, 128)  53504

residual_block_5 (ResidualBl    (None, 28, 28, 128)  53504

residual_block_6 (ResidualBl    (None, 28, 28, 128)  53504

conv2d (Conv2D)                 (None, 28, 28, 64)   8256

conv2d_1 (Conv2D)               (None, 28, 28, 1)    65
=================================================================
```

Figure 1.13 – The PixelCNN architecture, showing the layers and output shape

Residual blocks are used in many high-performance CNN-based models and were made popular by ResNet, which was invented by Kaiming He et al. in 2015. The following diagram illustrates a variant of residual blocks used in PixelCNN. The left path is called a **skip connection path**, which simply passes the features from the previous layer. On the right path are three sequential convolutional layers with filters of 1 x 1, 3 x 3, and 1 x 1. This path optimizes the residuals of the input features, hence the name **residual net**:

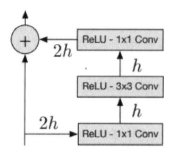

Figure 1.14 – The residual block where h is the number of filters. (Source: Aäron van den Oord et al., Pixel Recurrent Neural Networks)

Cross-entropy loss

Cross-entropy loss, also known as **log loss**, measures the performance of a model, where the output's probability is between 0 and 1. The following is the equation for binary cross-entropy loss, where there are only two classes, labels *y* can be either 0 or 1, and *p(x)* is the model's prediction. The equation is as follows:

$$BCE = -\frac{1}{N}\sum_{i=1}^{N} (y_i \log p(x) + (1 - y_i) \log(1 - p(x)))$$

Let's look at an example where the label is 1, the second term is zero, and the first term is the sum of *log p(x)*. The log in the equation is natural log ($\log_e$) but by convention the base of e is omitted from the equations. If the model is confident that *x* belongs to label 1, then *log(1)* is zero. On the other hand, if the model wrongly guesses it as label 0 and predicts a low probability of *x* being label *1*, say *p(x) = 0.1*. Then *-log (p(x))* becomes higher loss of *2.3*. Therefore, minimizing cross-entropy loss will maximize the model's accuracy. This loss function is commonly used in classification models but is also popular among generative models.

In PixelCNN, the individual image pixel is used as a label. In our binarized MNIST, we want to predict whether the output pixel is either 0 or 1, which makes this a classification problem with cross-entropy as the loss function.

There can be two output types:

- Since there can only be 0 or 1 in a binarized image, we can simplify the network by using `sigmoid()` to predict the probability of a white pixel, that is, $p(x_i = 1)$. The loss function is binary cross-entropy. This is what we will use in our PixelCNN model.

- Optionally, we could also generalize the network to accept grayscale or RGB images. We can use the `softmax()` activation function to produce N probabilities for each (sub)pixel. N will be *2* for binarized images, *256* for grayscale images, and *3 x 256* for RGB images. The loss function is sparse categorical cross-entropy or categorical cross-entropy if the label is one-hot encoded.

Finally, we are now ready to compile and train the neural network. As seen in the following code, we use binary cross-entropy for both `loss` and `metrics` and use RMSprop as the optimizer. There are many different optimizers to use, and their main difference comes in how they adjust the learning rate of individual variables based on past statistics. Some optimizers accelerate training but may tend to overshoot and not achieve global minima. There is no one best optimizer to use in all cases, and you are encouraged to try different ones.

However, the two optimizers that you will see a lot are **Adam** and **RMSprop**. The Adam optimizer is a popular choice in image generation for its fast learning, while RMSprop is used frequently by Google to produce state-of-the-art models.

The following is used to compile and fit the `pixelcnn` model:

```
pixelcnn = SimplePixelCnn()
pixelcnn.compile(
    loss = tf.keras.losses.BinaryCrossentropy(),
    optimizer=tf.keras.optimizers.RMSprop(learning_rate=0.001),
    metrics=[ tf.keras.metrics.BinaryCrossentropy()])
pixelcnn.fit(ds_train, epochs = 10, validation_data=ds_test)
```

Next, we will generate a new image from the preceding model.

Sample image

After the training, we can generate a new image using the model by taking the following steps:

1. Create an empty tensor with the same shape as the input image and fill it with zeros. Feed this into the network and get $p(x_1)$, the probability of the first pixel.

2. Sample from $p(x_1)$ and assign the sample value to pixel x_1 in the input tensor.

3. Feed the input to the network again and perform step 2 for the next pixel.

4. Repeat steps 2 and 3 until x_N has been generated.

One major drawback of the autoregressive model is that it is slow because of the need to generate pixel by pixel, which cannot be parallelized. The following images were generated by our simple PixelCNN model after 50 epochs of training. They don't look quite like proper digits yet, but they're starting to take the shape of handwriting strokes. It's quite amazing that we can now generate new images out of thin air (that is, with zero-input tensors). Can you generate better digits by training the model longer and doing some hyperparameter tuning?

Figure 1.15 – Some images generated by our PixelCNN model

With that, we have come to the end of the chapter!

Summary

Wow! I think we have learned a lot in this first chapter, from understanding pixel probability distribution to using it to build a probabilistic model to generate images. We learned how to build custom layers with TensorFlow 2 and use them to construct autoregressive PixelCNN models to generate images of handwritten digits.

In the next chapter, we will learn how to do representation with VAEs. This time, we will look at pixels from a whole new perspective. We will train a neural network to learn facial attributes, and you'll perform face edits, such as morphing a sad-looking girl into a smiling man with a mustache.

2
Variational Autoencoder

In the previous chapter, we looked at how a computer sees an image as pixels, and we devised a probabilistic model for pixel distribution for image generation. However, this is not the most efficient way to generate an image. Instead of scanning an image pixel by pixel, we first look at the image and try to understand what is inside. For example, a girl is sitting, wearing a hat, and smiling. Then we use that information to draw a portrait. This is how autoencoders work.

In this chapter, we will first learn how to use an autoencoder to encode pixels into latent variables that we can sample from to generate images. Then we will learn how to tweak it to create a more powerful model known as a **variational autoencoder** (**VAE**). Finally, we will train our VAE to generate faces and perform face editing. The following topics will be covered in this chapter:

- Learning latent variables with autoencoders
- Variational autoencoders
- Generating faces with VAEs
- Controlling face attributes

Technical requirements

The Jupyter notebooks and codes can be found at `https://github.com/PacktPublishing/Hands-On-Image-Generation-with-TensorFlow-2.0/tree/master/Chapter02`.

The notebooks used in this chapter are as follows:

- `ch2_autoencoder.ipynb`
- `ch2_vae_mnist.ipynb`
- `ch2_vae_faces.ipynb`

Learning latent variables with autoencoders

Autoencoders were first introduced in the 1980s, and one of the inventors is Geoffrey Hinton, who is one of the godfathers of modern deep learning. The hypothesis is that there are many redundancies in high-dimensional input space that can be compressed into some low-dimensional variables. There are traditional machine learning techniques such as **Principal Component Analysis (PCA)** for dimension reduction.

However, in image generation, we will also want to restore the low dimension space into high dimension space. Although the way to do it is quite different, you can think of it like image compression where a raw image is compressed into a file format such as JPEG, which is small and easy to store and transfer. Then the computer can restore the JPEG into pixels that we can see and manipulate. In other words, the raw pixels are compressed into low-dimensional JPEG format and restored to high-dimensional raw pixels for display.

Autoencoders are an *unsupervised machine learning* technique where no labels are needed to train the model. However, some call this *self-supervised* machine learning (*auto* means *self* in Latin) because we do need to use labels, and these labels are not annotated labels but the images themselves.

The basic building blocks of autoencoders are an **encoder** and a **decoder**. The encoder is responsible for reducing high-dimensional input into some low-dimensional latent (hidden) variables. Although it is not clear from the name, the decoder is the block that converts latent variables back into high dimensional space. The encoder-decoder architecture is also used in other machine learning tasks, such as **semantic segmentation**, where the neural network first learns about the image representation, then produces pixel-level labels. The following diagram shows the general architecture of an autoencoder:

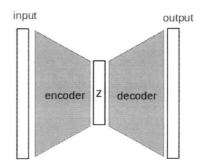

Figure 2.1 – General autoencoder architecture

In the preceding image, the **input** and **output** are images of the same dimension, and **z** is the low dimensional latent vector. The **encoder** compresses input into **z**, and the **decoder** reverses the process to generate the output image.

Having examined the overall architecture, let's look into how the encoder works.

Encoder

The encoder is made up of multiple neural network layers, and it is best illustrated by using fully connected (dense) layers. We will now jump straight into building an encoder for the MNIST dataset, which has a dimension of 28x28x1. We need to set the dimension of latent variables, which is a 1D vector. We will stick to the convention and name the latent variables as z, as seen in the following code.

The code can be found in ch2_autoencoder.ipynb:

```
def Encoder(z_dim):
    inputs  = layers.Input(shape=[28,28,1])
    x = inputs
    x = Flatten()(x)
    x = Dense(128, activation='relu')(x)
    x = Dense(64, activation='relu')(x)
    x = Dense(32, activation='relu')(x)
    z = Dense(z_dim, activation='relu')(x)

    return Model(inputs=inputs, outputs=z, name='encoder')
```

The size of the latent variable should be smaller than the input dimension. It is a hyperparameter, and we will first try with 10, which will give us a compression rate of *28*28/10 = 78.4.*

We will then use three fully connected layers with a decreasing number of neurons (128, 64, 32, and finally 10, which is our z dimension). We can see in the following model summary that the feature sizes got squeezed from 784 gradually down to 10 in the network's output:

```
Model: "encoder"

Layer (type)              Output Shape            Param #
=========================================================
input_1 (InputLayer)      [(None, 28, 28, 1)]     0

flatten (Flatten)         (None, 784)             0

dense (Dense)             (None, 128)             100480

dense_1 (Dense)           (None, 64)              8256

dense_2 (Dense)           (None, 32)              2080

dense_3 (Dense)           (None, 10)              330
=========================================================
Total params: 111,146
Trainable params: 111,146
Non-trainable params: 0
```

Figure 2.2 – Model summary of our encoder

This network topology forces the model to learn what is important and discard less important features from layer to layer, to finally come down to the 10 most important features. If you come to think of it, this looks very similar to the **CNN** classification, where the feature map size reduces gradually as it traverses to the top layers. **Feature map** refers to the first two dimensions (height, width) of the tensor.

As CNNs are more efficient and better suited for image inputs, we will build the encoder using **convolutional layers**. Old CNNs, such as **VGG**, used max pooling for feature map downsampling, but newer networks tend to achieve that by using stride of 2 in the convolutional layers. The following diagram illustrates the sliding of the convolutional kernel with a stride of 2 to produce a feature map that is half the size of the input feature map:

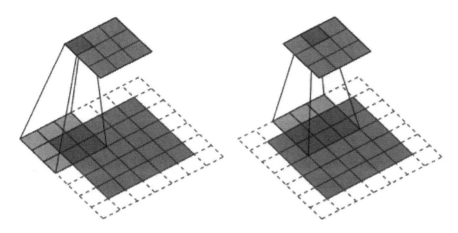

Figure 2.3 – From left to right, the figure illustrates a convolutional operation working with an input stride of 2

(Source: Vincent Dumoulin, Francesco Visin, "A guide to convolution arithmetic for deep learning" https://www.arxiv-vanity.com/papers/1603.07285/)

In this example, we will use four convolutional layers with 8 filters and include an input stride of 2 for downsampling, as follows:

```
def Encoder(z_dim):
    inputs  = layers.Input(shape=[28,28,1])
    x = inputs
    x = Conv2D(filters=8,  kernel_size=(3,3), strides=2,
              padding='same', activation='relu')(x)
    x = Conv2D(filters=8,  kernel_size=(3,3), strides=1,
              padding='same', activation='relu')(x)
    x = Conv2D(filters=8,  kernel_size=(3,3), strides=2,
              padding='same', activation='relu')(x)
    x = Conv2D(filters=8,  kernel_size=(3,3), strides=1,
              padding='same', activation='relu')(x)
    x = Flatten()(x)
    out = Dense(z_dim, activation='relu')(x)
    return Model(inputs=inputs, outputs=out, name='encoder')
```

In a typical CNN architectures, the number of filters increases while the feature map size decreases. However, our objective is to reduce the dimension, hence I have kept the filter size as constant. This is sufficient for simple data such as MNIST, and it is fine to change the filter sizes as we move toward the latent variables. Lastly, we flatten the output of the last convolutional layer and feed it to a dense layer to output our latent variables.

Decoder

If a decoder were a human, they would probably feel ill-treated. This is because the decoder does half of the work but only the encoder gets a place in the name. It should have been called auto-encoder-decoder!

The job of the decoder is essentially the reverse of the encoder, which is to convert low-dimensional latent variables into high-dimensional output to look like the input image. There is no need for layers in the decoder to look like the encoder in reverse order. You could use completely different layers, for instance, dense layers only in the encoder and convolutional layers only in the decoder. Anyway, we will still use convolutional layers in our decoder to upsample feature maps from 7x7 to 28x28. The following code snippet shows the construction of the decoder:

```
def Decoder(z_dim):
    inputs   = layers.Input(shape=[z_dim])
    x = inputs
    x = Dense(7*7*64, activation='relu')(x)
    x = Reshape((7,7,64))(x)
    x = Conv2D(filters=64, kernel_size=(3,3), strides=1,
                padding='same', activation='relu')(x)
    x = UpSampling2D((2,2))(x)
    x = Conv2D(filters=32, kernel_size=(3,3), strides=1,
                padding='same', activation='relu')(x)
    x = UpSampling2D((2,2))(x)
    x = Conv2D(filters=32, kernel_size=(3,3), strides=2,
                padding='same', activation='relu')(x)
    out = Conv2(filters=1, kernel_size=(3,3), strides=1,
                padding='same', activation='sigmoid')(x)
    return Model(inputs=inputs, outputs=out, name='decoder')
```

The first layer is a dense layer that takes in the latent variables and produces a tensor with a size of [7 x 7 x the number of filters] of our first convolutional layer. Unlike the encoder, the objective of the decoder is not to reduce dimensionality, thus we could and should use more filters to give it more generative capacity.

UpSampling2D interpolates the pixels to increase the resolution. It is an affine transformation (linear multiplications and additions), therefore it could **backpropagate**, but it uses fixed weights and is therefore is not trainable. Another popular upsampling method is to use the **transpose convolutional layer**, which is trainable, but it can create checkerboard-like artifacts in the generated image. You can read more at https://distill.pub/2016/deconv-checkerboard/.

The checkerboard artifacts are more obvious for low-dimension images or when you zoom into an image. The effect can be reduced by using an even-numbered convolutional kernel size, for example, 4 rather than the more popular size of 3. Therefore, recent image generative models tend to not use transpose convolution. We will be using `UpSampling2D` throughout the rest of the book. The following table shows the model summary of the decoder:

```
Model: "decoder"
```

Layer (type)	Output Shape	Param #
input_1 (InputLayer)	[(None, 10)]	0
dense (Dense)	(None, 3136)	34496
reshape (Reshape)	(None, 7, 7, 64)	0
conv2d (Conv2D)	(None, 7, 7, 64)	36928
up_sampling2d (UpSampling2D)	(None, 14, 14, 64)	0
conv2d_1 (Conv2D)	(None, 14, 14, 32)	18464
up_sampling2d_1 (UpSampling2	(None, 28, 28, 32)	0
conv2d_2 (Conv2D)	(None, 28, 28, 1)	289

```
Total params: 90,177
Trainable params: 90,177
Non-trainable params: 0
```

Figure 2.4 – Model summary of the decoder

> **Tips**
>
> When designing a CNN, it is important to know how to work out the convolutional layer's output tensor shape. If `padding='same'` is used, the output feature map will have the same size (height and width) as the input feature map. If `padding='valid'` is used instead, then the output size may be slightly smaller depending on the filter kernel dimension. When input `stride = 2` is used together with the same padding, the feature map size is halved. Lastly, the channel number of the output tensor is the same as the convolutional filter number. For example, if the input tensor has a shape of (28,28,1) and goes through `conv2d(filters=32, strides=2, padding='same')`, we know the output will have a shape of (14,14, 32).

Building an autoencoder

Now we are ready to put the encoder and decoder together to create an autoencoder. First, we instantiate the encoder and decoder separately. We then feed the encoder's output into the decoder's input, and we instantiate a `Model` using the encoder's input and the decoder's output as follows:

```
z_dim = 10
encoder = Encoder(z_dim)
decoder = Decoder(z_dim)
model_input = encoder.input
model_output = decoder(encoder.output)
autoencoder = Model(model_input, model_output)
```

A deep neural network can look complex and scary to build. However, we could break it down into smaller blocks or modules, then put them together later. The whole task becomes more manageable! For training, we will use L2 loss, this is implemented using **mean squared error** (**MSE**) to compare each of the pixels between the output and expected result. In this example, I have added in some callback functions that will be called after training every epoch as follows:

- `ModelCheckpoint(monitor='val_loss')` to save the model if the validation loss is lower than in earlier epochs.

- `EarlyStopping(monitor='val_loss', patience = 10)` to stop the training earlier if the validation loss has not improved for 10 epochs.

The image generated is as follows:

Figure 2.5 – The first row is the input image and the second row is generated by the autoencoder

As you can see, the first row is the input image and the second row is generated by our autoencoder. We can see that the generated images are a bit blurry; that is probably because we have compressed it too much and some data information is lost during the process.

To confirm our suspicion, we increase the latent variable dimension from 10 to 100 and generate the output and the result is as follows:

Figure 2.6 – Image generated by autoencoder with z_dim = 100

As you can see, the generated images now look a lot sharper!

Generating images from latent variables

So, how do we use an autoencoder? It is not very useful to have an AI model to convert an image into a blurrier version of itself. One of the first applications of autoencoders is image denoising, where we add some noise into the input image and train the model to produce a clean image. However, we are more interested in using it to generate images. So, let's see how we can do it.

Now that we have a trained autoencoder, we can ignore the encoder and use only the decoder to sample from the latent variables to generate images (See? The decoder deserves more recognition because it will still need to keep working after completing the training). The first challenge we face is working out how we sample from the latent variables. As we did not use any activation in the last layer before the latent variables, the latent space is unbounded and can be any real floating numbers, and there are hundreds of them!

To illustrate how this should work, we will train another autoencoder using `z_dim=2` so we can explore the latent space in two dimensions. The following graph shows the plot of the latent space:

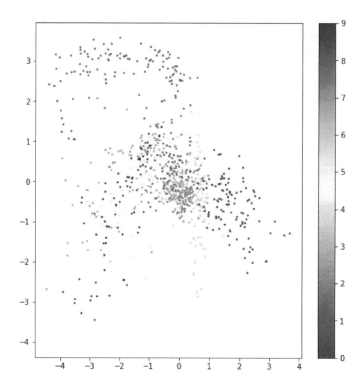

Figure 2.7 – Plot of latent space. A color version is available in the Jupyter notebook

The plot was generated by passing 1,000 samples into the trained encoder and plotting the two latent variables on the scatter plot. The color bar on the right indicates the intensity of the digit labels. We can observe the following from the plots:

- The latent variables sit roughly between **–5** and **+4**. We won't know the exact range unless we create this plot and look at it. This can change when you train the model again, and quite often the samples can scatter more widely beyond +-10.

- The classes are not distributed uniformly. You can see clusters in the top left and on the right that are well separated from other classes (refer to the color version in the Jupyter notebook). However, the classes at the center of the plot tend to be more densely packed and overlap with each other.

You might be able to see the non-uniformity better in the following images, which were generated by sweeping the latent variables from **–5** to **+5** with a 1.0 interval:

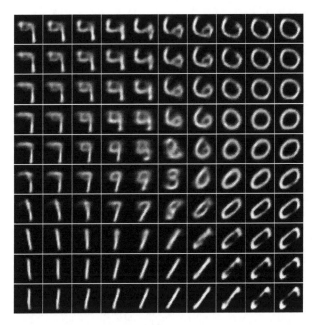

Figure 2.8 - Images generated by sweeping the two latent variables

We can see that digits 0 and 1 are well represented in the sample distribution and they are nicely drawn too. It is not the case for digits in the center, which are blurry, and some digits are even missing from the samples. The latter shows the shortcoming where there is very little variation in generated images for those classes.

It's not all bad. If you look closer, you can see how the digit 1 morphs into 7, then to 9 and 4, and that is interesting! It looks like the autoencoder has learned some relationship between the latent variables. It might be that the digits with round appearances are mapped into the latent space toward the top-right corner, while digits that look more like a stick sit on the left-hand side. That is good news!

> **Fun**
> There is a widget in the notebook that allows you to slide the latent variable bars to generate images interactively. Have fun!

In the coming section, we will see how we can use a VAE to solve the distribution issue in the latent space.

Variational autoencoders

In an autoencoder, the decoder samples directly from latent variables. **Variational autoencoders (VAEs)**, which were invented in 2014, differ in that the sampling is taken from a distribution parameterized by the latent variables. To be clear, let's say we have an autoencoder with two latent variables, and we draw samples randomly and get two samples of 0.4 and 1.2. We then send them to the decoder to generate an image.

In a VAE, these samples don't go to the decoder directly. Instead, they are used as a mean and variance of a **Gaussian distribution**, and we draw samples from this distribution to be sent to the decoder for image generation. As this is one of the most important distributions in machine learning, so let's go over some basics of Gaussian distributions before creating a VAE.

Gaussian distribution

A Gaussian distribution is characterized by two parameters – **mean** and **variance**. I think we are all familiar with the different bell curves shown in the following graph. The bigger the standard deviation (the square root of the variance), the larger the spread:

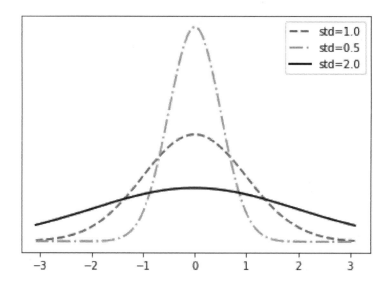

Figure 2.9 – Gaussian distribution probability density function with different standard deviations

We can use the $N(\mu, \sigma^2)$ notation to describe a univariate Gaussian distribution, where μ is the mean and σ is the standard deviation.

The mean tells us where the peak is: it is the value that has the highest probability density, in other words, the most frequent value. If we are to draw samples of pixel location (x,y) of an image, and each x and y have different Gaussian distributions, then we have a *multivariate* Gaussian distribution. In this case, it is a *bivariate* distribution.

The mathematical equations of a multivariate Gaussian distribution can look quite intimidating, so I'm not going to put them in here. The only thing we need to know is that we now incorporate standard deviations into the covariance matrix. The diagonal elements in the covariance matrix are simply the standard deviations of individual Gaussian distributions. The other elements measure the covariance between two Gaussian distributions, that is, the correlation between them.

The following graph shows us the bivariate Gaussian samples without correlation:

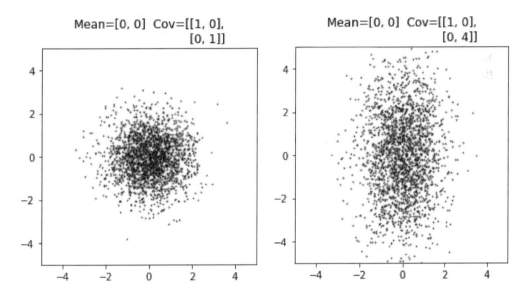

Figure 2.10 – Samples from a bivariate Gaussian distribution with no correlation

We can see that when the standard deviation of one dimension increases from 1 to 4, the spread increases only in that dimension (the *y* axis) without affecting the others. Here, we say the two Gaussian distributions are **identically and independently distributed** (abbreviated as **iid**).

Now, in the second example, the plot on the left shows that the covariance is non-zero and positive, which means when the density increases in one dimension, the other dimension will follow suit and they are correlated. The plot on the right shows a negative correlation:

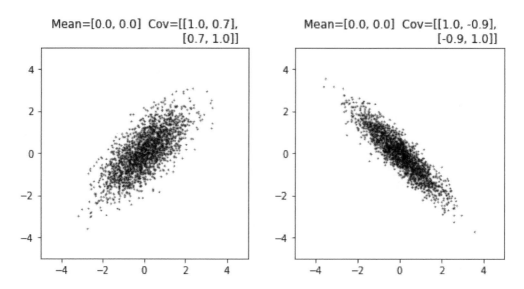

Figure 2.11 – Samples from a bivariate Gaussian distribution with correlation

Here is some good news for you: Gaussian distributions in VAEs are assumed to be iid and therefore do not require covariance matrix to describe the correlation between the variables. As a result, we need just n-pairs of mean and variance to describe our multivariate Gaussian distribution. What we hope to achieve is to create a nicely distributed latent space where latent variables' distributions for different data classes are as follows:

- Evenly spread so we have a better variation to sample from

- Overlap slightly with each other to create a continuous transition

This can be illustrated with the following plot:

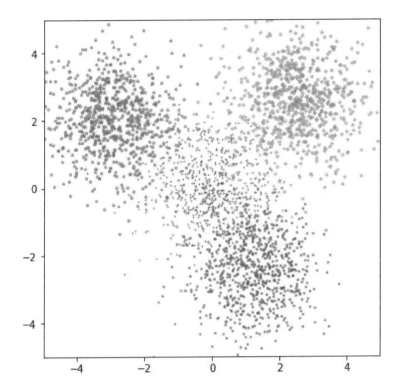

Figure 2.12 – Four samples drawn from a multivariate Gaussian distribution

Next, we will learn how to incorporate Gaussian distribution sampling into a VAE.

Sampling latent variables

When we train an autoencoder, the encoded latent variables go straight to the decoder. With a VAE, there is an additional sampling step between the encoder and the decoder. The encoder produces the mean and variance of Gaussian distributions as latent variables, and we draw samples from them to send to the decoder. The problem is, sampling is not back-propagatable and therefore is not trainable.

Backpropagation

For those who are not familiar with the fundamentals of deep learning, a neural network is trained using **backpropagation**. One of the steps is to calculate the gradients of the loss with respect to the network weights. Therefore, all operations must be differentiable for backpropagation to work.

To solve this, we can employ a simple *reparameterization trick* where we cast the Gaussian random variable *N* (mean, variance) into *mean + sigma * N(0, 1)*. In other words, we first sample from a standard Gaussian distribution of N(0,1), then multiply it with sigma then add mean to it. As you can see in the following diagram, the sampling becomes an affine transformation (which is composed of only add and multiplication operations) and the error could backpropagate from the output back to the encoder:

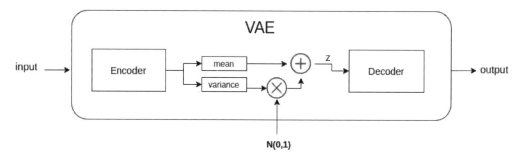

Figure 2.13 – Gaussian sampling in a VAE

The sampling from a standard Gaussian distribution **N(0,1)** can be seen as input to the VAE, and we do not need to backpropagate back to inputs. However, we will put the **N(0,1)** sampling inside our model. Now that we understand how sampling works, we can now go and build our VAE model.

Let's now implement the sampling as a custom layer, as shown in the following snippet:

```
class GaussianSampling(Layer):
    def call(self, inputs):
        means, logvar = inputs
        epsilon = tf.random.normal(shape=tf.shape(means),
                                   mean=0., stddev=1.)
        samples = means + tf.exp(0.5*logvar)*epsilon
        return samples
```

Note that we use log variance in the encoder space rather than variance for numerical stability. By definition, variance is a positive number, but unless we use an activation function such as `relu` to constrain it, the variance of latent variables can become negative. Furthermore, the variance can vary greatly, say from 0.01 to 100, which can make it difficult to train. However, the natural log of those values is -4.6 and +4.6, which is a smaller range. Nevertheless, we will need to convert the log variance into the standard deviation when doing sampling, hence the `tf.exp(0.5*logvar)` code.

Important note

There are a few ways to construct models in TensorFlow. One is to use the `Sequential` class to add layers sequentially. The input of the last layer goes into the next layer; therefore, you don't need to specify the input for the layer. While this is convenient, you can't use this on models that have branches. The next is to use the **Functional API**, where you start from the input, chain the layers, and specify the input to each layer. This is flexible and is what we used to build our autoencoder. However, `tf.random.normal()` will fail in eager execution mode, which is the default mode of TensorFlow 2 for creating a dynamic graph. This is because the function needs to know the batch size to generate the random numbers, but it is unknown as we create the layers. Thus, we would get an error in our Jupyter notebook when trying to draw a sample by passing in a size of `(None, 2)`. As a result, we will switch our model creation to using **subclassing**, which we have used to create custom layers. By the time `call()` is run, we will already know the batch size and hence complete the information of the shape.

Now we reconstruct our encoder using the **subclassing** method. The layers can be created in either `__init__()` or in `__built__()` if we need to use the input shape to construct the layers. Within the subclass, we use the `Sequential` class to create a block of convolutional layers conveniently as we don't need to read any intermediate tensors:

```python
class Encoder(Layer):
    def __init__(self, z_dim, name='encoder'):
        super(Encoder, self).__init__(name=name)
        self.features_extract = Sequential([
            Conv2D(filters=8, kernel_size=(3,3), strides=2,
                padding='same', activation='relu'),
            Conv2D(filters=8, kernel_size=(3,3), strides=1,
                padding='same', activation='relu'),
            Conv2D(filters=8, kernel_size=(3,3), strides=2,
                padding='same', activation='relu'),
            Conv2D(filters=8, kernel_size=(3,3), strides=1,
                padding='same', activation='relu'),
            Flatten()])
        self.dense_mean = Dense(z_dim, name='mean')
        self.dense_logvar = Dense(z_dim, name='logvar')
        self.sampler = GaussianSampling()
```

We then use two dense layers to predict the mean and log variance of z from the extracted features. Latent variables are sampled and return as output together with the mean and log variance for the loss calculation. The decoder is identical to the autoencoder except that we now re-write it using subclassing:

```
def call(self, inputs):
    x = self.features_extract(inputs)
    mean = self.dense_mean(x)
    logvar = self.dense_logvar(x)
    z = self.sampler([mean, logvar])
    return z, mean, logvar
```

Now the encoder block is completed. The decoder block design is unchanged from the autoencoder, so what is left to be done is to define a new loss function.

Loss function

We can now sample from a multivariate Gaussian distribution, but there is still no guarantee that the Gaussian blobs won't be far apart from each other and widely spread. The way VAEs do this is by putting in some regularization to encourage the Gaussian distribution to look like N(0,1). In other words, we want them to have a mean close to 0 to keep them close together, and variance close to 1 for a better variation to sample from. This is done by using **Kullback-Leibler divergence (KLD)**.

KLD is a measurement of how different one probability distribution is to another. For two distributions, P and Q, the KLD of P with respect to Q is the cross-entropy of P and Q minus the entropy of P. In information theory, entropy is a measure of information or the uncertainty of a random variable:

$$D_{KL}(P \parallel Q) = H(P, Q) - H(P)$$

Without going into the mathematical details, KLD is proportional to cross-entropy, hence minimizing cross-entropy will also minimize KLD. When KLD is zero, then the two distributions are identical. It suffices to say that there is a closed-form solution for KLD when the distribution to compare with is a standard Gaussian. This can be calculated directly from the following means and variances:

$$D_{KL}(N(\mu,\sigma) \parallel N(0,1)) = -0.5 \sum_{i=1}^{zdim} \log(\sigma_i^2) - \sigma_i^2 - \mu_i^2 + 1$$

We create custom loss function that takes in labels and network output to calculate the KL loss. I have used `tf.reduce_mean()` instead of `tf.reduce_sum()` to normalize it to the number of latent space dimensions. This doesn't really matter as the KL loss is multiplied by a hyperparameter, which we will discuss shortly:

```
def vae_kl_loss(y_true, y_pred):
    kl_loss =  - 0.5 * tf.reduce_mean(vae.logvar - tf.exp(vae.
logvar) - tf.square(vae.mean) - + 1)
    return kl_loss
```

The other loss function is what we have used in the autoencoder to compare the generated images with the label images. This is also called the **reconstruction loss**, which measures the difference in reconstructed images with the target image, hence the name. This can be either **binary cross-entropy** (**BCE**) or **mean squared error** (**MSE**). MSE tends to generate sharper images as it penalizes more severely for pixels that deviate from the label (by squaring the error):

```
def vae_rc_loss(y_true, y_pred):
    rc_loss = tf.keras.losses.MSE(y_true, y_pred)
    return rc_loss
```

Finally, we add the two losses together:

```
def vae_loss(y_true, y_pred):
    kl_loss = vae_kl_loss(y_true, y_pred)
    rc_loss = vae_rc_loss(y_true, y_pred)
    kl_weight_factor = 1e-2
    return kl_weight_factor*kl_loss + rc_loss
```

Now, let's talk about `kl_weight_factor`, which is an important hyperparameter that is often neglected in VAE examples or tutorials. As we can see, the total loss is made up of the KL loss and the reconstruction loss. The background of MNIST digits is black, and therefore the reconstruction loss is relatively low even though the network hasn't learned much and only outputs all zeroes.

Comparatively, the distribution of latent variables is all over the place at the beginning, and therefore the gain in reducing the KLD outweighs that of reducing the reconstruction loss. This encourages the network to ignore the reconstruction loss and optimize only for the KLD loss. As a result, the latent variables will have a perfect standard Gaussian distribution of $N(0,1)$ but the generated images will look nothing like the training images, and that is a disaster for a generative model!

> **Important note**
>
> The encoder is discriminative in that it tries to spot differences in the images. We can think of each latent variable as a feature. If we use two latent variables for MNIST digits, they could mean *round* or *straight*. When a decoder sees a digit, it predicts the likelihood of whether they are round or straight by using the means and variances. If a neural network is forced to make the KLD loss 0, the distribution of the latent variables will be identical – the center at 0 with a variance of 1. In other words, it is equally likely to be round and straight. Hence, the encoder loses its discriminative capacity. When this happens, you will see the decoder produces the same image every time and they look like the average pixel values.

Before we move on to the next part, I suggest you go to `ch2_vae_mnist.ipynb` and try a different `kl_weight_factor` with `VAE(z_dim=2)` to look at the latent variable distribution after training. You can also try to increase `kl_weight_factor` to see how it stops the VAE from learning to generate, and then look at the generated images and distributions again.

Generating faces with VAEs

Now that you have learned the theory of VAEs and have built one for MNIST, it is time to grow up, ditch the toy, and generate some serious stuff. We will use VAE to generate some faces. Let's get started! The code is in `ch2_vae_faces.ipynb`. There are a few face datasets available for training:

- Celeb A (`http://mmlab.ie.cuhk.edu.hk/projects/CelebA.html`). This is a popular dataset in academia as it contains annotations of face attributes, but unfortunately it is not available for commercial use.

- **Flickr-Faces-HQ Dataset** (**FFHQ**) (`https://github.com/NVlabs/ffhq-dataset`). This dataset is freely available for commercial use and contains high-resolution images.

In this exercise, we will only assume the dataset contains RGB images; feel free to use any dataset that suits your needs.

Network architecture

We reuse the **MNIST VAE** and training pipeline with some modifications given that the dataset is now different from MNIST. Feel free to reduce the layers, parameters, image size, epoch number, and batch size to suit your computing power. The modifications are as follows:

- Increase the latent space dimension to 200.

- The input shape is changed from (28,28,1) to (112,112,3) as we now have 3 color channels instead of grayscale. Why 112? Early CNNs such as VGG use the input size of 224x224 and set the standard for image classification CNNs. We don't want to use too-high resolutions now as we have not mastered the skills needed to generate high-resolution images. Therefore, I picked 224/2 = 112, but you could use any even values.

- Add image resizing in the pre-processing pipeline. We add more downsampling layers. In MNIST, the encoder downsamples twice, from 28 to 14 to 7. As we have a higher resolution to start with, we need to downsample four times in total.

- As the dataset is more complex, we increase the number of filters to increase the network capacity. Therefore, the convolutional layers in encoders are as follows. It is similar for the decoder but in the reverse direction. Instead of downsampling, the convolutional layers upsample the feature maps by striding:

a) `Conv2D(filters = 32, kernel_size=(3,3), strides = 2)`

b) `Conv2D(filters = 32, kernel_size=(3,3), strides = 2)`

c) `Conv2D(filters = 64, kernel_size=(3,3), strides = 2)`

d) `Conv2D(filters = 64, kernel_size=(3,3), strides = 2)`

> **Tips**
>
> Although we use the overall loss, that is, the KLD loss and the reconstruction loss in network training, we should only use the reconstruction loss as a metric to monitor when to save the model and early termination of the training. The KLD loss acts as regularization, but we are more interested in the reconstructed image's quality.

Facial reconstruction

Let's look at the following reconstructed images:

Figure 2.14 – Reconstructed images with a VAE

They do look good despite not being a perfect reconstruction. The VAE has managed to learn some features from the input image and use that to paint a new face. It looks like the VAE is better at reconstructing female faces. This is not surprising as we have seen the *mean face* in *Chapter 1, Getting Started with Image Generation Using TensorFlow*, which is of female appearance due to the higher proportion of females in the dataset. That is why mature men were given a younger, more feminine complexion.

The image background is also interesting. As the image backgrounds are so diverse, it was not possible for the encoder to encode every fine detail into low dimensions, so we can see the VAE encodes the background colors and the decoder creates a blurry backdrop based on those colors.

One fun thing to share with you, when the KL weight factor is too high and the VAE doesn't learn, then the *mean face* will come back to haunt you again. This is as if the VAE's encoder was blinded and told the decoder *"Hey, I can't see anything, just draw me a person"*, and then the decoder draws a portrait of what it thinks an average person looks like.

Generating new faces

To generate a new image, we create random numbers from the standard Gaussian distribution and feed it to the decoder, as shown in the following code snippet:

```
z_samples = np.random.normal(loc=0, scale=1, size=(image_num,
                                                      z_dim))
images = vae.decoder(z_samples.astype(np.float32))
```

And most of the generated faces look horrible!

Figure 2.15 – Faces generated with standard normal sampling

We can improve the image fidelity by using a **sampling trick**.

Sampling trick

We have just seen that the trained VAE could reconstruct the faces rather well. My suspicion was that there was something not quite right in samples generated by random sampling. To debug this problem, I fed in a few thousand images into the VAE decoder to collect the latent space means and variance. Then I plotted the average mean of each latent space variable, and the following is what I got:

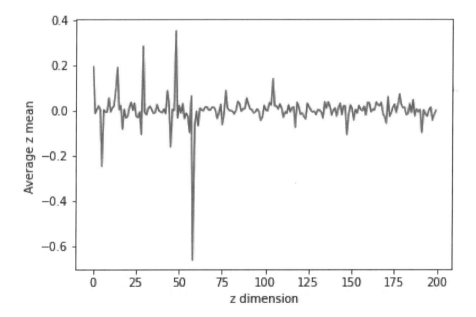

Figure 2.16 – Average mean of the latent variable

In theory, they should center at 0 and have a variance of 1, but they may not due to suboptimal KLD weight and stochasticity in the network training. Because of this, the randomly generated samples do not always match the distribution expected by the decoder. This is the trick I use to generate samples. Using steps similar to the preceding ones, I have collected the average standard deviation of latent variables (one scalar value), which I use for generating normally distributed samples (200 dimensions). Then I added the average mean (200 dimensions) to it.

Ta-da! Now they look a lot better and sharper!

Figure 2.17 – Faces generated with the sampling trick

Instead of generating random faces, in the next section we will learn how to perform face editing.

Controlling face attributes

Everything we have done in this chapter serves only one purpose: to prepare us for **face editing**! This is the climax of this chapter!

Latent space arithmetic

We have talked about the latent space several times now but haven't given it a proper definition. Essentially, it means every possible value of the latent variables. In our VAE, it is a vector of 200 dimensions, or simply 200 variables. As much as we hope each variable has a distinctive semantic meaning to us, such as $z[0]$ is for eyes, $z[1]$ dictates the eye color, and so on, things are never that straightforward. We will simply have to assume the information is encoded in all the latent vectors and we can use vector arithmetic to explore the space.

Before diving into high-dimensional space, let's try to understand it using a two-dimensional example. Imagine you are now at point *(0,0)* on a map and your home is at *(x,y)*. Therefore, the direction toward your home is *(x – 0 ,y - 0)* divided by the L2 norm of *(x,y)*, or let's denote the direction as *(x_dot, y_dot)*. Therefore, whenever you move *(x_dot, y_dot)*, you are moving toward your house; and when you move *(-2*x_dot, -2*y_dot)*, you are moving further away from home with twice as many steps.

Now, if we know the direction vector of the `smiling` attributes, we could add that to the latent variables to make the face smile:

```
new_z_samples = z_samples + smiling_magnitude*smiling_vector
```

`smiling_magnitude` is a scalar value that we set, so the next step is to work out the way to obtain `smiling_vector`.

Finding attribute vectors

Some datasets, such as Celeb A, come with annotations of facial attributes for each image. The labels are binary, meaning they indicate whether a certain attribute exists or not in the image. We will use the labels and the encoded latent variables to find our direction vectors! The idea is simple:

1. Use the test dataset or a few thousand samples from the training dataset and use the VAE decoder to generate the latent vectors.

2. Separate the latent vectors into two groups: with (positive) or without (negative) the one attribute we are interested in.

3. Calculate the average of the positive vectors and negative vectors separately.

4. Obtain the attribute direction vector by subtracting the average negative vector from the average positive vector.

The pre-processing function is modified to return the label of the attribute we are interested in. We then use a `lambda` function to map to the data pipeline:

```
def preprocess_attrib(sample, attribute):
    image = sample['image']
    image = tf.image.resize(image, [112,112])
    image = tf.cast(image, tf.float32)/255.
    return image, sample['attributes'][attribute]
ds = ds.map(lambda x: preprocess_attrib(x, attribute))
```

Not to be confused with the Keras Lambda layer that wraps arbitrary TensorFlow functions into a Keras layer, the `lambda` in the code is a generic Python expression. The `lambda` function is used as a small function but without the overhead code to define the function. The `lambda` function in the preceding code is equivalent to the following function:

```
def preprocess(x):
        return preprocess_attrib(x, attribute))
```

When chaining `map` to the dataset, the dataset object will read each image sequentially and call the `lambda` function equivalent to `preprocess(image)`.

Face editing

With the attribute vectors extracted, we can now do the magic:

1. First, we take an image from the dataset, which is the leftmost face from the following screenshot.

2. We encode the face into latent variables, then decode it to generate a new face, which we place in the middle of the row.

3. Then we add the attribute vector increasingly toward the right.

4. Similarly, we minus the attribute vector while going toward the left of the row.

The following screenshot shows the generated images by interpolating the latent vector for male, chubby, moustache, smiling, and glasses:

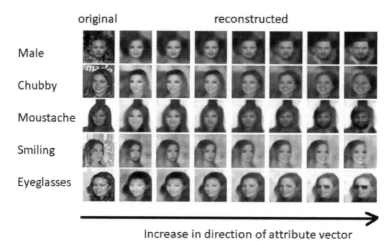

Figure 2.18 – Changing facial features by exploring latent space

The transitions were rather smooth. You should have noticed that these attributes are not exclusive to each other. For example, as we increase the moustache-ness of a female, the complexion and hair become more manlike, and the VAE even puts a tie on the person. This is totally reasonable, and in fact what we wanted. This shows that some latent variable distributions overlap.

Similarly, some latent variables do not overlap if we set the male vector to be the most negative. It will push the latent states to a place where traversing the moustache vector will not have an effect on growing a moustache on the face.

Next, we can try to change several face attributes together. The mathematics are similar; we now only need to add up all the attribute vectors. In the following screenshot, the image on the left was generated randomly and is used as a baseline. On the right is a new image after some latent space arithmetic, as shown in the bars preceding the images:

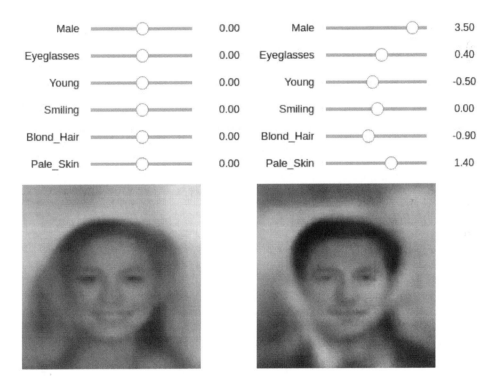

Figure 2.19 – Latent space exploration widget

The widget is available in the Jupyter notebook. Feel free to use it to explore the latent space and generate new faces!

Summary

We started this chapter by learning how to use an encoder to compress high-dimensional data into low-dimensional latent variables, then use a decoder to reconstruct the data from the latent variables. We learned that the autoencoder's limitation is not being able to guarantee a continuous and uniform latent space, which makes it difficult to sample from. Then we incorporated Gaussian sampling to build a VAE to generate MNIST digits.

Finally, we built a bigger VAE to train on the face dataset and had fun creating and manipulating faces. We learned the importance of the sampling distribution in the latent space, latent space arithmetic, and KLD, which lay the foundation for *Chapter 3, Generative Adversarial Network*.

Although GANs are more powerful than VAEs in generating photorealistic images, the earlier GANs were difficult to train. Therefore, we will learn about the fundamentals of GANs. By the end of the next chapter, you will have learned the fundamentals of all three main families of deep generative algorithms, which will prepare you for more advanced models in part two of the book.

Before we move on to GANs, I should stress that (variational) autoencoders are still being used widely. The variational encoding aspect has been incorporated into GANs. Therefore, mastering VAEs will help you master the advanced GAN models that we will cover in later chapters. We will cover the use of autoencoders to generate deep fake videos in *Chapter 9, Video Synthesis*. That chapter doesn't assume prior knowledge of GANs, therefore feel free to jump ahead to have a peek at how to use autoencoders to perform face swapping.

3
Generative Adversarial Network

Generative Adversarial Network, more commonly known as **GANs**, are currently the most prominent method in image and video generation. As the inventor of the convolutional neural network, Dr. Yann LeCun, said in 2016, *"...it is the most interesting idea in the last 10 years in machine learning."* The images generated using GANs are superior, in terms of realism, to other competing technologies and things have advanced tremendously since their invention in 2014 by then graduate student Ian Goodfellow.

In this chapter, we will first learn about the fundamentals of GANs and build a DCGAN to generate Fashion MNIST. We'll learn about the challenges in training GANs. Finally, we will learn how to build a WGAN and its variant, WGAN-GP, to resolve many of the challenges involved in generating faces.

In this chapter, we will cover the following topics:

- Understanding the fundamentals of GANs
- Building a Deep Convolutional GAN (DCGAN)
- Challenges in training GANs
- Building a Wasserstein GAN (WGAN)

Technical requirements

The Jupyter notebooks and code can be found here:

```
https://github.com/PacktPublishing/Hands-On-Image-Generation-
with-TensorFlow-2.0/tree/master/Chapter03
```

The notebooks used in the chapter are as follows:

- `ch3_dcgan.ipynb`
- `ch3_mode_collapse`
- `ch3_wgan_fashion_mnist.ipynb`
- `ch3_wgan_gp_fashion_mnist.ipynb`
- `ch3_wgan_gp_celeb_a.ipynb`

Understanding the fundamentals of GANs

The purpose of generative models is to learn a data distribution and to sample from it to generate new data. With the models that we looked at in the previous chapters, namely PixelCNN and VAE, their generative part gets to look at the image distribution during training. Thus, they are known as **explicit density models**. In contrast, the generative part in a GAN never gets to look at the images directly; rather, it is only told whether the generated images look real or fake. For this reason, GANs are categorized as **implicit density models**.

We could use an analogy to compare the explicit and implicit models. Let's say an art student, G, was given a collection of Picasso paintings and asked to learn how to draw fake Picasso paintings. The student can look at the collections as they learn to paint, so that is an explicit model. In a different scenario, we ask student G to forge Picasso paintings, but we don't show them any paintings and they don't know what a Picasso painting looks like. The only way they learn is from the feedback they get from student D, who is learning to spot fake Picasso paintings. The feedback is simple – the painting is either *fake* or *real*. That is our implicit density GAN model.

Perhaps one day they painted a twisted face by chance and learned from the feedback that it looked like a real Picasso painting. Then they start to draw in that style to fool student D. Students G and D are the two networks in a GAN, known as the **generator** and **discriminator**. This is the biggest difference in the network architecture compared with other generative models.

We will start this chapter by learning about the GAN building blocks, followed by the losses. The original GAN does not have reconstruction loss, which is another thing that sets it apart from other algorithms. Then, we will create custom training steps for a GAN, and we'll be ready to train our first GAN.

The architecture of a GAN

The word *adversarial* in Generative Adversarial Network means *involving opposition or disagreement* according to the dictionary definition. There are two networks, known as the generator and discriminator, that compete with each other. The generator, as the name implies, generates *fake* images; while the discriminator will look at the generated images to decide whether they are real or fake. Each network is trying to win the game – the discriminator wants to correctly identify every real and fake image and the generator wants to fool the discriminator into believing the fake images generated by it are real. The following diagram shows the architecture of a GAN:

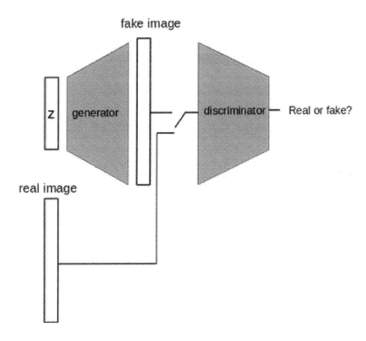

Figure 3.1 – Architecture of a GAN

The GAN architecture bears some resemblance to a VAE (see *Chapter 2, Variational Autoencoder*). In fact, you could rearrange the blocks in a VAE block diagram and add some lines and switches to produce this GAN block diagram. If a VAE was made up of two separate networks, we could think of:

- The GAN's generator as the VAE's decoder
- The GAN's discriminator as the VAE's encoder

The generator converts low-dimensional and simple distributions into high-dimensional images with a complex distribution, just like a decoder does. In fact, they are identical; we could simply copy and paste the decoder code and rename it as the generator, and vice versa, and it would just work. The input to the generator is usually samples from a normal distribution, despite some using uniform distribution.

We send real and fake images to the discriminator in different minibatches. Real images are those from the dataset while fake images are generated by the generator. The discriminator outputs a single value probability of whether the input is real or fake. It is a binary classifier and we could implement it using a CNN. Technically, the discriminator serves a different purpose than the encoder but they both reduce the dimensionality of their inputs.

Well, it turns out having two networks in a model is not that scary after all. The generator and discriminator are our old friends in disguise and under new names. We already know how to build those models, therefore let's not worry about the details of constructing them now. In fact, the original GAN paper used only a multilayer perceptron, which is made up of some basic dense layers.

Value functions

The value function captures the fundamentals of how a GAN works. The equation is as follows:

$$min_G \; max_D V(D, G) = \mathrm{E}_{x \sim P_{data}(x)}[\log D(x)] + \mathrm{E}_{z \sim P_z(z)}[\log(1 - D(G(z)))]$$

Here:

- D stands for discriminator.
- G is the generator.
- x is input data and z is a latent variable.

We will also use the same notation in the code. This is the function that the generator tries to minimize while the discriminator wants to maximize it.

When you understand it, the code implementation will be a lot easier and will make a lot of sense. Furthermore, much of our later discussion about the challenges of GANs and improvements to it revolves around the loss function. Therefore, it is well worth your time studying it. The GAN loss function is also known as **adversarial loss** in some literature. It looks rather complex now, but I'll break it down and show you step by step how it can be converted into simple loss functions that we can implement.

Discriminator loss

The first right-hand term of the value function is the value to classify a real image correctly. From the left-hand term, we know the discriminator wants to maximize it. **Expectation** is a mathematical term that is the sum of the weighted average of every sample of a random variable. In this equation, the weight is the probability of data, and the variable is the log of the discriminator output as follows:

$$E_X(logD(x)) = \sum_{i=1}^{N} p(x)logD(x) = \frac{1}{N}\sum_{i=1}^{N} logD(x)$$

In a minibatch of size N, p(x) is 1/N. This is because x is a single image. Instead of trying to maximize it, we can change the sign to minus and try to minimize it instead. This can be done with the help of the following equation, called the **log loss**:

$$min_D V(D) = -\frac{1}{N}\sum_{i=1}^{N} logD(x) = -\frac{1}{N}\sum_{i=1}^{N} y_i \log p(y_i)$$

Here:

- y_i is the label, which is *1* for real images.
- $p(y_i)$ is the probability of the sample being real.

The second right-hand term of the value function is about fake images; z is random noise and G(z) is generated fake images. D(G(z)) is the discriminator's confidence score of how likely the image is to be real. If we use a label of 0 for fake images, we can use the same method to cast it into the following equation:

$$-E_{z\sim P_z(z)}[\log(1 - D(G(z)))] = -\frac{1}{N}\sum_{i=1}^{N} (1 - y_i)\log(1 - p(y_i))$$

Now, putting everything together, we have our discriminator loss function, which is binary cross-entropy loss:

$$min_D V(D) = -\frac{1}{N}\sum_{i=1}^{N} y_i \log p(y_i) + (1 - y_i)\log(1 - p(y_i))$$

The following code shows how to implement the discriminator loss. You can find the code in Jupyter notebook `ch3_dcgan.ipynb`:

```
import tf.keras.losses.binary_crossentropy as bce
def discriminator_loss(pred_fake, pred_real):
    real_loss = bce(tf.ones_like(pred_real), pred_real)
    fake_loss = bce(tf.zeros_like(pred_fake), pred_fake)
    d_loss = 0.5 *(real_loss + fake_loss)
    return d_loss
```

In our training, we do a forward pass on real and fake images separately using the same minibatch size. Therefore, we compute the binary cross-entropy loss for them separately and take the average as the loss.

Generator loss

The generator is only involved when the model is evaluating fake images, thus we only need to look at the second right-hand term of the value function and simplify it to this:

$$min_G V(G) = E_{z \sim P_z(z)}[\log(1 - D(G(z)))]$$

At the beginning of the training, the generator is not good at generating images, therefore the discriminator is confident in classifying it as *0* all the time, making *D(G(z))* always *0*, and so is *log (1 – 0)*. When the error in the model output is always *0*, then there is no gradient to backpropagate. As a result, the generator's weights are not updated, and the generator is not learning. This phenomenon is known as **saturating gradient** due to there being almost no gradient in the discriminator's sigmoid output. To avoid this problem, the equation is cast from minimizing *1-D(G(z))* to maximizing *D(G(z))* as follows:

$$max_G V(G) = E_{z \sim P_z(z)}[\log(D(G(z)))]$$

GANs that use this function are also known as **Non-Saturating GANs (NS-GANs)**. In fact, almost every implementation of **Vanilla GAN** uses this value function rather than the original GAN function.

> **Vanilla GAN**
>
> The interest of researchers in GANs exploded soon after their invention and many researchers gave their GAN a name. Some tried to keep track of all the named GANs over the years, but the list got too long. Vanilla GAN is the name used to loosely refer to the first basic GAN without fancy flavors. Vanilla GAN is usually implemented with two or three hidden dense layers.

We can derive the generator loss using the same mathematical steps for the discriminator, which will eventually lead to the same discriminator loss function except that labels of one is used for real images. It can be confusing to beginners as to why to use real labels for fake images. It will be clear if we derive the equation, or we can also understand it as we want to fool the discriminator into assuming that those generated images are real, thus we use the real labels. The code is as follows:

```
def generator_loss(pred_fake):
    g_loss = bce(tf.ones_like(pred_fake), pred_fake)
    return g_loss
```

Congratulations, you have turned the most complex equation in a GAN into simple binary cross-entropy loss and implemented it in a few lines of code! Now let's look at the GAN training pipeline.

GAN training steps

To train a conventional neural network in TensorFlow or any other high-level machine learning framework, we specify the model, loss function, optimizer, and then call `model.fit()`. TensorFlow will do all the work for us – we just sit there and wait for the loss to drop. Unfortunately, we cannot chain the generator and discriminator to be a single model, like we did for the VAE, and call `model.fit()` to train the GAN.

Before delving into the GAN problem, let's take a pause and refresh ourselves on what happens underneath the hood when doing a single training step:

1. Perform a forward pass to compute the loss.
2. From the loss, backpropagate the gradients backward with respect to the variables (weights and biases).
3. Then, it's the variables update step. The optimizer will scale the gradients and add them to the variables, which completes one training step.

These are the generic training steps in a deep neural network. The various optimizers differ only in how they calculate the scaling factors.

Now come back to the GAN and look at the flow of gradients. When we train with real images, only the discriminator is involved – the network input is a real image and the output is a label of *1*. The generator plays no role here and therefore we can't use `model.fit()`. However, we could still fit the model using the discriminator only, that is, `D.fit()` so that it is not the blocking issue. The problem arises when we use fake images and the gradients backpropagate to the generator via the discriminator. So, what is the problem? Let's take the generator loss and discriminator loss for the fake image and put them side by side:

```
g_loss = bce(tf.ones_like(pred_fake), pred_fake)
# generator
fake_loss = bce(tf.zeros_like(pred_fake), pred_fake)
# generator
```

If you try to spot the difference between them, then you'll find that their labels are opposite signs! This means, using generator loss to train the entire model will make the discriminator move in the opposite direction and not learn to discriminate. This is counterproductive and we don't want to have an untrained discriminator that will discourage the generator from learning. For this reason, we must train the generator and discriminator separately. We will freeze the discriminator's variables when training the generator.

There are two ways to design a GAN training pipeline. One is to use the high-level Keras model, which needs less code and therefore looks more elegant. We'll only need to define the model once, and call `train_on_batch()` to perform all the steps, including the forward pass, backpropagation, and weights update. However, it is less flexible when it comes to implementing more complex loss functions.

The other method is to use low-level code so we can control every step. For our first GAN, we will use a low-level custom training step function from the official TensorFlow GAN tutorial (`https://www.tensorflow.org/tutorials/generative/dcgan`), as shown in the following code:

```
def train_step(g_input, real_input):
    with tf.GradientTape() as g_tape,\
        tf.GradientTape() as d_tape:
        # Forward pass
        fake_input = G(g_input)
        pred_fake = D(fake_input)
        pred_real = D(real_input)
        # Calculate losses
```

```
d_loss = discriminator_loss(pred_fake, pred_real)
g_loss = generator_loss(pred_fake)
```

`tf.GradientTape()` is used to record the gradients of a single pass. You may have seen another API, `tf.Gradient()`, that has a similar function, but the latter does not work in TensorFlow eager execution. We will see how the three procedural steps mentioned previously get implemented in `train_step()`. The preceding code snippet shows the first step to carry out a forward pass to calculate the losses.

The second step is to calculate the gradient of the generator and discriminator from their respective losses using a tape gradient:

```
gradient_g = g_tape.gradient(g_loss,\
                    G.trainable_variables)
gradient_d = d_tape.gradient(d_loss,\
                    D.trainable_variables)
```

The third and final step is to use the optimizer to apply the gradients to the variables:

```
G_optimizer.apply_gradients(zip(gradient_g,
                    self.G.trainable_variables))
D_optimizer.apply_gradients(zip(gradient_d,
                    self.D.trainable_variables))
```

You have now learned everything you need to train a GAN. What is left to be done is to set up the input pipeline, generator, and discriminator, and we will go over that in the coming section.

Custom model fit

After TensorFlow 2.2, it is now possible to create a custom `train_step()` for a Keras model without re-writing the entire training pipeline. Then, we can use `model.fit()` in the usual way. This will also enable the use of multiple GPUs for training. Unfortunately, this new feature was not released in time to make it into the code in this book. However, do check out the TensorFlow tutorial at `https://www.tensorflow.org/guide/keras/customizing_what_happens_in_fit` and feel free to modify the GAN's code to use a custom model fit.

Building a Deep Convolutional GAN (DCGAN)

Although Vanilla GAN has proven itself as a generative model, it suffers from a few training problems. One of them is the difficulty in scaling networks to make them deeper in order to increase their capacities. The authors of **DCGAN** incorporated a few recent advancements in CNNs at that time to make networks deeper and stabilize the training. These include the removal of the **maxpool** layer, replacing it with strided convolutions for downsampling, and the removal of fully connected layers. This has since become the standard way of designing a new CNN.

Architecture guidelines

DCGAN is not strictly a fixed neural network that has layers pre-defined with a fixed set of parameters such as kernel size and the number of layers. Instead, it is more like architecture design guidelines. The use of batch normalization, activation, and upsampling in DCGAN has influenced the development of GANs. We will therefore look into them more, which should provide guidance in designing our own GAN.

Batch normalization

Batch normalization is informally called **batchnorm** within the machine learning community. In the early days of deep neural network training, a layer updated its weights after backpropagation to produce outputs that are closer to the targets. However, the weights of the subsequent layers have also changed, so it is like a moving goal, and this makes the training of deep networks difficult. Batchnorm solves this by normalizing the input to every layer to have zero mean and unity variance, hence stabilizing the training. These are operations that happen within batchnorm:

- Calculate the mean μ and standard deviation σ of tensor x in a minibatch for every channel (hence the name *batch* normalization).
- Normalize the tensor: $x' = (x - \mu) / \sigma$.
- Perform an affine transformation: $y = \alpha * x' + \beta$, where α and β are trainable variables.

In a DCGAN, batchnorm is added to both the generator and discriminator, except for the first layer of the discriminator and the last layer of the generator. One thing to note is that newer researches show that batchnorm is not the best normalization technique to use for image generation as it removes some of the important information. We will look at other normalization techniques in later chapters, but we will keep using batchnorm in our GAN until then. One thing that we should know is that in order to use batchnorm, we will have to use a large minibatch, otherwise, the batch statistics can vary greatly from batch to batch and make the training unstable.

Activations

The following figure shows the activations that we will use in DCGAN:

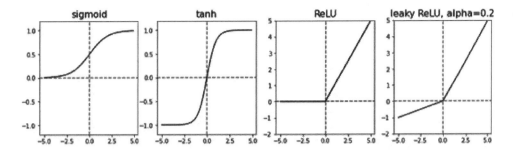

Figure 3.2 – ReLU and leaky ReLU are used in intermediate layers of the generator and discriminator

As the discriminator's job is to be a binary classifier, we use sigmoid to squeeze the output to within the range of *0* (fake) and *1* (real). On the other hand, the generator's output uses *tanh*, which bounds the images between *-1* and *+1*. Therefore, we will need to scale our images to this range in the preprocessing step.

For intermediate layers, the generator uses ReLU in all layers, but the discriminator uses leaky ReLU instead. In standard ReLU, the activation increases linearly with positive input but is zero for all negative input values. This limits the gradient flow when it is negative and thus the generator does not receive gradients in order to update its weights and learn. Leaky ReLU alleviates that problem by allowing small gradients to flow when the activation is negative.

As we can see in the preceding figure, for input above and equal to *0*, it is identical to ReLU where the output equals input with a slope of *1*. For input below *0*, the output is scaled to *0.2* of the input. The default slope of leaky ReLU in TensorFlow is *0.3* while the DCGAN uses *0.2*. It is just a hyperparameter and you are free to try any other values.

Upsampling

In DCGAN, upsampling in the generator is performed using the transpose convolutional layer. However, it has been shown that this will produce a checkerboard pattern in the generated image, especially in images with strong colors. As a result, we replace it with `UpSampling2D`, which performs conventional image resizing methods by using bilinear interpolation.

Building a DCGAN for Fashion-MNIST

The Jupyter notebook for this exercise is `ch3_dcgan.ipynb`.

MNIST has been used in many introductory machine learning tutorials and we are all familiar with it. With recent advancements in machine learning, this dataset began to look a bit trivial for deep learning. As a result, a new dataset, Fashion-MNIST, has been created as a direct drop-in replacement for the MNIST dataset. It has exactly the same number of training and test examples, 28x28 grayscale images of 10 classes. This is what we will train our DCGAN with.

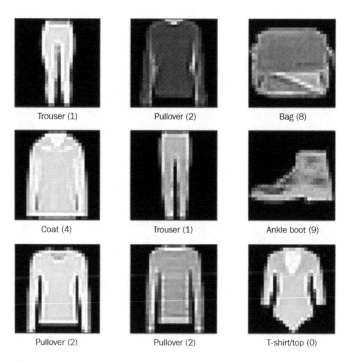

Figure 3.3 – Examples of images from the Fashion-MNIST dataset

Generator

The design of the generator can be broken into two parts:

- Convert the 1D latent vector into a 3D activation map.

- Double the activation map's spatial resolution until it matches the target image.

The first thing to do is to work out the number of upsampling stages. As the images have a shape of 28x28, we can use two upsampling stages to increase the dimension from 7->14->28.

For simple data, we can use one convolution layer per upsampling stage, but we could also use more layers. This method is similar to CNNs in that you have several convolution layers working on the same spatial resolution before downsampling.

Next, we will decide the channel numbers of the first convolutional layer. Let's say we use [512, 256, 128, 1], where the last channel number is the image channel number. With this information, we know the neuron numbers in first dense layer to be 7 x 7 x 512. The 7x7 is the spatial resolution we worked out and 512 is the filter number in the first convolutional layer. After the dense layer, we reshape it to (7,7,512) so it can be fed into a convolutional layer. Then, we only need to define the filter number of convolutional layers and add the batchnorm and ReLU, as shown in the following code:

```python
def Generator(self, z_dim):
    model = tf.keras.Sequential(name='Generator')
    model.add(layers.Input(shape=[z_dim]))
    model.add(layers.Dense(7*7*512))
    model.add(layers.BatchNormalization(momentum=0.9))
    model.add(layers.LeakyReLU())
    model.add(layers.Reshape((7,7,512)))
    model.add(layers.UpSampling2D((2,2),
                interpolation="bilinear"))
    model.add(layers.Conv2D(256, 3, padding='same'))
    model.add(layers.BatchNormalization(momentum=0.9))
    model.add(layers.LeakyReLU())
    model.add(layers.UpSampling2D((2,2),
                interpolation="bilinear"))
    model.add(layers.Conv2D(128, 3, padding='same'))
    model.add(layers.LeakyReLU())
    model.add(layers.Conv2D(image_shape[-1], 3,
                padding='same', activation='tanh'))
    return model
```

The model summary for the generator is as follows:

```
Model: "Generator"
```

Layer (type)	Output Shape	Param #
dense_1 (Dense)	(None, 25088)	2533888
batch_normalization_2 (Batch	(None, 25088)	100352
leaky_re_lu (LeakyReLU)	(None, 25088)	0
reshape (Reshape)	(None, 7, 7, 512)	0
up_sampling2d (UpSampling2D)	(None, 14, 14, 512)	0
conv2d_2 (Conv2D)	(None, 14, 14, 256)	1179904
batch_normalization_3 (Batch	(None, 14, 14, 256)	1024
leaky_re_lu_1 (LeakyReLU)	(None, 14, 14, 256)	0
up_sampling2d_1 (UpSampling2	(None, 28, 28, 256)	0
conv2d_3 (Conv2D)	(None, 28, 28, 128)	295040
leaky_re_lu_2 (LeakyReLU)	(None, 28, 28, 128)	0
conv2d_4 (Conv2D)	(None, 28, 28, 1)	1153

```
Total params: 4,111,361
Trainable params: 4,060,673
Non-trainable params: 50,688
```

Figure 3.4 – DCGAN generator model summary

The generator's model summary shows the activation map shapes that are doubling in spatial resolution (7×7 to 14×14 to 28×28) while halving in the channel numbers (512 to 256 to 128).

Discriminator

The design of the discriminator is straightforward, just like a simple classifier CNN but with leaky ReLU as activation. As a matter of fact, the discriminator architecture was not even mentioned in the DCGAN paper. As a rule of thumb, the discriminator should have fewer or an equal number of layers as the generator, so it doesn't overpower the generator to stop the latter from learning. The following is the code to create the discriminator:

```python
def Discriminator(self, input_shape):
    model = tf.keras.Sequential(name='Discriminator')
    model.add(layers.Input(shape=input_shape))
    model.add(layers.Conv2D(32, 3, strides=(2,2),
                            padding='same'))
```

```
model.add(layers.BatchNormalization(momentum=0.9))
model.add(layers.ReLU())
model.add(layers.Conv2D(64, 3, strides=(2,2),
                        padding='same'))
model.add(layers.BatchNormalization(momentum=0.9))
model.add(layers.ReLU())
model.add(layers.Flatten())
model.add(layers.Dense(1, activation='sigmoid'))
return model
```

The model summary of the discriminator, which is a simple CNN classifier, is shown as follows:

```
Model: "Discriminator"

Layer (type)                    Output Shape              Param #
=================================================================
conv2d (Conv2D)                 (None, 14, 14, 32)        320

batch_normalization (BatchNo    (None, 14, 14, 32)        128

re_lu (ReLU)                    (None, 14, 14, 32)        0

conv2d_1 (Conv2D)               (None, 7, 7, 64)          18496

batch_normalization_1 (Batch    (None, 7, 7, 64)          256

re_lu_1 (ReLU)                  (None, 7, 7, 64)          0

flatten (Flatten)               (None, 3136)              0

dense (Dense)                   (None, 1)                 3137
=================================================================
Total params: 22,337
Trainable params: 22,145
Non-trainable params: 192
```

Figure 3.5 – DCGAN discriminator model summary

Training our DCGAN

Now we can start training our first GAN. The following diagram shows the samples generated during different steps in the training:

Figure 3.6 – Generated images during DCGAN training

The first row of samples is generated right after network weight initialization and before any training steps. As we can see, they are just some random noise. As training progresses, the generated images become better. However, the generator loss is higher than when it was only generating random noise.

The loss is not an absolute measurement of generated image quality; it merely provides relative terms to compare the performance of the generator relative to the discriminator and vice versa. The generator loss was low simply because the discriminator had not learned to do its job well. This is one of the challenges of a GAN where the loss does not give sufficient information about the model's quality.

The following graphs show the discriminator loss and generator loss during training:

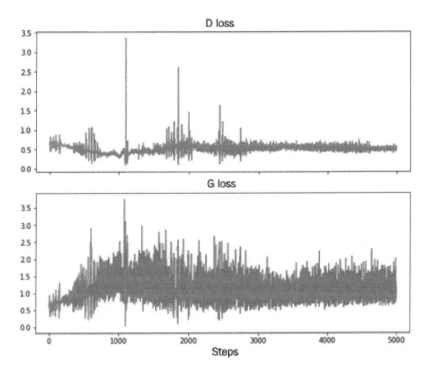

Figure 3.7 – Discriminator and generator training losses

We can see that the equilibrium achieved in the first 1,000 steps and the loss remain roughly stable after that. However, the loss isn't definitive in gauging when to stop training. For now, we can save the weights every few epochs and eyeball to select the one that generates the best-looking images!

In theory, the global optimal for the discriminator is achieved when *pdiscriminator* = *pdata*. In other words, if *pdata* = *0.5* as half of the data is real and half is fake, then *pdiscriminator* = *0.5* will mean it can no longer distinguish between the two classes and the prediction is no better than flipping a coin.

Challenges in training GANs

GANs are notoriously difficult to train. We'll discuss some of the main challenges in training a GAN.

Uninformative loss and metrics

When training a CNN for classification or detection tasks, we can look at the shape of the loss plots to tell whether the network has converged or is overfitting and we'll know when to stop training. Then the metrics will correlate with the loss. For example, classification accuracy is normally the highest when the loss is the lowest. However, we can't do the same with GAN loss, as it doesn't have a minimum but fluctuates around some constant values after training for a while. We also could not correlate the generated image quality with the loss. A few metrics were invented to address this in the early days of GANs and one of them is the **inception score.**

A classification CNN known as **inception** is used to predict the confidence score of an image belonging to one of 1,000 categories in the ImageNet dataset. If high confidence is recorded for a class, it is more likely to be a real image. There is another metric known as the **Fréchet inception distance**, which measures the variety of generated images. These metrics are normally used only in academic papers to make a comparison with other models (so they can claim their models are superior), so we will not cover them in detail in this book. Human visual inspection is still the most reliable way of assessing the quality of generated images.

Instability

GANs are extremely sensitive to any change in hyperparameters, including learning rate and filter kernel size. Even after a lot of hyperparameter tuning, and the correct architecture, there are instances while retraining the model where the following can occur:

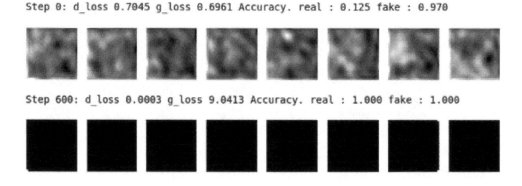

Figure 3.8 – Generator stuck in local minima

If the network weights are unfortunately randomly initialized to some bad values, the generator could get stuck in some bad local minima and may never recover, while the discriminator keeps improving. As a result, the generator gives up and produces only nonsensical images. This is also known as **convergence failure**, where the losses fail to converge. We'll need to stop the training, re-initialize the network, and restart the training. This is also the reason why I haven't chosen a more complex dataset such as CelebA to introduce GANs, but don't worry, we'll get there before the chapter ends.

Vanishing gradient

One reason for instability is the vanishing gradient of the generator. As we've already mentioned, when we train the generator, the gradient will flow through the discriminator. If the discriminator is confident that the images are fake, then there will be little or even zero gradient to backpropagate to the generator. The following points are some of the methods of mitigation:

- Reformulating the value function from minimizing log *(1-D(G(z))* to maximizing log *D(G(z))*, which we already did. In practice, this alone is still not enough.

- Using activation functions that allow more gradients to flow, such as leaky ReLU.

- Balancing between the generator and the discriminator by reducing the discriminator's network capacity or increasing the training steps for the generator.

- Using *one-sided label smoothing,* where the label of the real image is decreased from *1* to, say, *0.9* to reduce the discriminator's confidence.

Mode collapse

Mode collapse happens when the generator is producing images that look like each other. This is not to be confused with convergence failure where the GAN produces only garbage images.

Mode collapse can happen even when the generated images look great but are limited to small subsets of classes (inter-class mode collapse) or a few of the same images within the class (intra-class mode collapse). We can demonstrate mode collapse by training a Vanilla GAN on a mixture of two Gaussian distributions, which you could run in the ch3_mode_collapse notebook.

The following figure shows the shape of the generated samples during training taking the form of two Gaussian blobs. One sample is round and the other is elliptical:

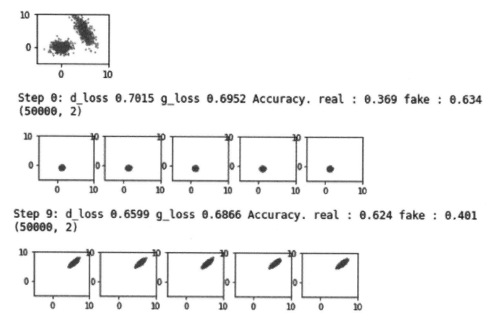

Figure 3.9 – The top figure is the real samples. The bottom figures show generated samples in two different epochs during training

As the Vanilla GAN trains, the generated samples can look like one of two modes in a minibatch but never two modes at the same time. For Fashion-MNIST, it may be that the generator is producing shoes that look the same every time, regardless. After all, the objective of the generator is to produce realistic-looking images, and it is not penalized for showing the same shoes every time as long as the discriminator deems the images to be real. As proven in the original GAN paper mathematically, after the discriminator achieved optimality, the generator will work toward optimizing for **Jensen-Shannon divergence (JSD)**.

For our purposes, we only need to know that JSD is a symmetrical version of **Kullback-Leibler divergence (KLD)** with an upper bound of *log(2)* rather than an infinite upper bound. Unfortunately, JSD is also the cause of mode collapse, as can be illustrated in the following figure:

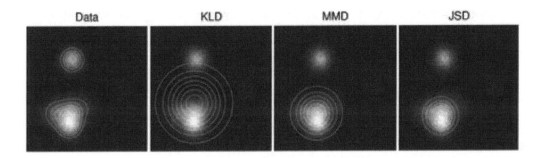

Figure 3.10 – A standard Gaussian distribution fit on data drawn from a mixture of Gaussians by minimizing KLD, MMD, and JSD (Source: L. Theis et al, 2016, "A Note On The Evaluation of Generative Models," https://arxiv.org/abs/1511.01844)

We will not talk about **maximum mean discrepancy** (**MMD**), which is not used in a GAN. The data is two Gaussian distributions where one has more mass density than the other. A single Gaussian is fitted on the data. In other words, we try to estimate one best mean and standard deviation to describe the two type of Gaussian distribution. With KLD, we see that although the fitted Gaussian leans toward the bigger Gaussian blob, it still provides some coverage to the smaller Gaussian blob. This is not the case for JSD, where it is fitted to only the most prominent Gaussian blob. This explains mode collapse in a GAN – when the probability of some particular generated images is high, when these few modes are *locked* by the optimizer.

Building a Wasserstein GAN

Many have attempted to solve the instability of GAN training by using heuristic approaches such as trying different network architectures, hyperparameters, and optimizers. One major breakthrough happened in 2016 with the introduction of **Wasserstein GAN (WGAN)**.

WGAN alleviates or even eliminates many of the GAN challenges we've discussed altogether. It no longer requires careful design of network architecture nor careful balancing of the discriminator and the generator. The mode collapse problem is also reduced drastically.

The biggest fundamental improvement from the original GAN is the change of the loss function. The theory is that if the two distributions are disjointed, JSD will no longer be continuous, hence not differentiable, resulting in a zero gradient. WGAN solves this by using a new loss function that is continuous and differentiable everywhere!

The notebook for this exercise is ch3_wgan_fashion_mnist.ipynb.

> **Tips**
>
> It is alright to not learn how to implement the code in this section, particularly WGAN-GP, which is more complex. Although theoretically superior, we could still train GANs stably using a simpler loss function with carefully designed model architecture and hyperparameters. However, you should try to understand the term Lipschitz constraint as it was used in the development of several advanced techniques, which we will cover in later chapters.

Understanding Wasserstein loss

Let's remind ourselves of the non-saturating value function:

$$E_{X \sim P_{data}(x)}[\log D(x)] + E_{z \sim P_z(z)}[\log D(G(z))]$$

WGAN uses a new loss function known as the **Earth mover's distance** or just Wasserstein distance. It measures the distance or the effort needed to transform one distribution into another. Mathematically, it is the minimum distance for every joint distribution between real and generated images, which is intractable, with some mathematical assumptions that are outside the scope of this book, and the value function becomes:

$$E_{X \sim P_{data}(x)}[D(x)] - E_{z \sim P_z(z)}[D(G(z))]$$

Now, let's compare the preceding equation with NS loss and use that to derive the loss function. The most prominent change is that the *log()* is gone, and another is the sign of the fake image term changes. The loss function of the first term is therefore:

$$-\frac{1}{N}\sum_{i=1}^{N} D(x) = -\frac{1}{N}\sum_{i=1}^{N} y_i D(x)$$

This is the average of the discriminator output, multiplied by -1. We can also generalize it by using y_i as labels where *+1 is for real images*, and *-1 is for fake images*. Thus, we can implement Wasserstein loss as a TensorFlow Keras custom loss function as follows:

```
def wasserstein_loss(self, y_true, y_pred):
    w_loss = -tf.reduce_mean(y_true*y_pred)
    return w_loss
```

As this loss function is no longer binary cross-entropy, the discriminator's objective is no longer classifying or discriminating between real and fake images. Instead, it aims to maximize the score for real images with respect to fake images. For this reason, in WGAN, the discriminator is given a new name of **critic**.

The generator and discriminator architecture stays the same. The only change is that the sigmoid is removed from the discriminator's output. Therefore, the critic's prediction is unbounded and can be very large positive and negative values. This is put in check by implementing the **1-Lipschitz** constraint.

Implementing the 1-Lipschitz constraint

The mathematical assumption mentioned in Wasserstein loss is the **1-Lipschitz function**. We say the critic $D(x)$ is *1-Lipschitz* if it satisfies the following inequality:

$$|D(x_1) - D(x_2)| \leq |x_1 - x_2|$$

For two images, x_1 and x_2, their absolute critic's output difference must be smaller or equal to their average pixel-wise absolute difference. In other words, the critic's outputs should not differ too much for different images – be it real images or fakes. When WGAN was invented, the authors could not think of a proper implementation to enforce inequality. Therefore, they came up with a hack, which is to clip the critic's weights to some small values. By doing that, the layers' outputs and eventually the critics' outputs are capped to some small values. In the WGAN paper, the weights are clipped to the range of *[-0.01, 0.01]*.

Weight clipping can be implemented in two ways. One way is to write a custom constraint function and use that in instantiating a new layer as follows:

```
class WeightsClip(tf.keras.constraints.Constraint):
    def __init__(self, min_value=-0.01, max_value=0.01):
        self.min_value = min_value
        self.max_value = max_value
    def __call__(self, w):
        return tf.clip_by_value(w, self.min,
                                self.max_value)
```

We can then pass the function to layers that accept constraint functions as follows:

```
model = tf.keras.Sequential(name='critics')
model.add(Conv2D(16, 3, strides=2, padding='same',
                 kernel_constraint=WeightsClip(),
```

```
                bias_constraint=WeightsClip()))
model.add(BatchNormalization(
                beta_constraint=WeightsClip(),
            gamma_constraint=WeightsClip()))
```

However, adding the constraint code in every layer creation can make the code look bloated. As we don't need to cherry-pick which layer to clip, we can use a loop to read the weights and clips and write them back as follows:

```
for layer in critic.layers:
    weights = layer.get_weights()
    weights = [tf.clip_by_value(w, -0.01, 0.01) for
            w in weights]
    layer.set_weights(weights)
```

This is the method we use in the code example.

Restructuring training steps

In the original GAN theory, the discriminator is supposed to be trained optimally before the generator. That was not possible in practice due to the vanishing gradient of the generator as the discriminator gets better. Now, with the Wasserstein loss function, the gradient is derivable everywhere and we don't have to worry about the critic being too good to compare with the generator.

Therefore, in WGAN, the critic is trained for five steps for every one training step for the generator. In order to do this, we will split the critic training step into a separate function, which we can then loop through multiple times:

```
for _ in range(self.n_critic):
    real_images = next(data_generator)
    critic_loss = self.train_critic(real_images,
                            batch_size)
```

We will also need to rework the generator training step. In our DCGAN code, we use two models – the generator and discriminator. To train the generator, we also use gradient tape to update the weights. All these are rather cumbersome. There is another way of implementing the training step for the generator by merging the two models into one as follows:

```
self.critic = self.build_critic()
self.critic.trainable = False
```

```
self.generator = self.build_generator()
critic_output = self.critic(self.generator.output)
self.model = Model(self.generator.input, critic_output)
self.model.compile(loss = self.wasserstein_loss,
                optimizer = RMSprop(3e-4))
self.critic.trainable = True
```

In the preceding code, we freeze the critic layers by setting `trainable=False`, and we chain that to the generator to create a new model and compile it. After that, we can set the critic to be trainable again, which will not affect the model that we have already compiled.

We use the `train_on_batch()` API to perform a single training step that will automatically do the forward pass, loss calculation, backpropagation, and weights update:

```
g_loss = self.model.train_on_batch(g_input,
                                real_labels)
```

For this exercise, we resize the image shape to 32x32 so we can use deeper layers in the generator to upscale the image. The WGAN generator and discriminator architecture are shown in the following model summaries:

```
Model: "Generator"

Layer (type)                 Output Shape              Param #
=================================================================
dense_1 (Dense)              (None, 8192)              1056768

batch_normalization_2 (Batch (None, 8192)              32768

re_lu (ReLU)                 (None, 8192)              0

reshape (Reshape)            (None, 4, 4, 512)         0

up_sampling2d (UpSampling2D) (None, 8, 8, 512)         0

conv2d_3 (Conv2D)            (None, 8, 8, 256)         3277056

batch_normalization_3 (Batch (None, 8, 8, 256)         1024

re_lu_1 (ReLU)               (None, 8, 8, 256)         0

up_sampling2d_1 (UpSampling2 (None, 16, 16, 256)       0

conv2d_4 (Conv2D)            (None, 16, 16, 128)       819328

batch_normalization_4 (Batch (None, 16, 16, 128)       512

re_lu_2 (ReLU)               (None, 16, 16, 128)       0

up_sampling2d_2 (UpSampling2 (None, 32, 32, 128)       0

conv2d_5 (Conv2D)            (None, 32, 32, 1)         3201
=================================================================
Total params: 5,190,657
Trainable params: 5,173,505
Non-trainable params: 17,152
```

Figure 3.11 – Model summary of the WGAN's generator

The generator architecture follows the usual design with decreasing channel numbers as the feature map's size doubles. The following is the model summary of the WGAN's critic:

```
Model: "critics"

Layer (type)                    Output Shape            Param #
=================================================================
conv2d (Conv2D)                 (None, 16, 16, 128)     3328

leaky_re_lu (LeakyReLU)         (None, 16, 16, 128)     0

conv2d_1 (Conv2D)               (None, 8, 8, 256)       819456

batch_normalization (BatchNo    (None, 8, 8, 256)       1024

leaky_re_lu_1 (LeakyReLU)       (None, 8, 8, 256)       0

conv2d_2 (Conv2D)               (None, 4, 4, 512)       3277312

batch_normalization_1 (Batch    (None, 4, 4, 512)       2048

leaky_re_lu_2 (LeakyReLU)       (None, 4, 4, 512)       0

flatten (Flatten)               (None, 8192)            0

dense (Dense)                   (None, 1)               8193
=================================================================
Total params: 4,111,361
Trainable params: 4,109,825
Non-trainable params: 1,536
```

Figure 3.12 – Model summary of the WGAN's critic

Despite the improvement over DCGAN, I found it difficult to train a WGAN and the image quality produced is no more superior than DCGAN. We'll now implement a WGAN variant that trains faster and produces sharper images.

Implementing gradient penalty (WGAN-GP)

Weight clipping is not an ideal way to enforce a Lipschitz constraint, as acknowledged by the WGAN authors. There are two drawbacks: capacity underuse and exploding/vanishing gradients. As we limit the weights, we also limit the critic's ability to learn. It was found that weight clipping forces the network to learn only simple functions. Therefore, the neural network's capacity becomes underused.

Secondly, the clipping values require careful tuning. If set too high, the gradients will explode, hence violating the Lipschitz constraint. If set too low, gradients will vanish as we move the network back. Also, the weight clipping will push the gradients to the two limits, as shown in the following diagram:

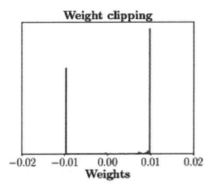
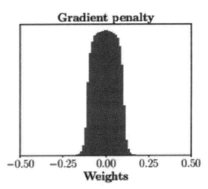

Figure 3.13 – Left: Weight clipping pushes weights toward two values. Right: Gradients produced by gradient penalty. Source: I. Gulrajani et al, 2017, Improved Training of Wasserstein GANs

As a result, **gradient penalty (GP)** is proposed to replace weight clipping to enforce the Lipschitz constraint as follows:

$$Gradient\ penalty = \lambda\ E_{\hat{x}}[(\|\nabla_{\hat{x}} D(\hat{x})\|_2 - 1)^2]$$

We will look at each of the variables in the equation and implement them in the code. The Jupyter notebook for this exercise is `ch3_wgan_gp_fashion_mnist.ipynb`.

We normally use x to denote a real image, but there is now an $\hat{x}$ in the equation. This $\hat{x}$ is pointwise interpolation between a real image and a fake image. The ratio of the images, or the epsilon, is drawn from a uniform distribution of *[0,1]*:

```
epsilon = tf.random.uniform((batch_size,1,1,1))
interpolates = epsilon*real_images + \
                    (1-epsilon)*fake_images
```

There is mathematical proof that the *"optimal critic contains straight lines with gradient norm 1 connecting coupled points from Pr and Pg"*, as quoted from the WGAN-GP paper *Improved Training of Wasserstein GANs* (`https://arxiv.org/pdf/1704.00028.pdf`). For our purposes, we can understand it as the gradient comes from the mixture of both real and fake images and we don't need to calculate the penalty for real and fake images separately.

The term $\nabla_{\hat{x}} D(\hat{x})$ is the gradient of the critic's output with respect to the interpolation. We can again use gradient tape to get the gradient:

```
with tf.GradientTape() as gradient_tape:
    gradient_tape.watch(interpolates)
    critic_interpolates = self.critic(interpolates)
    gradient_d = gradient_tape.gradient(
```

```
                                   critic_interpolates,
                                   [interpolates])
```

The next step is to calculate the L2-norm:

$$\|\nabla_x D(x)\|_2$$

We square every value, add them together, then do a square root as follows:

```
grad_loss = tf.square(grad)
```

```
grad_loss = tf.reduce_sum(grad_loss,
                          axis=np.arange(1,
                              len(grad)loss.shape)))
```

```
graid_loss = tf.sqrt(grad_loss)
```

When doing `tf.reduce_sum()`, we exclude the first dimension in the axis as that dimension is the batch size. The penalty aims to bring the gradient norm close to `1`, and this is the last step to calculate the gradient loss:

```
grad_loss = tf.reduce_mean(tf.square(grad_loss - 1))
```

The lambda in the equation is the ratio of the gradient penalty to other critic losses and is set to 10 in the paper. Now we add all the critic losses and gradient penalty to backpropagate and update weights:

```
total_loss = loss_real + loss_fake + LAMBDA * grad_loss
```

```
gradients = total_tape.gradient(total_loss,
                                self.critic.variables)
```

```
self.optimizer_critic.apply_gradients(zip(gradients,
                                   self.critic.variables))
```

That is everything you'll need to add to the WGAN to make it WGAN-GP. There are two things to remove though:

- Weight clipping

- Batch normalization in the critic

The gradient penalty is to penalize the norm of the critic's gradient with respect to each input independently. However, batch normalization changes the gradients with the batch statistics. To avoid this problem, batch normalization was removed from the critic and it was found that it still works well. This has since become a common practice in GANs.

The critic architecture is the same as WGAN, less the batch normalization:

```
Model: "critics"

Layer (type)                Output Shape              Param #
=================================================================
conv2d_6 (Conv2D)           (None, 16, 16, 128)       3200

leaky_re_lu_3 (LeakyReLU)   (None, 16, 16, 128)       0

conv2d_7 (Conv2D)           (None, 8, 8, 256)         819200

leaky_re_lu_4 (LeakyReLU)   (None, 8, 8, 256)         0

conv2d_8 (Conv2D)           (None, 4, 4, 512)         3276800

leaky_re_lu_5 (LeakyReLU)   (None, 4, 4, 512)         0

flatten_1 (Flatten)         (None, 8192)              0

dense_2 (Dense)             (None, 1)                 8193
=================================================================
Total params: 4,107,393
Trainable params: 0
Non-trainable params: 4,107,393
```

Figure 3.14 – Model summary of WGAN-GP

The following are the samples generated by a trained WGAN-GP:

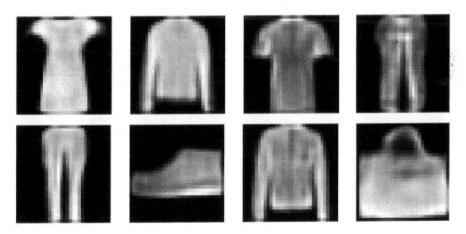

Figure 3.15 – Samples generated by WGAN-GP

They look sharp and pretty, much like samples from the Fashion-MNIST dataset. The training was very stable and converged quickly! Next, we will put WGAN-GP to the test by training it on CelebA!

Tweaking WGAN-GP for CelebA

We will make some small tweaks to WGAN-GP to train on the CelebA dataset. First, as we will use a larger image size of 64 compared to 32 previously, we will need to add another stage of upsampling. Then we replace the batch normalization with **layer normalization** as suggested by the WGAN-GP authors. The following figure shows different types of normalization for tensors with a dimension of **(N, H, W, C)** where the notations stand for batch size, height, width, and channel respectively:

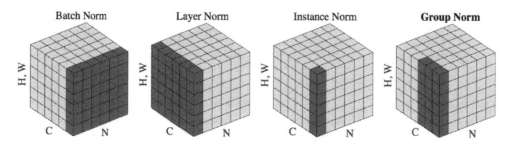

Figure 3.16 – Different types of normalizations used in deep learning. (Source: Y. Wu, K. He, 2018, Group Normalization)

Batch normalization calculates statistics across **(N, H, W)** to produce one statistic for each channel. In contrast, layer normalization calculates statistics across all tensors within one sample, that is, **(H,W,C)** and therefore does not correlate between samples and hence works better for image generation. It is a drop-in replacement for batch normalization where we replace the word *Batch* with *Layer*:

```
model.add(layers.BatchNormalization())
model.add(layers.LayerNormalization())
```

The Jupyter notebook for this exercise is ch3_wgan_gp_celeb_a.ipynb. The following are the images generated by our WGAN-GP. Although the training time of WGAN-GP is longer due to the additional step to do gradient penalty, the training is able to converge faster:

Figure 3.17 – Celebrity faces generated by WGAN-GP

They don't look quite perfect compared to the VAE, partly because there wasn't reconstruction loss to make sure the facial features stay in the places they belong. Nonetheless, this encourages the GAN to be more imaginative and, as a result, more varieties of faces were generated. I also did not notice mode collapse. WGAN-GP is a milestone to achieve the training stability of a GAN. Many subsequent GANs use Wasserstein loss and gradient penalty, and that includes the Progressive GAN, to generate high-resolution images, which we will talk about in detail in *Chapter 7, High Fidelity Face Generation.*

Summary

We have definitely learned a lot in this chapter. We started by learning about the theory and loss functions of GANs, and how to translate the mathematical value function into the code implementation of binary cross-entropy loss. We implemented DCGAN with convolutional layers, batch normalization layers, and leaky ReLU to make the networks go deeper. However, there are still challenges in training GANs, which include instability and being prone to mode collapse due to Jensen-Shannon divergence.

Many of these problems were solved by WGAN with Wasserstein distance, weight clipping, and the removal of the sigmoid at the critic's output. Finally, WGAN-GP introduces gradient penalty to properly enforce the 1-Lipztschitz constraint and give us a framework for stable GAN training. We then replaced batch normalization with layer normalization to train on the CelebA dataset successfully to generate a good variety of faces.

This concludes part 1 of the book. Well done to you for making it this far! By now, you have learned about using different families of generative models to generate images. That includes autoregressive models like PixelCNN in *Chapter 1, Getting Started with Image Generation Using TensorFlow*, in *Chapter 2, Variational Autoencoder* and GANs in this chapter. You are now familiar with the concept of distribution, loss functions, and how to construct neural networks for image generation.

With this solid foundation, we will explore some interesting applications in part 2 of the book, where we will also get to learn about some advanced techniques and cool applications. In the next chapter, we will learn how to perform image-to-image translation with GANs.

Section 2: Applications of Deep Generative Models

In this section, you'll learn about some interesting applications of image generation models. This includes translating a horse into a zebra and using neural style transfer to convert photos into artistic paintings.

This section comprises the following chapters:

- *Chapter 4, Image-to-Image Translation*
- *Chapter 5, Style Transfer*
- *Chapter 6, AI Painter*

4
Image-to-Image Translation

In part one of the book, we learned to generate photorealistic images with VAE and GANs. The generative models can turn some simple random noise into high-dimensional images with complex distribution! However, the generation processes are unconditional, and we have fine control over the images to be generated. If we use MNIST as an example, we will not know which digit will be generated; it is a bit of a lottery. Wouldn't it be nice to be able to tell GAN what we want it to generate? This is what we will learn in this chapter.

We will first learn to build a **conditional GAN (cGAN)** that allows us to specify the class of images to generate. This lays the foundation for more complex networks that follow. We will learn to build a GAN known as **pix2pix** to perform **image-to-image translation**, or **image translation** for short. This will enable a lot of cool applications such as converting sketches to real images. After that, we will build **CycleGAN**, an upgrade from pix2pix that could turn a horse into a zebra and then back to a horse! Finally, we will build **BicyleGAN**, to translate not only high quality but also diversified images with different styles. The following topics will be covered in this chapter:

- Conditional GANs
- Image translation with pix2pix
- Unpaired image translation with CycleGAN
- Diversifying translation with BicycleGAN

The following topics will be covered in this chapter:

In this chapter, we will reuse code and network blocks from *Chapter 3, Generative Adversarial Network*, such as upsampling and downsampling blocks of DCGAN. This will allow us to focus on higher-level architectures of new GANS and to cover more GANs in this chapter. The latter three GANs were created in chronological order and share many common blocks. Thus, you should read them in order, beginning with pix2pix, followed by CycleGAN, and finishing with BicycleGAN, which will make a lot more sense than jumping to BicycleGAN, which is the most complex model in this book so far.

Technical requirements

The Jupyter notebooks can be found at the following link:

`https://github.com/PacktPublishing/Hands-On-Image-Generation-with-TensorFlow-2.0/tree/master/Chapter04`.

The notebooks used in this chapter are as follows:

- `ch4_cdcgan_mnist.ipynb`
- `ch4_cdcgan_fashion_mnist.ipynb`
- `ch4_pix2pix.ipynb`
- `ch4_cyclegan_facade.ipynb`
- `ch4_cyclegan_horse2zebra.ipynb`
- `ch4_bicycle_gan.ipynb`

Conditional GANs

The first goal of a generative model is to be able to produce good quality images. Then we would like to be able to have some control over the images that are to be generated.

In *Chapter 1, Getting Started with Image Generation Using TensorFlow*, we learned about conditional probability and generated faces with certain attributes using a simple conditional probabilistic model. In that model, we generated a smiling face by forcing the model to only sample from the images that had a smiling face. When we condition on something, that thing will always be present and will no longer be a variable with random probability. You can also see that the probability of having those conditions is set to *1*.

To enforce the condition on a neural network is simple. We simply need to show the labels to the network during training and inference. For example, if we want the generator to generate the digit 1, we will need to present the label of 1 in addition to the usual random noise as input to the generator. There are several ways of implementing it. The following diagram shows one implementation as it appeared in the *Conditional Generative Adversarial Nets* paper that first introduced the idea of cGAN:

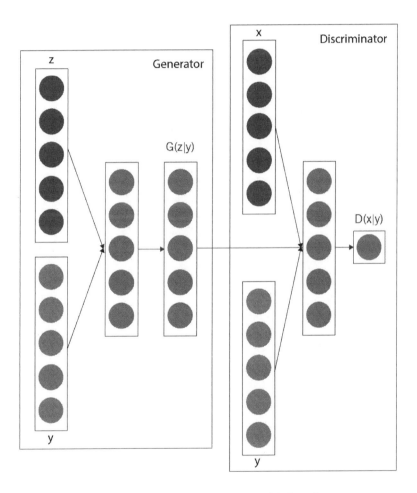

Figure 4.1 – Condition by concatenating labels and inputs
(Redrawn from: M. Mirza, S. Osindero, 2014, Conditional Generative Adversarial Nets – https://arxiv.
org/abs/1411.1784)

In unconditional GAN, the generator input is only the latent vector z. In conditional GAN, the latent vector z joins with a one-hot encoded input label y to form a longer vector, as shown in the preceding diagram. The following table shows one-hot encoding using `tf.one_hot()`:

Class Label	One-hot Vector
0	[1,0,0,0,0,0,0,0,0,0]
1	[0,1,0,0,0,0,0,0,0,0]
2	[0,0,1,0,0,0,0,0,0,0]
3	[0,0,0,1,0,0,0,0,0,0]
4	[0,0,0,0,1,0,0,0,0,0]
5	[0,0,0,0,0,1,0,0,0,0]
6	[0,0,0,0,0,0,1,0,0,0]
7	[0,0,0,0,0,0,0,1,0,0]
8	[0,0,0,0,0,0,0,0,1,0]
9	[0,0,0,0,0,0,0,0,0,1]

Figure 4.2 – Table showing one-hot encoding for classes of 10 in TensorFlow

One-hot encoding converts a label into a vector with dimensions equal to the number of classes. The vectors have all zeros, apart from one unique position that is filled with 1. Some machine learning frameworks use a different order of 1 in the vector; for example, class label 0 is encoded as 0000000001 where the 1 is in the right-most position. The order doesn't matter as long as they are consistently used in both training and inference. This is because one-hot encoding is only used to represent categorical classes and does not have semantic meaning.

Implementing a conditional DCGAN

Now, let's implement a conditional DCGAN on MNIST. We have implemented a DCGAN in *Chapter 2, Variational Autoencoder*, and therefore we extend the network by adding the conditional bits. The notebook for this exercise is ch4_cdcgan_mnist.ipynb.

Let's first look at the generator:

The first step is to one-hot encode the class label. As tf.one_hot([1], 10) will create a shape of (1, 10), we'll need to reshape it to a 1D vector of (10) so that we can concatenate with the latent vector z:

```
input_label = layers.Input(shape=1, dtype=tf.int32,
                            name='ClassLabel')
one_hot_label = tf.one_hot(input_label,
                           self.num_classes)
one_hot_label = layers.Reshape((self.num_classes,))
                               (one_hot_label)
```

The next step is to join the vectors together by using the Concatenate layer. By default, concatenation happens across the last dimension (axis=-1). Therefore, concatenating latent variables with a shape of (batch_size, 100) with one-hot labels of (batch_size, 10) will produce a tensor shape of (batch_size, 110). The code is as follows:

```
input_z = layers.Input(shape=self.z_dim,
                        name='LatentVector')
generator_input = layers.Concatenate()([input_z,
                                         one_hot_label])
```

That is the only change required for the generator. As we have already covered the details of DCGAN architecture, I won't be repeating them in here. For a quick recap, the input will go through a dense layer, followed by several upsampling and convolutional layers to generate an image with a shape of (32, 32, 3), as shown in the following model diagram:

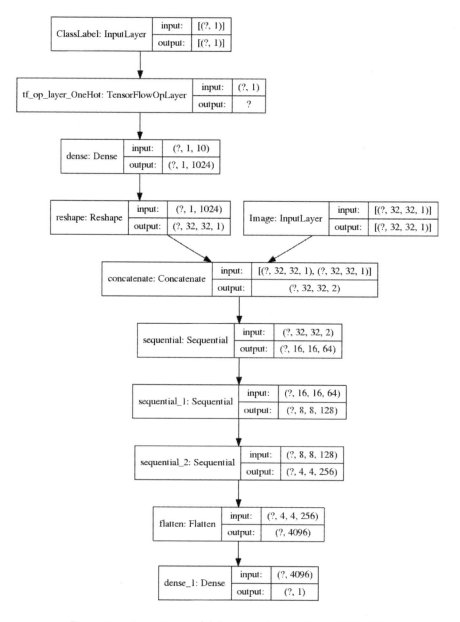

Figure 4.3 – Generator model diagram of a conditional DCGAN

The next step is to inject the label into the discriminator as it is not enough that the discriminator is able to tell whether the image is real or fake, but also to tell whether it is the correct image.

The original cGAN uses only dense layers in the network. The input image is flattened and concatenates with a one-hot encoded class label. However, this doesn't work well with DCGAN as the first layer of the discriminator is a convolutional layer that is expecting a 2D image as input. If we use the same approach, we will end up with an input vector of 32×32×1 + 10 = 1,034, and that can't be reshaped to a 2D image. We will need another way to project the one-hot vector into a tensor of the correct shape.

One way to do this is to use a dense layer to project the one-hot vector into the shape of an input image (32,32,1), and concatenate it to produce a shape of (32, 32, 2). The first color channel will be our grayscale image, and the second channel will be the projected one-hot labels. Again, the rest of the discriminator network is unchanged, as shown in the following model summary:

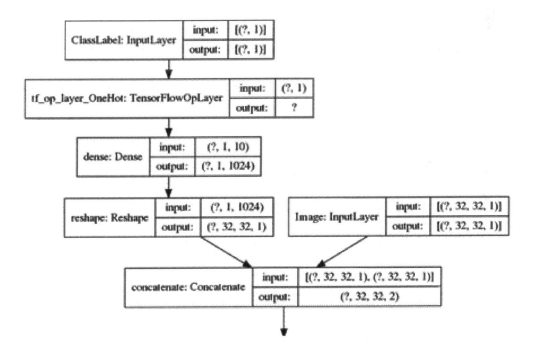

Figure 4.4 – Inputs to discriminator of a conditional DCGAN

As we have seen, the only change made to networks is by adding another path that takes class labels as input. The last remaining bit to do before starting the model training is to add the additional label class into the model's input. To create a model with multiple inputs, we pass a list of input layers as follows:

```
discriminator = Model([input_image, input_label], output]
```

Similarly, we pass a list of `images` and `labels` in the same order when performing a forward pass:

```
pred_real = discriminator([real_images, class_labels])
```

During training, we create random labels for the generator as follows:

```
fake_class_labels = tf.random.uniform((batch_size),
                                minval=0, maxval=10,
                                dtype=tf.dtypes.int32)
fake_images = generator.predict([latent_vector,
                                fake_class_labels])
```

We use a DCGAN training pipeline and loss function. Here are samples of the digits generated by conditioning on the input labels from 0 to 9:

Figure 4.5 – Hand-written digits generated by a conditional DCGAN

We can also train cDCGAN on Fashion-MNIST without any change. The result samples are as follows:

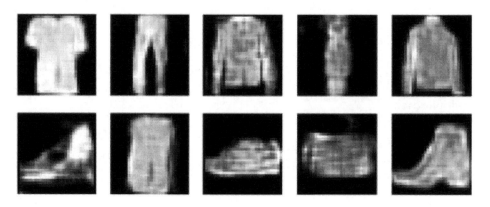

Figure 4.6 – Image generated by a conditional DCGAN

Conditional GAN works really well on MNIST and Fashion-MNIST! Next, we will look at different ways of applying the class conditions on GANs.

Variants of cGAN

We implemented conditional DCGAN by one-hot encoding the labels, passing it through a dense layer (for discriminator), and concatenating the input layer. The implementation is simple and gives good results. We will introduce a few other popular methods of implementing conditional GANs and you are encouraged to implement the code on your own to try them out.

Using the embedding layer

One popular implementation is to replace one-hot encoding and the dense layer with the `embedding` layer. The embedding layer takes categorical values as input, and the output is a vector, such as a dense layer. In other words, it has the same input and output shapes as the `label->one-hot-encoding->dense` block. The code snippet is shown here:

```
encoded_label = tf.one_hot(input_label, self.num_classes)

embedding = layers.Dense(32 * 32 * 1, activation=None)\
                        (encoded_label)

embedding = layers.Embedding(self.num_classes,
                              32*32*1)(input_label)
```

Both methods produce similar results, albeit the `embedding` layer is more computationally efficient as the size of the one-hot vector can grow quickly for large numbers of classes. Embedding is used extensively to encode words due to a large number of vocabularies. For small classes such as MNIST, the computational advantage is negligible.

Element-wise multiplication

Concatenating a latent vector with an input image increases the dimensions and the first layer of the network. Instead of concatenating, we could also perform element-wise multiplication of the label embedding with the original network input and keep the original input shape. The origin of this approach is unclear. However, a few industry experts carried out experiments on **Natural Language Processing** tasks and found this method to outperform that of one-hot encoding. The code snippet to perform element-wise multiplication between an image and embedding is as follows:

```
x = layers.Multiply()([input_image, embedding])
```

Combining the preceding code with the embedding layer gives us the following graph, as implemented in `ch4_cdcgan_fashion_mnist.ipynb`:

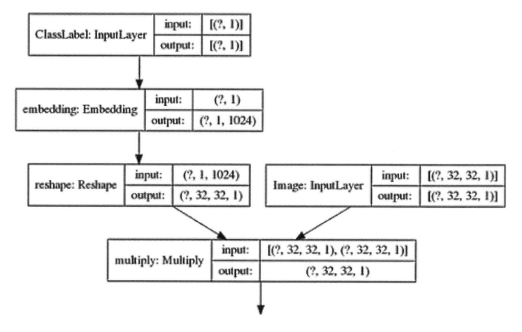

Figure 4.7 – Implementation of cDCGAN using embedding and element-wise multiplication

Next, we will see why inserting labels into the intermediate layer is popular.

Inserting labels in the intermediate layer

Instead of inserting the label into the first layer of the network, we can choose to do this in the intermediate layer. This approach is popular for generators with encoder-decoder architectures, where the label is inserted into a layer that is close to the end of the encoder with the smallest dimensions. Some insert the label embedding toward the discriminator output, so the majority of the discriminator can focus on deciding whether the images look real. The only part of the last few layers' capacity is used in deciding whether the image matches the label.

We will learn how to insert label embedding into intermediate and normalization layers when we implement advanced models in *Chapter 8, Self-Attention for Image Generation*. We have now understood how to use class labels conditioned to generate images. For the rest of the chapter, we will use an image as a condition to perform image-to-image translation.

Image translation with pix2pix

The introduction of pix2pix in 2017 caused quite a stir, not only within the research community, but also the wider population. This can be attributed in part to the `https://affinelayer.com/pixsrv/` website, which puts the models online and allows people to translate their sketches into cats, shoes, and bags. You should try it too! The following screenshot is taken from their website to give you a glimpse of how it works:

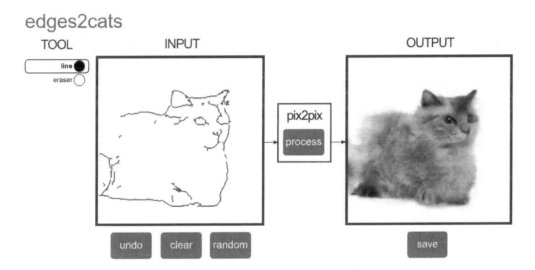

Figure 4.8 – Application of turning a sketch of a cat into a real image
(Source: https://affinelayer.com/pixsrv/)

Pix2pix came from a research paper entitled *Image-to-Image Translation with Conditional Adversarial Networks*. From the paper title, we can tell that pix2pix is a conditional GAN that performs image-to-image translation. The model can be trained to perform general image translation, but we will need to have image pairs in the dataset. In our pix2pix implementation, we will translate masks of building façades into realistic-looking building façades, as shown here:

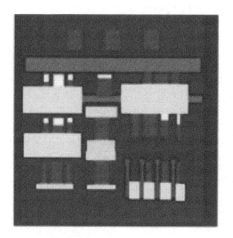

Figure 4.9 – Mask and real image of a building façade

In the preceding screenshot, the picture on the left shows an example of the semantic segmentation mask used as input of pix2pix where the building parts are encoded in different colors. On the right is the target real image of a building façade.

Discarding random noise

In all the GANs we have learned so far, we always sample from random distribution as input to the generator. We require that randomness, otherwise the generator will produce deterministic outputs and fail to learn data distribution. Pix2pix breaks away from that tradition by removing random noise from GANs. As the authors pointed out in the *Image-to-Image Translation with Conditional Adversarial Networks* paper, they could not get the conditional GAN to work with an image and noise as input as the GAN would simply ignore the noise.

As a result, the authors turned to the use of dropout in generator layers to provide randomness. A side effect is that this is minor randomness; hence, little variations are seen in the output and they tend to look similar in styles. This problem is overcome with BicycleGAN, which we will learn about later.

U-Net as a generator

The notebook for this tutorial is `ch4_pix2pix.ipynb`. The architecture of generators and discriminators is rather different from DCGAN and we will go through each of them in detail. Without the use of random noise as input, all that is left to the generator input is the input image that is used as the condition. Thus, both the input and output are an image of the same shape, which is (256, 256, 3) in our examples. Pix2pix uses U-Net, which is an encoder-decoder-like architecture similar to an autoencoder, but with skip connections between the encoder and decoder. Following is the architecture diagram of the original U-Net:

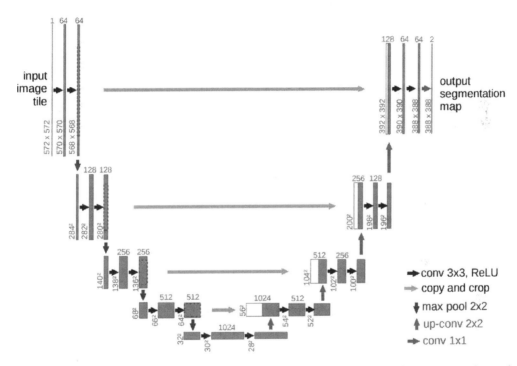

Figure 4.10 – Original U-Net architecture (Source: O. Ronneberger et al., 2015, "U-Net: Convolutional Networks for Biomedical Image Segmentation" – https://arxiv.org/abs/1505.04597)

In *Chapter 2, Variational Autoencoder,* we saw how an autoencoder downsamples a high-dimension input image into low-dimension latent variables before upsampling it back to the original size. During the downsampling process, the high frequency content of images (the texture details) is lost. As a result, the restored image can appear to be blurry. By passing the high spatial resolution content from an encoder to a decoder via the skip connections, the decoder could capture and generate those details to make the images look sharper. As a matter of fact, U-Net was first used to translate medical images into semantic segmentation masks, which is the reverse of what we are trying to do in this chapter.

To make the construction of the generator easier, we first write a function to create a block for downsampling with a default stride of 2. This consists of convolution and optional normalization, `activation`, and `dropout` layers, as follows:

```python
def downsample(self, channels, kernels, strides=2,
            norm=True, activation=True, dropout=False):
    initializer = tf.random_normal_initializer(0., 0.02)
    block = tf.keras.Sequential()
    block.add(layers.Conv2D(channels, kernels,
            strides=strides, padding='same',
            use_bias=False,
            kernel_initializer=initializer))
    if norm:
        block.add(layers.BatchNormalization())
    if activation:
        block.add(layers.LeakyReLU(0.2))
    if dropout:
        block.add(layers.Dropout(0.5))
    return block
```

The `upsample` block is similar, but with an additional `UpSampling2D` before `Conv2D` and has strides of `1`, as follows:

```python
def upsample(self, channels, kernels, strides=1,
            norm=True, activation=True, dropout=False):
    initializer = tf.random_normal_initializer(0., 0.02)
    block = tf.keras.Sequential()
    block.add(layers.UpSampling2D((2,2)))
    block.add(layers.Conv2D(channels, kernels,
            strides=strides, padding='same',
            use_bias=False,
```

```
                        kernel_initializer=initializer))
    if norm:
        block.add(InstanceNormalization())
    if activation:
        block.add(layers.LeakyReLU(0.2))
    if dropout:
        block.add(layers.Dropout(0.5))
    return block
```

We will first construct the downsampling path, where the feature map sizes are halved after every downsampling block as follows. It is important to note the output shapes as we will need to match those with the upsampling path for skip connections as follows:

```
input_image = layers.Input(shape=image_shape)
down1 = self.downsample(DIM, 4, norm=False)(input_image) # 128
down2 = self.downsample(2*DIM, 4)(down1) # 64
down3 = self.downsample(4*DIM, 4)(down2) # 32
down4 = self.downsample(4*DIM, 4)(down3) # 16
down5 = self.downsample(4*DIM, 4)(down4) # 8
down6 = self.downsample(4*DIM, 4)(down5) # 4
down7 = self.downsample(4*DIM, 4)(down6) # 2
```

In the upsampling path, we concatenate the previous layer's output with a skip connection from the downsampling path to form input to the upsample block. We use dropout in the first three layers as follows:

```
up6 = self.upsample(4*DIM, 4, dropout=True)(down7) # 4,4*DIM
concat6 = layers.Concatenate()([up6, down6])
up5 = self.upsample(4*DIM, 4, dropout=True)(concat6)
concat5 = layers.Concatenate()([up5, down5])
up4 = self.upsample(4*DIM, 4, dropout=True)(concat5)
concat4 = layers.Concatenate()([up4, down4])
up3 = self.upsample(4*DIM, 4)(concat4)
concat3 = layers.Concatenate()([up3, down3])
up2 = self.upsample(2*DIM, 4)(concat3)
concat2 = layers.Concatenate()([up2, down2])
up1 = self.upsample(DIM, 4)(concat2)
concat1 = layers.Concatenate()([up1, down1])
```

```
output_image = tanh(self.upsample(3, 4, norm=False,
                         activation=None)(concat1))
```

This last layer of the generator is Conv2D, with a channel size of 3 to match the image channel numbers. Like DCGAN, we normalize the images to the range of [-1, +1], using `tanh` as the activation function, and binary cross-entropy as the loss function.

Loss functions

Pix2pix uses standard GAN loss functions of binary cross-entropy for both the generator and discriminator, just like DCGAN. Now that we have a target image to generate, we can therefore add L1 reconstruction loss to the generator. In the paper, the ratio of the reconstruction loss to binary cross-entropy is set to 100:1. The following code snippet shows how to compile combined generator-discriminator with losses:

```
LAMBDA = 100
self.model.compile(loss = ['bce','mae'],
                   optimizer = Adam(2e-4, 0.5, 0.9999),
                   loss_weights=[1, LAMBDA])
```

`bce` stands for **binary cross-entropy loss**, while `mae` stands for **mean absolute entropy loss**, or is more commonly known as **L1 loss**.

Implementing a PatchGAN discriminator

Researchers found that L2 or L1 loss produces blurry results on image generation problems. Although they fail to encourage high-frequency crispness, they can capture low-frequency content well. We can see low-frequency information as content, such as the building structures, while high-frequency information provides the style information, such as the fine-detail textures and colors of building façades. To capture high-frequency information, a new discriminator known as PatchGAN was used. Don't be misled by its name; PatchGAN is not a GAN but a **Convolutional Neural Network (CNN)**.

The conventional GAN discriminator looks at the entire image and judges whether that entire image is real or fake. Instead of looking at the entire image, PatchGAN looks at patches of images, hence the name. The receptive field of a convolutional layer is the number of input points that are mapped to one output point or, in other words, represents the size of the convolutional kernel. For a kernel size of N×N, each output of the layer is mapped to N×N pixels of the input tensor.

As we go deeper along the network, the next layer gets to see a larger patch of input images and the effective receptive field of the output increases. The default PatchGAN is designed to have an effective field of 70×70. The original PatchGAN has an output shape of 30×30 due to the careful padding, but we will use only the 'same' padding to give the output shape of 29×29. Each of the 29×29 patches looks at different and overlapping 70x70 patches of input images.

In other words, the discriminator tries to predict whether each of the patches is real or fake. By zooming into local patches, the discriminator is encouraged to look at high-frequency information of the images. To summarize, we use L1 reconstruction loss to capture the low-frequency content, and PatchGAN to encourage high-frequency-style details.

PatchGAN is simply a CNN and can be implemented using several downsampling blocks as shown in the following code. We will use the notation A to refer to the input (source) image, and B for the output (target) image. Like cGAN, the discriminator requires two inputs – the condition, which is image A, and the output image B, which can be a real one from the dataset or a fake one from the generator. We concatenate the two images together at the beginning of the discriminator, hence, PatchGAN looks at both image A (condition) and image B (output image or fake image) together to decide whether it is real or fake. The code is as follows:

```
def build_discriminator(self):
    DIM = 64
    model = tf.keras.Sequential(name='discriminators')
    input_image_A = layers.Input(shape=image_shape)
    input_image_B = layers.Input(shape=image_shape)
    x = layers.Concatenate()([input_image_A,
                              input_image_B])
    x = self.downsample(DIM, 4, norm=False)(x)
    x = self.downsample(2*DIM, 4)(x)
    x = self.downsample(4*DIM, 4)(x)
    x = self.downsample(8*DIM, 4, strides=1)(x)
    output = layers.Conv2D(1, 4, activation='sigmoid')(x)
    return Model([input_image_A, input_image_B], output)
```

The discriminator model summary is as follows:

```
Model: "model"

Layer (type)                   Output Shape           Param #    Connected to
==================================================================================
input_1 (InputLayer)           [(None, 256, 256, 3)   0

input_2 (InputLayer)           [(None, 256, 256, 3)   0

concatenate (Concatenate)      (None, 256, 256, 6)    0          input_1[0][0]
                                                                 input_2[0][0]

sequential (Sequential)        (None, 128, 128, 64)   6144       concatenate[0][0]

sequential_1 (Sequential)      (None, 64, 64, 128)    131328     sequential[0][0]

sequential_2 (Sequential)      (None, 32, 32, 256)    524800     sequential_1[0][0]

sequential_3 (Sequential)      (None, 32, 32, 512)    2098176    sequential_2[0][0]

conv2d_4 (Conv2D)              (None, 29, 29, 1)      8193       sequential_3[0][0]
==================================================================================
Total params: 2,768,641
Trainable params: 2,768,641
Non-trainable params: 0
```

Figure 4.11 – Discriminator model summary

Note that the output layer has the shape of *(29, 29, 1)*. Therefore, we will create labels that match its output shape as follows:

```
real_labels = tf.ones((batch_size, self.patch_size,
                       self.patch_size, 1))

fake_labels = tf.zeros((batch_size, self.patch_size,
                        self.patch_size, 1))

fake_images = self.generator.predict(real_images_A)

pred_fake = self.discriminator([real_images_A,
                                fake_images])

pred_real = self.discriminator([real_images_A,
                                real_images_B])
```

Now we are ready to train pix2pix.

Training pix2pix

It was well known as a result of the invention of pix2pix that batch normalization is bad for image generation as the statistics from the batch of images tend to make the generated images look more similar and blurrier. The pix2pix authors noticed that generated images look better when the batch size is set to 1. When the batch size is 1, batch normalization becomes a special case of **instance normalization**, but the latter can be applied for any batch size. To recap on normalization, for an image batch with a shape of (N, H, W, C), batch normalization uses statistics across (N, H, W), while instance normalization uses statistics from individual images across dimensions (H,W). This prevents the statistics from other images from creeping in.

Therefore, to get good results, we can either use batch normalization with a batch size of 1, or we replace it with instance normalization. Instance normalization is not available as a standard Keras layer at the time of writing, perhaps this hasn't gained mainstream usage beyond image generation. However, instance normalization is available from the `tensorflow_addons` module. After importing from the module, it is a drop-in replacement for batch normalization:

```
from tensorflow_addons.layers import InstanceNormalization
```

We train pix2pix using a DCGAN pipeline and it is surprisingly easy to train compared with DCGAN. This is because the probability distribution to cover an input image is narrower than the one from random noise. The following images show the image samples after 100 epochs of training. The image on the left is the segmentation mask, the middle one is the ground truth, and the one on the right is generated:

Figure 4.12 – Images generated by pix2pix after 100 epochs of training. Left: Input mask. Middle: Ground truth. Right: Generated image

Images generated by pix2pix capture the image content correctly due to the large weight (lambda=100) of reconstruction loss. For example, the doors and windows are almost always in the correct places and correct shapes. However, it lacks variation in styles as the generated buildings have mostly the same color, as are the styles of windows. This is due to the absence of random noise in the model as mentioned earlier and acknowledged by the authors. Nevertheless, pix2pix opens the floodgates for image-to-image translation using GAN.

Unpaired image translation with CycleGAN

CycleGAN was created by the same research group who invented pix2pix. CycleGAN could train with unpaired images using two generators and two discriminators. However, by using pix2pix as a foundation, CycleGAN is actually quite simple to implement once you understand how the cycle consistency loss works. Before this, let's try to understand the advantage of CycleGAN over pix2pix in the following sections.

Unpaired dataset

One drawback of pix2pix is that it requires a paired training dataset. For some applications, we can create a dataset rather easily. A grayscale-to-color images dataset and vice-versa is probably the simplest to create using any image processing software libraries such as OpenCV or Pillow. Similarly, we could also easily create sketches from real images using edge detection techniques. For a photo-to-artistic-painting dataset, we can use neural style transfer (we'll cover this in *Chapter 5*, *Style Transfer*) to create artistic painting from real images.

However, there are some datasets that cannot be automated, such as day-to-night scenes. Some have to be labeled manually, which can be expensive to do, such as the segmentation masks for building façades. Then, some image pairs are simply impossible to collect or create, such as a horse-to-zebra image translation. This is where CycleGAN excels as it does not require paired data. CycleGAN could train on unpaired datasets and then translate images in either direction!

Cycle consistency loss

In a generative model, the generator translates from domain A (source) to domain B (target), for example, from orange to apple. By conditioning on the image from A (orange), the generator creates images with pixel distributions of B (apple). However, this does not guarantee that those images are paired in a meaningful way.

We will use language translation as an analogy. Let's assume you are tourist in a foreign country and you ask a local to help translate an English sentence into the local language and she replies with a beautifully sounding sentence. OK, it does sound real, but is the translation correct? You walk down the street and ask another person to explain that sentence into English. If that translation matches your original English sentence, then we know the translation was correct.

Using the same concept, CycleGAN adopts a translation cycle to ensure that the mapping is correct in both directions. The following diagram shows the architecture of CycleGAN that forms a cycle between two generators:

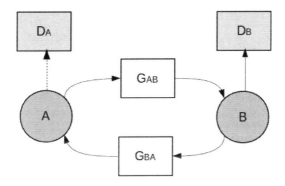

Figure 4.13 – Architecture of CycleGAN. (The solid arrows show the flow of the forward cycle, while the dashed arrow path is not used in the forward cycle but is drawn to show the overall connections between blocks.)

In the preceding diagram, we have image domain **A** on the left and domain **B** on the right. The procedure that is followed is listed here:

GAB is a generator that translates from **A** to fake **B**; the generated image then goes to the discriminator **DB**. This is the standard GAN data path. Next, the fake image **B** is translated back into domain **A** via **GBA** and that completes the forward path. At this point, we have a reconstructed image, **A**. If the translations went perfectly, then it should look identical to the source image **A**.

We also come across **cycle consistency loss**, which is an L1 loss between the source image and the reconstructed image. Similarly, for the backward path, we start the cycle by translating from domain **B** to **A**.

In training, we show CycleGAN with two images from domains **A** and **B**, respectively. It performs forward and backward paths to learn bidirectional translation. We will be looking at how to implement CycleGAN from scratch in the ch4_cyclegan_facade. ipynb notebook.

CycleGAN also uses what is known as **identity loss**, which is equivalent to the reconstruction loss of pix2pix. **GAB** translates image **A** into the fake **B**, while the forward identity loss is the L1 distance between the fake **B** and the real **B**. Similarly, there is also a backward identity loss in the reverse direction. With façade datasets, the weight of identity loss should be set to low. This is because some of the real images in this dataset have parts of their images blacked out. This dataset was meant to let a machine learning algorithm guess the missing pixels. Thus, we use a low weight to discourage the network from translating the blackout.

Building CycleGAN models

We will now build the discriminators and generators of CycleGAN. The discriminator is PatchGAN, like pix2pix, with two changes. First, the discriminator only sees the images from its domain and thus, only one image inputs into discriminators rather than both images from A and B. In other words, the discriminators only need to judge whether the images are real or fake in their own domain.

Second, sigmoid is removed from the output layer. This is because CycleGAN uses a different adversarial loss function called **least-squares loss**. We haven't covered LSGAN in this book, but it is sufficient to know that this loss is more stable than **log-loss**, and we can implement it using the Keras **mean squared loss** (**MSE**) function. We train discriminators with the usual training step as follows:

```
def build_discriminator(self):
    DIM = 64
    input_image = layers.Input(shape=image_shape)
    x = self.downsample(DIM, 4, norm=False)(input_image) # 128
    x = self.downsample(2*DIM, 4)(x) # 64
    x = self.downsample(4*DIM, 4)(x) # 32
    x = self.downsample(8*DIM, 4, strides=1)(x) # 29
    output = layers.Conv2D(1, 4)(x)
```

For the generator, the original CycleGAN uses a residual block for improved performance, but we will reuse U-Net from pix2pix, so we can focus more on CycleGAN's high-level architecture and training steps.

Now, let's instantiate two pairs of generators and discriminators:

```
self.discriminator_B = self.build_discriminator()
self.discriminator_A = self.build_discriminator()
self.generator_AB = self.build_generator()
self.generator_BA = self.build_generator()
```

Here comes the core of CycleGAN, which is to implement the combined model to train generators. All we need to do is to follow the arrows in the architecture diagram to feed input into the generator to generate a fake image that goes to the discriminator and cycles back as follows:

```
image_A = layers.Input(shape=input_shape)
image_B = layers.Input(shape=input_shape)
# forward
fake_B = self.generator_AB(image_A)
discriminator_B_output = self.discriminator_B(fake_B)
reconstructed_A = self.generator_BA(fake_B)
# backward
fake_A = self.generator_BA(image_B)
discriminator_A_output = self.discriminator_A(fake_A)
reconstructed_B = self.generator_AB(fake_A)
# identity
identity_B = self.generator_AB(image_A)
identity_A = self.generator_BA(image_B)
```

The final step is to create a model with those inputs and outputs:

```
self.model = Model(inputs=[image_A, image_B],
                   outputs=[discriminator_B_output,
                            discriminator_A_output,
                            reconstructed_A,
                            reconstructed_B,
                            identity_A, identity_B
                           ])
```

Then, we need to assign correct losses and weights to them. As mentioned earlier, we use mae (L1 loss) for cycle consistency loss and mse (mean squared error) for adversarial loss, as follows:

```
self.LAMBDA = 10
self.LAMBDA_ID = 5
self.model.compile(loss = ['mse','mse', 'mae','mae',
                           'mae','mae'],
                   optimizer = Adam(2e-4, 0.5),
                   loss_weights=[1, 1,
                                 self.LAMBDA, self.LAMBDA,
                                 self.LAMBDA_ID,
                                 self.LAMBDA_ID]).
```

In each training step, we first train both discriminators in both directions, from A to B and from B to A. The train_discriminator() function includes training with fake and real images as follows:

```
# train discriminator
d_loss_AB = self.train_discriminator("AB", real_images_A,
                                      real_images_B)
d_loss_BA = self.train_discriminator("BA", real_images_B,
                                      real_images_A)
```

This is followed by training generators. The inputs are real images A and B. With regard to the labels, the first pair is real/fake labels, the second pair is the cycle reconstructed images, and the last pair is for identity loss:

```
# train generator
combined_loss = self.model.train_on_batch(
                    [real_images_A, real_images_B],
                    [real_labels, real_labels,
                     real_images_A, real_images_B,
                     real_images_A, real_images_B
                    ])
```

Then we can start training.

Analysis of CycleGAN

The following are some of the building façades generated by CycleGAN:

Figure 4.14 – Building façades generated by CycleGAN

Although they look good, they are not necessarily better than pix2pix. The strength of CycleGAN compared to pix2pix lies in its ability to train on unpaired data. In order to test this, I have created `ch4_cyclegan_horse2zebra.ipynb` to train it on unpaired horse and zebra images. Just so you know, training on unpaired images is a lot harder. Therefore, have fun trying! The following images show image-to-image translation between horses and zebras:

Figure 4.15 – Translation between horse and zebra

(Source: J-Y. Zhu et al., "Unpaired Image-to-Image Translation Using Cycle-Consistent Adversarial Networks" – https://arxiv.org/abs/1703.10593)

Pix2pix and CycleGAN are popular GANs that are used by many. However, they both have one shortcoming; that is the image outputs almost always look identical. For example, if we were to perform zebra-to-horse translation, the horse will always have the same skin color. This is due to the inherent nature of GANs that learns to reject the randomness of noise. In the next section, we will look at how BicycleGAN solves this problem to generate richer variations of images.

Diversifying translation with BicyleGAN

Both Pix2pix and CycleGAN came from the **Berkeley AI Research (BAIR)** laboratory at UC Berkeley. They are popular and have a number of tutorials and blogs about them online, including on the official TensorFlow site. BicycleGAN is what I see as the last of the image-to-image translation trilogy from that research group. However, you don't find a lot of example code online, perhaps due to its complexity.

In order to build the most advanced network in this book up to this point, we will throw in all the knowledge you have acquired in this chapter, plus the last two chapters. Maybe that is why it is regarded as advanced by many. Don't worry; you already have all the prerequisite knowledge. Let's jump in!

Understanding architecture

Before jumping straight into implementation, let me give you an overview of BicycleGAN. From the name, you may naturally think that BicycleGAN is an upgrade of CycleGAN by adding another cycle (from unicycle to bicycle). No, it is not! It has nothing to do with CycleGAN; it is rather an improvement to pix2pix.

As mentioned earlier, pix2pix is a one-to-one mapping where the output is always the same for a given input. The authors tried to add noise to the generator input, but it simply ignores the noise and fails to create variations in the output image. Therefore, they searched for a method where the generator does not ignore the noise, but instead uses the noise to generate diversified images, hence, one-to-many mapping.

In the following screenshot, we can see different models and configurations related to BicycleGAN. Diagram *(a)* is the configuration for inference where image **A** is combined with input noise to generate image **B**. This is essentially the cGAN at the beginning of the chapter, except for the role reversal between image **A** and noise. In cGAN, noise plays the leading role, with 100 dimensions and a condition of 10 class labels. In BicycleGAN, image **A** with a shape of (256, 256, 3) is the condition, while the noise sampled from latent *z* has a dimension of 8. *Figure (b)* is the training configuration for *pix2pix + noise*. The two configurations at the bottom of the diagram are used by BicycleGAN, and we will look at these shortly:

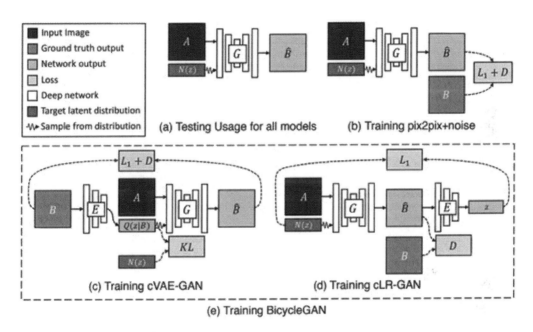

Figure 4.16 – Models within BicycleGAN

(Source: J-Y. Zhu, "Toward Multimodal Image-to-Image Translation" – https://arxiv.org/abs/1711.11586)

The main concept of BicycleGAN is to find a relation between the latent code *z* and the target image **B**, so the generator can learn to generate a different image **B** when given a different *z*. BicycleGAN does it by combining the two methods, **cVAE-GAN** and **cLR-GAN**, as shown in the preceding diagram.

cVAE-GAN

Let's go over some background to **VAE-GAN**. The authors of VAE-GAN argue that L1 loss is not a good metric for measuring the visual perception of an image. If the image moves a few pixels to the right, it may look no different to the human eye, but can result in a large L1 loss. Why not let a network learn what is the appropriate objective function to use? Indeed, they use GAN's discriminator to learn the objective function to tell whether the fake image looks real and use VAE as a generator. As a result, the generated images appear sharper. If we look at *Figure (c)* from the preceding diagram and ignore image **A**, that is a VAE-GAN. With **A** as a condition, it becomes a conditional cVAE-GAN. The training steps are as follows:

1. The VAE encodes the real image **B** into latent code of a multivariate Gaussian mean and log variance, and then samples from them to create noise input. This flow is the standard VAE workflow. Please refer to *Chapter 2, Variational Autoencoder*, for a refresher.

2. Now with the condition **A**, the noise sampled from the latent vector z is used to generate a fake image **B**.

The information flow is $B \rightarrow z \rightarrow \hat{B}$ (the solid lined arrow in *Figure (c)*). There are three loses:

-   $\mathcal{L}_{GAN}^{VAE}$: Adversarial loss
-   $\mathcal{L}_{1}^{VAE}$: L1 reconstruction loss
-   $\mathcal{L}_{KL}$: KL divergence loss

cLR-GAN

The theory behind Conditional Latent Regressor GAN is beyond the scope of this book. However, we will focus on how this is applied in BicycleGAN. In cVAE-GAN, we encode a real image B to provide the ground truth of a latent vector and sample from it. However, cLR-GAN does things differently by first letting the generator generate a fake image B from random noise, and then encoding the fake image B and seeing how it deviates from the input random noise.

The forward steps are as follows:

1. Like cGAN, we randomly generate some noise, and then concatenate with image A to generate a fake image B.

2. Then we use the same encoder from VAE-GAN to encode the fake image B into latent vectors.

3. We then sample z from encoded latent vectors, and compute the point loss with the input noise z.

The flow is $z \rightarrow \hat{B} \rightarrow \hat{z}$ (solid lined arrow in *Figure (d)*). There are two losses as follows:

- $\mathcal{L}_{GAN}$: Adversarial loss
- $\mathcal{L}_1^{latent}$: L1 loss between noise $N(z)$ and the encoded mean

By combining these two flows, we got a bijection cycle between the output and the latent space. The *bi* in BicycleGAN comes from *bijection*, which is a mathematical term that roughly means one-to-one mapping and is reversible. In this case, BicycleGAN maps the output to a latent space, and similarly from the latent space to the output. The total loss is as follows:

$$\text{Bicycle loss} = \mathcal{L}_{GAN}^{VAE} + \mathcal{L}_{GAN} + \lambda \mathcal{L}_1^{VAE} + \lambda_{latent} \mathcal{L}_1^{latent} + \lambda_{KL} \mathcal{L}_{KL}$$

Where $\lambda=10$, $\lambda_{latent} = 0.5$, and $\lambda_{latent}=0.01$ are used in the default configuration.

Now that we understand the BicycleGAN architecture and loss functions, we can now go on to implement them.

Implementing BicycleGAN

We will use the ch4_bicycle_gan.ipynb notebook here. There are three types of networks in BicycleGAN – the generator, discriminator, and encoder. We will reuse the discriminator (PatchGAN) from pix2pix and the encoder from VAE from *Chapter 2, Variational Autoencoder*. The encoder is bulked up with more filters and deeper layers as the input image size is larger. The code can look slightly different, but essentially the concept is the same as before. The original BicycleGAN uses two PatchGANs with effective receptive fields of 70x70 and 140x140.

For simplicity, we'll use only one 70x70 PatchGAN. Using a separate discriminator for cVAE-GAN and cLR-GAN improves image quality, meaning we have four networks in total – the generator, encoder, and two discriminators.

Inserting latent code into the generator

The authors tried two methods of inserting latent code into the generator, one involving concatenating with the input image, and the other involving inserting it into other layers in the downsampling path of the generator, as shown in the following diagram. It was found that the former works well. Let's implement this simple method:

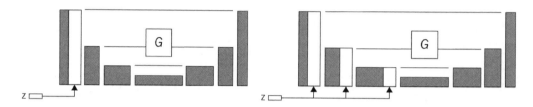

Figure 4.17 – Different ways of injecting z into the generator (Redrawn from: J-Y. Zhu, "Toward Multimodal Image-to-Image Translation" – https://arxiv.org/abs/1711.11586)

As we have learned at the beginning of this chapter, there are several ways to join the input and conditions of different shapes. BicycleGAN's method is to repeat the latent code multiple times and concatenate with the input image.

Let's use a concrete example. In BicycleGAN, the latent code length is 8. We draw 8 samples from noise distribution, and each sample is repeated H×W times to form a tensor with the shape of (H,W,8). In other words, in each of the 8 channels, its (H, W) feature map is made up of the same repeated number from that channel. The following is the code snippet of `build_generator()`, which shows the tiling and concatenation of latent code. The remainder of the code is the same as the pix2pix generator:

```
input_image = layers.Input(shape=image_shape,
                            name='input_image')
input_z = layers.Input(shape=(self.z_dim,), name='z')
z = layers.Reshape((1,1, self.z_dim))(input_z)
z_tiles = tf.tile(z, [self.batch_size, self.input_shape[0],
                      self.input_shape[1], self.z_dim])
x = layers.Concatenate()([input_image, z_tiles])
```

The next step is to create two models, cVAE-GAN and cLR-GAN, to incorporate the networks and create the forward path flow.

cVAE-GAN

Here is the code to create a model for cVAE-GAN. This is the implementation of the forward pass, as mentioned earlier:

```
images_A_1 = layers.Input(shape=input_shape,
                          name='ImageA_1')

images_B_1 = layers.Input(shape=input_shape,
                          name='ImageB_1')

z_encode, self.mean_encode, self.logvar_encode = \
                          self.encoder(images_B_1)

fake_B_encode = self.generator([images_A_1, z_encode])

encode_fake = self.discriminator_1(fake_B_encode)

encode_real = self.discriminator_1(images_B_1)

kl_loss =  - 0.5 * tf.reduce_sum(1 + self.logvar_encode - \
                          tf.square(self.mean_encode) - \
                          tf.exp(self.logvar_encode))

self.cvae_gan = Model(inputs=[images_A_1, images_B_1],
                      outputs=[encode_real, encode_fake,
fake_B_encode, kl_loss])
```

We include the KL divergence loss in the model as opposed to that in the custom loss function. This is simpler and more efficient as `kl_loss` can be calculated directly from the mean and log variance without needing external labels to be passed in from a training step.

cLR-GAN

Here is the implementation of cLR-GAN. One thing to note is that this has different inputs to images A and B that are separate from cVAE-GAN:

```
images_A_2 = layers.Input(shape=input_shape,
                          name='ImageA_2')

images_B_2 = layers.Input(shape=input_shape,
                          name='ImageB_2')

z_random = layers.Input(shape=(self.z_dim,), name='z')

fake_B_random = self.generator([images_A_2, z_random])

_, mean_random, _ = self.encoder(fake_B_random)

random_fake = self.discriminator_2(fake_B_random)

random_real = self.discriminator_2(images_B_2)

self.clr_gan = Model(inputs=[images_A_2, images_B_2,
```

```
                              z_random],
                 outputs=[random_real, random_fake,
                 mean_random])
```

Alright, we now have the models defined. The next step is to implement the training step.

Training step

Both models train together in one step, but with different image pairs. Therefore, in each training step, we fetch the data twice, once for each model. Some do it by creating data pipelines that load the batch size twice and then split them into two halves, as shown in the following code snippet:

```
images_A_1, images_B_1 = next(data_generator)
images_A_2, images_B_2 = next(data_generator)
self.train_step(images_A_1, images_B_1, images_A_2,
                images_B_2)
```

Previously, we used two different methods to perform the training step. One is to define and compile a Keras model with an optimizer and loss function, and then call `train_on_batch()` to perform the training step. This is simple and works well on well-defined models. Alternatively, we can also use `tf.GradientTape` to allow finer control of the gradients and update. We have been using both of them in our models, where we use `train_on_batch()` for the generator and `tf.GradientTape` for the discriminator.

The purpose was to familiarize ourselves with both methods so that if we need to implement complex training steps with low-level code, we know how to do it, and now is the time. BicycleGAN has two models that share a generator and encoder, but we update them using different combinations of loss functions, which make the `train_on_batch` method unfeasible without modifying the original settings. Therefore, we will combine both the generator and discriminator of both models into a single training step using `tf.GradientTape` as follows:

1. The first step is to perform a forward pass and collect the outputs from both models:

```
    def train_step(self, images_A_1, images_B_1,
                   images_A_2, images_B_2):
        z = tf.random.normal((self.batch_size,
                             self.z_dim))
        real_labels = tf.ones((self.batch_size,
                             self.patch_size,
                             self.patch_size, 1))
        fake_labels = tf.zeros((self.batch_size,
```

```
                                  self.patch_size,
                                  self.patch_size, 1))
```

```
with tf.GradientTape() as tape_e,
     tf.GradientTape() as tape_g,\
     tf.GradientTape() as tape_d1,\
     tf.GradientTape() as tape_d2:
```

```
encode_real, encode_fake, fake_B_encode,\
    kl_loss = self.cvae_gan([images_A_1,
                             images_B_1])
```

```
random_real, random_fake, mean_random = \
      self.clr_gan([images_A_2, images_B_2, z])
```

2. Next, we backpropagate and update the discriminators:

```
self.d1_loss = self.mse(real_labels, encode_real) + \
               self.mse(fake_labels, encode_fake)
```

```
gradients_d1 = tape_d1.gradient(self.d1_loss,
        self.discriminator_1.trainable_variables)
```

```
self.optimizer_d1.apply_gradients(zip(gradients_d1,
        self.discriminator_1.trainable_variables))
```

```
self.d2_loss = self.mse(real_labels, random_real) +\
               self.mse(fake_labels, random_fake)
```

```
gradients_d2 = tape_d2.gradient(self.d2_loss,
        self.discriminator_2.trainable_variables)
```

```
self.optimizer_d2.apply_gradients(zip(gradients_d2,
        self.discriminator_2.trainable_variables))
```

3. Then we calculate the losses from the models' outputs. Similar to CycleGAN, BicycleGAN also uses the LSGAN loss function, which is the mean squared error:

```
self.LAMBDA_IMAGE = 10
```

```
self.LAMBDA_LATENT = 0.5
```

```
self.LAMBDA_KL = 0.01
```

```
self.gan_1_loss = self.mse(real_labels, encode_fake)
```

```
self.gan_2_loss = self.mse(real_labels, random_fake)
```

```
self.image_loss = self.LAMBDA_IMAGE * self.mae(
                          images_B_1, fake_B_encode)
```

```
self.kl_loss = self.LAMBDA_KL*kl_loss
```

```
self.latent_loss = self.LAMBDA_LATENT *self.mae(z,
                                     mean_random)
```

4. Finally, there is the update to the generator's and encoder's weights. The L1 latent code loss is only used to update the generator, and not the encoder. It was found that optimizing them simultaneously for the loss would encourage them to hide information relating to the latent code and not learn meaningful modes. Therefore, we calculate separate losses for the generator and encoder and update the weights accordingly:

```
encoder_loss = self.gan_1_loss + self.gan_2_loss +\
                self.image_loss + self.kl_loss

generator_loss = encoder_loss + self.latent_loss

gradients_generator = tape_g.gradient(generator_loss,
                self.generator.trainable_variables)

self.optimizer_generator.apply_gradients(zip(
                gradients_generator,
                self.generator.trainable_variables))

gradients_encoder = tape_e.gradient(encoder_loss,
                self.encoder.trainable_variables)

self.optimizer_encoder.apply_gradients(zip(
                gradients_encoder,
                self.encoder.trainable_variables))
```

There you go. You can now train your BicycleGAN. There are two datasets you can choose from in the notebook – building façades or edges to shoes. The shoe dataset has simpler images and therefore is easier to train. The following images are examples from the original BicycleGAN paper. The first real image on the left is the ground truth and the four images on the right are generated ones:

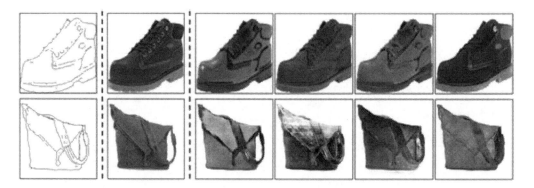

Figure 4.18 – Examples of transforming sketches to images with a variety of styles. Source: J-Y. Zhu, "Toward Multimodal Image-to-Image Translation"

You may struggle to notice the difference between them on this grayscale page because their differences are mainly in color. It captures the structure of the shoes and bags almost perfectly, but not so much in terms of the fine details.

Summary

We began this chapter by learning how the basic cGAN enforces the class label as a condition to generate MNIST. We implemented two different ways of injecting the condition, one being to one-hot encode the class labels to a dense layer, reshape them to match the channel dimensions of the input noise, and then concatenate them together. The other way is to use the embedding layer and element-wise multiplication.

Next, we learned to implement pix2pix, a special type of condition GAN for image-to-image translation. It uses PatchGAN as a discriminator, which looks at patches of images to encourage fine details or high-frequency components in the generated image. We also learned about a popular network architecture, U-Net, that has been used for various applications. Although pix2pix can generate high-quality image translation, the image is one-to-one mapping without diversification of the output. This is due to the removal of input noise. This was overcome by BicycleGAN, which learned the mapping between the latent code and the output image so that the generator doesn't ignore the input noise. With that, we are one step closer toward multimodal image translation.

In the timeline between pix2pix and BicycleGAN, CycleGAN was invented. Its two generators and two discriminators use the cycle consistency loss to allow training with unpaired data. In total, we have implemented four GANs in this chapter and they are not easy ones. Well done! In the next chapter, we will look at style transfer, which entangles an image into content code and style code. This has had a profound influence on the development of new GANs.

5
Style Transfer

Generative models such as VAE and GAN are great at generating realistic looking images. But we understand very little about the latent variables, let alone how to control them with regard to image generation. Researchers began to explore ways to better represent images aside from pixel distribution. It was found that an image could be disentangled into **content** and **style**. Content describes the composition in the image such as a tall building in the middle of the image. On the other hand, style refers to the fine details, such as the brick or stone textures of the wall or the color of the roof. Images showing the same building at different times of the day have different hues and brightness and can be seen as having the same content but different styles.

In this chapter, we will start by implementing some seminal work in **neural style transfer** to transfer the artistic style of an image. We will then learn to implement **feed-forward neural style transfer**, which is a lot faster in terms of speed. Then we will implement **adaptive instance normalization (AdaIN)** to perform style transfer with arbitrary numbers of styles. AdaIN has been incorporated into some state-of-the-art GANs, which are collectively known as **style-based GANs**. This includes **MUNIT** for image translation and **StyleGAN**, which is famous for generating realistic looking, high-fidelity faces. We will learn about their architecture in the final section of the chapter. This wraps up the evolution of style-based generative models.

By the end of this chapter, you will have learned how to perform artistic neural style transfer to convert a photo into painting. You will have a good understanding of how style is used in advanced GANs.

In this chapter, we will cover the following topics:

- Neural style transfer

- Improving style transfer

- Arbitrary style transfer in real time

- Introduction to style-based generative models

Technical requirements

The Jupyter notebooks and codes can be found at the following link:

`https://github.com/PacktPublishing/Hands-On-Image-Generation-with-TensorFlow-2.0/tree/master/Chapter05`

The notebooks used in the chapter are as follows:

- `ch5_neural_style_transfer.ipynb`

- `ch5_arbitrary_style_transfer.ipynb`

Neural style transfer

When **convolutional neural networks (CNNs)** outperformed all other algorithms in the ImageNet image classification competition, people started to realize the potential of it and began exploring it for other computer vision tasks. In the *A Neural Algorithm of Artistic Style* paper published in 2015 by Gatys et al., they demonstrated the use of CNNs to transfer the artistic style of one image to another, as shown in the following examples:

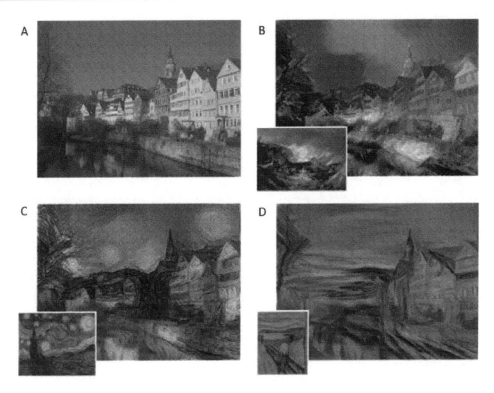

Figure 5.1 – (A) Content image. (B)-(D) Bottom image is the style image and the bigger pictures are stylized images

(Source: Gatys et al., 2015, "A Neural Algorithm of Artistic Style" https://arxiv.org/abs/1508.06576)

Unlike most deep learning trainings that require tons of training data, neural style transfer requires only two images – content and style images. We can use pre-trained CNN such as VGG to transfer the style from the style image to the content image.

As shown in the preceding image, (**A**) is the content image and (**B**) – (**D**) are the style and stylized images. The results were so impressive that they blew people's minds! Some even use the algorithm to create and sell art paintings. There are websites and apps that let people upload photos to perform style transfer without having to know the underlying theory and coding. Of course, as technical folks, we want to implement things by ourselves.

We will now look into the details in terms of how to implement neural style transfer, starting with extracting image features with CNNs.

Extracting features with VGG

Classification CNNs, like VGG, can be divided into two parts. The first part is known as **feature extractor** and is made up of mainly convolutional layers. The latter part consists of several dense layers that give the scores of classes. This is known as **classifier head**. It was found that a CNN pre-trained on ImageNet for classification tasks can be used for other tasks as well.

For example, if you want to create classification CNNs for other datasets that have only 10 classes instead of ImageNet's 1,000 classes, then you could keep the feature extractor and only swap out the classifier head with a new one. This is known as **transfer learning**, where we could transfer or reuse some learned knowledge to new networks or applications. Many deep neural networks for computer vision tasks include a feature extractor, either reusing weights or training from scratch. This includes **object detection** and **pose estimation**.

In a CNN, as we go deeper toward the output, it increasingly learns representation of the content of the image compared to its detailed pixel values. To understand this better, we will build a network to reconstruct the image that the layers see. The two steps for image reconstruction are as follows:

1. Forward pass the image through a CNN to extract the features.

2. With randomly initialized input, we *train the input* so that it recreates the features that best match the reference features from *step 1*.

Let me elaborate on *step 2*. In normal network training, the input image is fixed and the backpropagated gradients are used to update the network weights.

In neural style transfer, all network layers are frozen, and we use the gradients to change the input instead. The original paper uses VGG19 and Keras does have a pre-trained model that we could use. The feature extractor part of VGG is made up of five blocks and there is one downsampling at the end of each block. Every block has between two and four convolutional layers and the entire VGG19 has 16 convolutional layers and 3 dense layers, hence the number 19 in VGG19 stands for 19 layers with trainable weights. The following table shows different VGG configurations:

ConvNet Configuration					
A	A-LRN	B	C	D	E
11 weight layers	11 weight layers	13 weight layers	16 weight layers	16 weight layers	19 weight layers
input (224 × 224 RGB image)					
conv3-64	conv3-64 **LRN**	conv3-64 **conv3-64**	conv3-64 conv3-64	conv3-64 conv3-64	conv3-64 conv3-64
maxpool					
conv3-128	conv3-128	conv3-128 **conv3-128**	conv3-128 conv3-128	conv3-128 conv3-128	conv3-128 conv3-128
maxpool					
conv3-256 conv3-256	conv3-256 conv3-256	conv3-256 conv3-256	conv3-256 conv3-256 **conv1-256**	conv3-256 conv3-256 **conv3-256**	conv3-256 conv3-256 conv3-256 **conv3-256**
maxpool					
conv3-512 conv3-512	conv3-512 conv3-512	conv3-512 conv3-512	conv3-512 conv3-512 **conv1-512**	conv3-512 conv3-512 **conv3-512**	conv3-512 conv3-512 conv3-512 **conv3-512**
maxpool					
conv3-512 conv3-512	conv3-512 conv3-512	conv3-512 conv3-512	conv3-512 conv3-512 **conv1-512**	conv3-512 conv3-512 **conv3-512**	conv3-512 conv3-512 conv3-512 **conv3-512**
maxpool					
FC-4096					
FC-4096					
FC-1000					
soft-max					

Figure 5.2 – Different configurations of VGG

(Source: K. Simonyan, A. Zisserman, "Very Deep Convolutional Networks For Large-Scale Image Recognition" – https://arxiv.org/abs/1409.1556)

The Jupyter notebook for this is ch5_neural_style_transfer.ipynb, which is the complete neural style transfer solution.

However, in the following text, I'll use a simpler code to show content reconstruction, which will be expanded to perform style transfer. The following is the code for using a pretrained VGG to extract the output layer of block4_conv2:

```
vgg = tf.keras.applications.VGG19(include_top=False,
                                  weights='imagenet')
content_layers = ['block4_conv2']
```

```
content_outputs = [vgg.get_layer(x).output for x in
                                        content_layers]
model = Model(vgg.input, content_outputs)
```

Pre-trained Keras CNN models are grouped into two parts. The bottom part is made up of convolutional layers, commonly known as the **feature extractor**, while the top part is the classifier head made up of dense layers. As we only want to extract the features and not bother about the classification, we will set `include_top=False` when instantiating the VGG model.

VGG pre-processing

A Keras pre-trained model expects an input image to be in BGR in the range [0, 255]. Thus, the first step is to reverse the color channel to convert RGB into BGR. VGG uses different mean values for different color channels. Inside `preprocess_input()`, the pixel values are subtracted by the values of 103.939, 116.779, and 123.68 for the B, G, and R channels, respectively.

The following is the forward pass code where the image is first pre-processed before feeding into the model to return the content feature. We then extract the content features and use them as our target:

```
def extract_features(image):
    image = tf.keras.applications.vgg19.\
                preprocess_input(image *255.)
    content_ref = model(image)
    return content_ref
content_image = tf.reverse(content_image, axis=[-1])
content_ref = extract_features(content_image)
```

Note that the image is normalized to [0., 1.] and so we need to restore that to [0., 255.] by multiplying it by 255. We then create a randomly initialized input that will also become the stylized image:

```
image = tf.Variable(tf.random.normal(
                            shape=content_image.shape))
```

Next, we will use backpropagation to reconstruct the image from the content features.

Reconstructing content

In the training step, we feed an image to the frozen VGG to extract the content features and we use L2 loss to measure against the target content features. The following is the custom `loss` function to calculate the L2 loss of each feature layer:

```
def calc_loss(y_true, y_pred):
    loss = [tf.reduce_sum((x-y)**2) for x, y in
                        zip(y_pred, y_true)]
    return tf.reduce_mean(loss)
```

The following training step uses `tf.GradientTape()` to calculate the gradients. In normal neural network training, the gradients are applied to the trainable variables, that is, the weights of the neural network. However, in neural style transfer, the gradients are applied to the image. After that, we clip the image value between [0., 1.] as follows:

```
for i in range(1,steps+1):
    with tf.GradientTape() as tape:
        content_features = self.extract_features(image)
        loss = calc_loss(content_features, content_ref)
    grad = tape.gradient(loss, image)
    optimizer.apply_gradients([(grad, image)])
    image.assign(tf.clip_by_value(image, 0., 1.))
```

We train it for 1,000 steps, and this is what the reconstructed content looks like:

Figure 5.3 – Image reconstructed from content layers
(Source: https://www.pexels.com/. (Left): Original content image, (Right): Content of 'block1_1')

We could reconstruct the image almost perfectly with the first few convolutional layers similar to *block1_1*, as shown in the image above:

Figure 5.4 – Image reconstructed from content layers
(Left): Content of 'block4_1'. (Right): Content of 'block5_1'

As we go deeper into *block4_1*, we start to lose fine details, such as the window frames and the words on the building. As we go deeper into *block5_1*, we see that all the details are gone and filled with some random noise. If we look carefully, the building structure and edges are still intact and in places where they should be. Now we have extracted just the content and omitted the style. After extracting the content features, the next step is to extract the style features.

Reconstructing styles with the Gram matrix

As we have seen with the style reconstruction, the feature maps, especially the first few layers, contain both style and content. So how do we extract the style representation from the image? Gats et al. uses the **Gram matrix**, which computes the correlations between the different filter responses. Let's say the activation of convolutional layer l has a shape of (H, W, C), where H and W are the spatial dimensions and C is the number of channels, which equals the number of filters. Each filter detects different image features; they can be horizontal lines, diagonal lines, colors, and so on.

Humans perceive things as having the same textures when they share some common features, such as a color and an edge. For instance, if we feed an image of a grass field into a convolutional layer, the filters that detect *vertical lines* and *green color* will produce bigger responses in their feature maps. Hence, we can use the correlation between feature maps to represent textures in the image.

To create a Gram matrix from activations with a shape of (H, W, C), we will first reshape it into C number of vectors. Each vector is a flattened feature map with a size of H×W. We perform an inner product on these C vectors to get a symmetric C×C Gram matrix. The detailed steps for calculating a Gram matrix in TensorFlow are as follows:

1. Use `tf.squeeze()` to remove the batch dimension (1, H, W, C) to (H, W, C) as the batch size is always 1.

2. Transpose the tensor to transform the shape from (H, W, C) to (C, H, W).

3. Flatten the final two dimensions to become (C, H×W).

4. Perform the dot product of the features to create a Gram matrix with a shape of (C, C).

5. Normalize by dividing the matrix by the number of points (H×W) in each flattened feature map.

The code to calculate a Gram matrix from a single convolution layer activation is as follows:

```
def gram_matrix(x):
    x = tf.transpose(tf.squeeze(x), (2,0,1));
    x = tf.keras.backend.batch_flatten(x)
    num_points = x.shape[-1]
    gram = tf.linalg.matmul(x, tf.transpose(x))/num_points
    return gram
```

We can use this function to obtain Gram matrices for each VGG layer that we designated as a style layer. We then use L2 loss on Gram matrices from the target and reference images. The loss function and the rest of the code is identical to content reconstruction. The code to create a list of the Gram matrices is as follows:

```
def extract_features(image):
    image = tf.keras.applications.vgg19.\
                   preprocess_input(image *255.)
    styles = self.model(image)
    styles = [self.gram_matrix(s) for s in styles]
    return styles
```

The following images are reconstructed from style features from the different VGG layers:

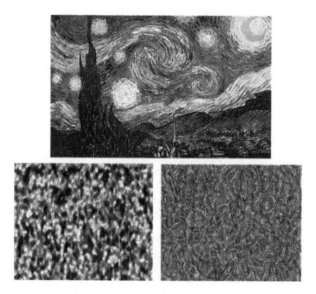

Figure 5.5 – (Top) Style image: Vincent Van Goh's Starry Night. (Bottom Left) Reconstructed style from 'block1_1'. (Bottom Right) Reconstructed style from 'block3_1'

In the style image reconstructed from *block1_1*, the content information is completely gone, showing only high spatial frequency texture details. The higher layer, *block3_1*, shows some curly shapes that seem to capture the higher hierarchy of the style in the input image. The loss function for the Gram matrix is the sum of **squared error** instead of **mean squared error**. Hence, higher hierarchy style layers have higher intrinsic weights. This allows the transfer of higher style representations, such as brush strokes. If we use mean squared error, low-level style features such as texture will be more prominent visually and may appear like high frequency noise.

Performing neural style transfer

We can now merge the code from both the content and style reconstruction to perform neural style transfer.

We first create a model that extracts two blocks of features, one for content and the other for style. We use only one layer of `block5_conv1` for the content, and five layers, from `block1_conv1` to `block5_conv1`, to capture styles from different hierarchies as follows:

```
vgg = tf.keras.applications.VGG19(include_top=False,
                                  weights='imagenet')
```

```
default_content_layers = ['block5_conv1']
default_style_layers = ['block1_conv1',
                        'block2_conv1',
                        'block3_conv1',
                        'block4_conv1',
                        'block5_conv1']
content_layers = content_layers if content_layers else default_
content_layers
style_layers = style_layers if style_layers else default_style_
layers
self.content_outputs = [vgg.get_layer(x).output for x in
content_layers]
self.style_outputs = [vgg.get_layer(x).output for x in style_
layers]
self.model = Model(vgg.input, [self.content_outputs,
                              self.style_outputs])
```

Before the start of the training loop, we extract content and style features from respective images to use as the targets. While we can use randomly initialized input for content and style reconstruction, it would be faster to train by starting from the content image as follows:

```
content_ref, _ = self.extract_features(content_image)
_, style_ref = self.extract_features(style_image)
```

Then, we weigh the content and style loss and add them. The code snippet is as follows:

```
def train_step(self, image, content_ref, style_ref):
    with tf.GradientTape() as tape:
        content_features, style_features = \
                        self.extract_features(image)
        content_loss = self.content_weight*self.calc_loss(
                            content_ref, content_features)
        style_loss = self.style_weight*self.calc_loss(
                            style_ref, style_features)
        loss = content_loss + style_loss
    grad = tape.gradient(loss, image)
    self.optimizer.apply_gradients([(grad, image)])
    image.assign(tf.clip_by_value(image, 0., 1.))
    return content_loss, style_loss
```

The following are the two stylized images produced using different weights and content layers:

Figure 5.6 – Stylized images using neural style transfer

Feel free to change the weights and layers to create the styles that you want. I hope you now have a better understanding of content and style representation, which will come in handy when we explore advanced generative models. Next, we will look at ways to improve the neural style transfer.

Improving style transfer

The research community and industry were excited about neural style transfer and wasted no time in putting it to use. Some set up websites to allow users to upload photos to perform style transfer, while some used that to create merchandise to sell. Then people realized some of the shortcomings of the original neural style transfer and worked to improve it.

One of the biggest limitations is that style transfer takes all the style information, including the color and brush strokes of the entire style image, and transfers it to the whole of the content image. Using the examples that we just did in the previous section, the blueish color from the style image was transferred into both the building and background. Wouldn't it be nice if we had the choice to transfer only the brush stroke but not the color, and just to the preferred regions?

The lead author of neural style transfer and his team produced a new algorithm to address these issues. The following diagram shows the control the algorithm can give and an example of the results:

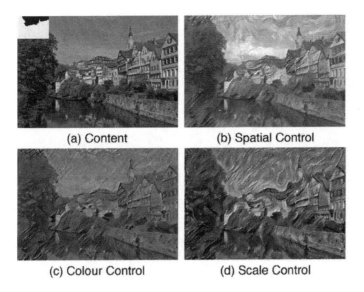

(a) Content   (b) Spatial Control

(c) Colour Control   (d) Scale Control

Figure 5.7 – Different control methods of neural style transfer. (a) Content image (b) The sky and ground are stylized using different style images (c) The color of the content image is preserved (d) The fine scale and coarse scale are stylized using different style images
(Source: L. Gatys, 2017, "Controlling Perceptual Factors in Neural Style Transfer", https://arxiv.org/abs/1611.07865)

The controls proposed in this paper are as follows:

- **Spatial control**: This controls the spatial location of style transfer in both the content and style images. This is done by applying a spatial mask to style features before calculating the Gram matrix.

- **Color control**: This can be used to preserve the color of the content image. To do this, we will convert the RGB format into color space such that HCL separates the luminance (brightness) from other color channels. We can think of the luminance channel as a grayscale image. We then perform style transfer only in the luminance channel and then merge it with color channels from the original style image to give the final stylized image.

- **Scale control**: This manages the granularity of the brush strokes. The process is more involved as it requires multiple runs of style transfers and different layers of style features to be chosen in order to compute the Gram matrix.

These perceptual controls are useful for creating better stylized images that suit your requirements. I'll leave it as an exercise for you to implement those controls if you desire, because we have more important things to cover.

The following are the two major themes associated with improving style transfer that had a big influence on the development of GANs:

- Improving speed
- Improving style variations

Let's go through some of these developments to lay some foundations for the next project that we will implement – performing arbitrary style transfer in real time.

Faster style transfer with a feed-forward network

Neural style transfer is based on optimization that is akin to neural network training. It is slow and takes several minutes to run even with the use of a GPU. This limited its potential applications on mobile devices. As a result, researchers were motivated to develop faster algorithms for style transfer and **feed-forward style transfer** was born. The following diagram shows one of the first networks that employed such an architecture:

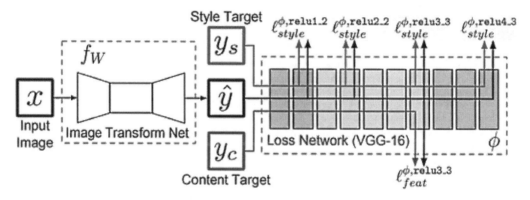

Figure 5.8 – Block diagram of a feed-forward convolutional neural network for style transfer.
(Redrawn from: J. Johnson et al., 2016 "Perceptual Losses for Real-Time Style Transfer and Super-Resolution" – https://arxiv.org/abs/1603.08155)

The architecture is simpler than the how the block diagram looks. There are two networks in this architecture:

- A **trainable convolutional network** (normally known as a **style transfer network**) to translate an input image into a stylized image. This can be implemented as an encoder-decoder-like architecture, like that of U-Net or VAE.
- A **fixed convolutional network**, usually a pretrained VGG, that measures the content and style losses.

Similar to the original neural style transfer, we first extract the content and style targets with VGG. Instead of training the input image, we now train a convolutional network to translate a content image into a stylized image. The content and style features of the stylized image are extracted by VGG, and losses are measured and backpropagated to the trainable convolutional network. We train it like a normal feed-forward CNN. During inference, we only need to perform one forward pass to translate the input image into a stylized image, which is 1,000 times faster than before!

Alright, the speed problem is now solved, but there is still a problem. Such a network could only learn one style to transfer. We'll need to train one network for each of the styles we want to perform, which is a lot less flexible than the original style transfer. Then people started working on that, and as you may have guessed, that got solved too! We'll go over that shortly.

A different style feature

The original neural style transfer paper didn't explain why the Gram matrix is effective as a style feature. Many subsequent improvements to style transfers, such as the feed-forward style transfer, continued using the Gram matrix solely as style features. That's changed with the *Demystifying Neural Style Transfer* paper published by Y, Li et al. in 2017. It was found that the style information is intrinsically represented by the *distributions of activations* in a CNN. They have shown that matching Gram matrices of activations are equivalent to minimizing the **maximum mean discrepancy** (**MMD**) of activation distributions. Therefore, we can perform style transfer by matching the activation distribution of an image to those of the style image.

Therefore, the Gram matrix is not the only way in which to implement style transfer. We could use adversarial loss, too. Let's recall that GANs such as pix2pix (*Chapter 4, Image-to-Image Translation*) could perform style transfer by matching the pixel distribution of a generated image with the real (style) images. The difference is that GANs try to minimize the discrepancy in pixel distribution, while style transfer does it to the layer activation's distributions.

Later, researchers found that we can use just the basic statistics of the mean and variance of the activations to represent the styles. In other words, if we feed two images that are similar in style into VGG, their layer activations will have a similar mean and variance. We can therefore train a network to perform style transfer by minimizing the difference in the mean and variance of activations between a generated image and a style image. This leads to the development of using a normalization layer to control the style.

Controlling styles with a normalization layer

A simple but effective way of controlling the activation statistics is by changing the gamma γ and beta β in the normalization layer. In other words, we could change the style by using different affine transform parameters (gamma and beta). As a reminder, both batch normalization and instance normalization share the same equation, as follows:

$$BN(x) = IN(x) = \gamma \left(\frac{x - \mu(x)}{\sigma(x)}\right) + \beta$$

The difference is that batch normalization (*BN*) calculates the mean μ and standard deviation σ across (N, H, W) dimensions, while instance normalization (*IN*) calculates only from (H, W).

However, there is only one gamma and beta pair per normalization layer, which limits the network to learning only one style. How do we make the network learn multiple styles? Well, we could use multiple sets of gammas and betas where each set remembers one style. This is exactly what **conditional instance normalization** (**CIN**) does.

It builds upon instance normalization but has multiple sets of gamma and beta pairs. Each gamma and beta set is used to train a particular style; in other words, they are conditioned on the style images. The equation of conditional instance normalization is as follows:

$$CIN(x; s) = \gamma^s \left(\frac{x - \mu(x)}{\sigma(x)}\right) + \beta^s$$

Say we have S different style images, then we have S gammas and S betas in normalization layers for each of the styles. In addition to the content image, we also feed in the one-hot encoded style label into the style transfer network. In practice, gamma and beta are implemented as matrices with a shape of (S×C). We retrieve the gamma and beta for that style by performing matrix multiplication of a one-hot encoded label (1×S) with matrices (S×C) to get γ^s and β^s for each (1×C) channel. It is easier to understand when we implement the code. However, we will defer implementation to *Chapter 9, Video Synthesis*, when we use it to perform class condition normalization. We are introducing CIN now to prepare ourselves for the upcoming section.

Now, with style encoded into the embedding spaces of gammas and betas, we could perform style interpolation by interpolating gammas and betas as shown in the following image:

Figure 5.9 – Combination of artistic styles by interpolating the gammas and betas of two different styles (Source: V. Dumoulin et al., 2017 "A Learned Representation for Artistic Style" – https://arxiv.org/abs/1610.07629)

This is all good, but the network is still limited to the fixed N styles that are used in training. Next, we will learn and implement an improvement that allows any arbitrary styles!

Arbitrary style transfer in real time

In this section, we will learn how to implement a network that could perform arbitrary style transfer in real time. We have already learned how to use a feed-forward network for faster inference and that solves the real-time part. We have also learned how to use conditional instance normalization to transfer a fixed number of styles. Now, we will learn one further normalization technique that allows for any arbitrary style, and then we are good to go in terms of implementing the code.

Implementing adaptive instance normalization

Like CIN, **AdaIN** is also instance normalization, meaning that the mean and standard deviation are calculated across (H, W) per image, and per channel, as opposed to batch normalization, which calculates across (N, H, W). In CIN, the gammas and betas are trainable variables, and they learn the means and variances that are needed for different styles. In AdaIN, gammas and betas are replaced by standard deviations and means of style features, as follows:

$$AdaIN(x, y) = \sigma(y)\left(\frac{x - \mu(x)}{\sigma(x)}\right) + \mu(y)$$

AdaIN can still be understood as a form of conditional instance normalization where the conditions are the style features rather than the style labels. In both training and inference time, we use VGG to extract the style layer outputs and use their statistics as the style conditions. This avoids the need to pre-define a fixed set of styles. We can now implement AdaIN in TensorFlow. The notebook for this is `ch5_arbitrary_style_transfer.ipynb`.

We will use TensorFlow's subclassing to create a custom `AdaIN` layer as follows:

```python
class AdaIN(layers.Layer):
    def __init__(self, epsilon=1e-5):
        super(AdaIN, self).__init__()
        self.epsilon = epsilon
    def call(self, inputs):
        x = inputs[0] # content
        y = inputs[1] # style
        mean_x, var_x = tf.nn.moments(x, axes=(1,2),
                                      keepdims=True)
        mean_y, var_y = tf.nn.moments(y, axes=(1,2),
                                      keepdims=True)
        std_x = tf.sqrt(var_x+self.epsilon)
        std_y = tf.sqrt(var_y+self.epsilon)
        output = std_y*(x - mean_x)/(std_x) + mean_y
        return output
```

This is a straightforward implementation of the equation. One thing that deserves a bit of explanation is the use of `tf.nn.moments`, which is also used in the TensorFlow batch normalization implementation. It calculates the mean and variance of the feature maps, where the axes 1, 2 refer to H, W of the feature maps. We also set `keepdims=True` to keep the results in four dimensions with a shape of (N, 1, 1, C) as opposed to the default (N, C). The former allows TensorFlow to perform broadcast arithmetic with the input tensor that has a shape of (N, H, W, C). Here, broadcast refers to repeating one value in bigger dimensions.

To be more precise, when we subtract *x* from the calculated mean for a particular instance and channel, the single mean value will first be repeated into the shape of (H, W) before the subtraction. We will now look at how to incorporate AdaIN into style transfer.

Style transfer network architecture

The following diagram shows the architecture of a style transfer network and the training pipeline:

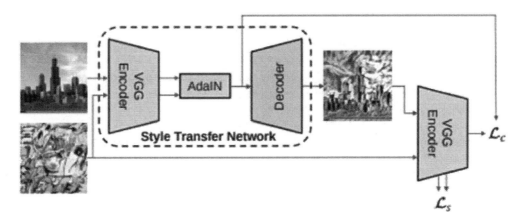

Figure 5.10 – Overview of style transfer with AdaIN

(Redrawn from: X. Huang, S. Belongie, 2017, "Arbitrary Style Transfer in Real Time with Adaptive Instance Normalization" – https://arxiv.org/abs/1703.06868)

The **style transfer network** (**STN**) is an encoder-decoder network where the encoder encodes the content and style features with fixed VGG. AdaIN then encodes the style features into the statistics of content features and the decoder takes these new features to generate the stylized image.

Building the encoder

The following is the code to build the encoder from VGG:

```
def build_encoder(self, name='encoder'):
    self.encoder_layers = ['block1_conv1',
                           'block2_conv1',
                           'block3_conv1',
                           'block4_conv1']
    vgg = tf.keras.applications.VGG19(include_top=False,
                                      weights='imagenet')
    layer_outputs = [vgg.get_layer(x).output for x in
                     self.encoder_layers]
    return Model(vgg.input, layer_outputs, name=name)
```

This is similar to neural style transfer, except that we use the last style layer, `'block4_conv1'`, as our content layer. Thus, we don't need to define the content layer separately. We will now make a small but important improvement to the convolutional layer to improve the appearance of generated images.

Reducing block artifacts with reflection padding

Normally, when we apply padding to an input tensor in a convolutional layer, constant zeros are padded around the tensor. However, the sudden drop in value at a border creates high frequency components and results in block artefacts in the generated image. One way to reduce these frequency components is by adding *total variation loss* as the regularizer in the network training.

To do that, we first calculate the high frequency components simply by shifting the image by one pixel, and then subtract by the original image to create a matrix. Total variation loss is the L1 norm or the sum of absolute values. Therefore, the training will try to minimize this loss function so as to reduce the high-frequency component.

There is another alternative, which is to replace the constant zeros in padding with reflective values. For example, if we pad an array of [10, 8, 9] with zeros, this will give [0, 10, 8, 9, 0]. We can then see a sudden change in values between 0 and its neighbors.

If we use reflective padding, the padded array will be [8, 10, 8, 9, 8], which provides a smoother transition toward the border. However, Keras Conv2D doesn't support reflective padding, so we will have to create a custom Conv2D using TensorFlow subclassing. The following code snippet (the code has been curtailed for brevity; please check out GitHub for the entire code) shows how to add reflective padding to the input tensor prior to the convolution:

```
class Conv2D(layers.Layer):
    @tf.function
    def call(self, inputs):
        padded = tf.pad(inputs, [[0, 0], [1, 1], [1, 1],
                                 [0, 0]], mode='REFLECT')
        # perform conv2d using low level API
        output = tf.nn.conv2d(padded, self.w, strides=1,
                              padding="VALID") + self.b
        if self.use_relu:
            output = tf.nn.relu(output)
        return output
```

The preceding code is taken from *Chapter 1, Getting Started with Image Generation Using TensorFlow*, but with an added low-level tf.pad API to pad the input tensor.

Building the decoder

Although we use 4 VGG layers (`block1_conv1` to `block4_conv1`) in the encoder code, only the last layer, `block4_conv1`, from the encoder is used by AdaIN. Therefore, the input tensor to the decoder has the same activation as `block4_conv1`. The decoder architecture is not too dissimilar to the ones we have implemented in earlier chapters. It consists of convolutional and upsampling layers, as shown in the following code:

```
def build_decoder(self):
    block = tf.keras.Sequential([\
            Conv2D(512, 256, 3),
            UpSampling2D((2,2)),
            Conv2D(256, 256, 3),
            Conv2D(256, 256, 3),
            Conv2D(256, 256, 3),
            Conv2D(256, 128, 3),
            UpSampling2D((2,2)),
            Conv2D(128, 128, 3),
            Conv2D(128, 64, 3),
            UpSampling2D((2,2)),
            Conv2D(64, 64, 3),
            Conv2D(64, 3, 3, use_relu=False)],
                        name='decoder')
    return block
```

The preceding code uses custom `Conv2D` with reflective padding. All layers use the ReLU activation function, except the output layer, which does not have any non-linearity activation function. We have now completed AdaIN, the encoder, and the decoder, and can move on to the image pre-processing pipeline.

VGG processing

Like the neural style transfer we built earlier, we will need to pre-process the image by inverting the color channel to BGR and then subtracting the color means. The code is as follows:

```
def preprocess(self, image):
    # rgb to bgr
    image = tf.reverse(image, axis=[-1])
    return tf.keras.applications.vgg19.preprocess_input(image)
```

We could do the same in post-processing, that is, adding back the color means and reversing the color channel. However, this is something that could be learned by the decoder as color means is equivalent to the biases in the output layer. We will let the training do the job and all we need to do is to clip the pixels to range of [0, 255], as follows:

```
def postprocess(self, image):
    return tf.clip_by_value(image, 0., 255.)
```

We now have all the building blocks ready and all that is left to do is to put them together to create the STN and training pipeline.

Building the style transfer network

Constructing the **STN** is straightforward and simply involves connecting the encoder, AdaIN, and decoder, as shown in the preceding architectural diagram. The STN is also the model we will use to perform inference. The code to do this is as follows:

```
content_image = self.preprocess(content_image_input)
style_image = self.preprocess(style_image_input)
self.content_target = self.encoder(content_image)
self.style_target = self.encoder(style_image)
adain_output = AdaIN()([self.content_target[-1],
                        self.style_target[-1]])
self.stylized_image = self.postprocess(
                        self.decoder(adain_output))
self.stn = Model([content_image_input,
                  style_image_input],
                 self.stylized_image)
```

The content and style images are pre-processed and fed into the encoder. The last feature layer, that is, `block4_conv1` from both images, goes to `AdaIN()`. The stylized feature then goes into the decoder to generate the stylized image in RGB.

Arbitrary style transfer training

Like neural and feed-forward style transfer, content loss and style loss are computed from an activation extracted by the fixed VGG. The content loss is also an L2 norm, but the generated stylized image's content features are now compared against AdaIN's output rather than the features from the content image, as shown in the following code. The authors of the paper found that this makes convergence faster:

```
content_loss =  tf.reduce_sum((output_features[-1]-\
                               adain_output)**2)
```

For style loss, the commonly used Gram matrix is replaced with the L2 norm of the activation statistics of mean and variance. This produces similar results to the Gram matrix but is conceptually cleaner. The following is the style loss function equation:

$$\mathcal{L}_s = \sum_{i=1}^{L} \|\mu(\phi_i(stylized)) - \mu(\phi_i(style))\|_2 + \|\sigma(\phi_i(stylized)) - \sigma(\phi_i(style))\|_2$$

Here, φ^i denotes a layer in VGG-19 used to compute the style loss.

We use `tf.nn.moments` as in the AdaIN layer to calculate the statistics and the L2 norm between the features from stylized and style images. Each style layer carries the same weight, and hence we average the content layer losses as follows:

```
def calc_style_loss(self, y_true, y_pred):
    n_features = len(y_true)
    epsilon = 1e-5
    loss = []
    for i in range(n_features):
        mean_true, var_true = tf.nn.moments(y_true[i],
                                   axes=(1,2), keepdims=True)
        mean_pred, var_pred = tf.nn.moments(y_pred[i],
                                   axes=(1,2), keepdims=True)
        std_true, std_pred = tf.sqrt(var_true+epsilon),
                                   tf.sqrt(var_pred+epsilon)
        mean_loss = tf.reduce_sum(tf.square(
                                   mean_true-mean_pred))
        std_loss = tf.reduce_sum(tf.square(
                                   std_true-std_pred))
        loss.append(mean_loss + std_loss)
    return tf.reduce_mean(loss)
```

The final step is to write the training step, as shown here:

```
def train_step(self, train_data):
    with tf.GradientTape() as tape:
        adain_output, output_features, style_target = \
                            self.training_model(train_data)
        content_loss = tf.reduce_sum(
                    (output_features[-1]-adain_output)\
                                            **2)
        style_loss = self.style_weight * \
                        self.calc_style_loss(
                            style_target, output_features)
        loss =  content_loss + style_loss
        gradients = tape.gradient(loss,
                        self.decoder.trainable_variables)
        self.optimizer.apply_gradients(zip(gradients,
                        self.decoder.trainable_variables))
    return content_loss, style_loss
```

Instead of tweaking weights to both the content and style, we fix the content weight to be 1 and adjust just the style weight. In this example, we set the content weight to 1 and the style weight to 1e-4. In *Figure 5.10*, it may look like there are three networks to train but two of them are fixed VGG, so the only trainable network is the decoder. Therefore, we only track and apply gradients to the decoder.

> **Tips**
>
> The preceding training step can be replaced by Keras' `train_on_batch()` function (see *Chapter 3, Generative Adversarial Network*), which uses fewer code lines. I'll leave this to you as an additional exercise.

In this example, we'll use faces as content images, and `cyclegan/vangogh2photo` for the styles. Although Van Gogh's paintings are of one artistic style, from the style transfer perspective, each style image is a unique style. The `vangoh2photo` dataset contains 400 style images, meaning we are training the network with 400 different styles! The following diagram shows examples of images produced by our network:

Figure 5.11 – Arbitrary style transfer. (Left) Style image (Middle) Content image (Right) Stylized image

The images in the preceding diagram shows the style transfers in inference time using style images that were not previously seen by the network. Each style transfer happens only with a single forward pass, which is a lot faster than the iterative optimization of the original neural style transfer algorithm. Having understood various techniques to perform style transfer, we are now in a good position to learn how to design GANs in style (pun intended).

Introduction to style-based GANs

The innovations in style transfer made their way into influencing the development of GANs. Although GANs at that time could generate realistic images, they were generated by using random latent variables, where we had little understanding in terms of what they represented. Even though multimodal GANs could create variations in generated images, we did not know how to control the latent variables to achieve the outcome that we wanted.

In an ideal world, we would love to have some knobs to independently control the features we would like to generate, as in the face manipulation exercise in *Chapter 2, Variational Autoencoder*. This is known as **disentangled representation**, which is a relatively new idea in deep learning. The idea of disentangled representation is to separate an image into independent representation. For example, a face has two eyes, a nose, and a mouth, with each of them being a representation of a face. As we have learned in style transfer, an image can be disentangled into content and style. So researchers brought that idea into GANs.

In the next section, we will look at a style-based GAN known as **MUNIT**. As we are limited by the number of pages in the book, we won't be writing the detailed code, but will go over the overall architecture to understand how style is used in these models.

Multimodal Unsupervised Image-to-Image Translation (MUNIT)

MUNIT is an image-to-image translation model similar to BicycleGAN (*Chapter 4, Image-to-Image Translation*). Both can generate multimodal images with continuous distributions, but BicycleGAN needs to have paired data while MUNIT does not. BicycleGAN generates multimodal images by using two models that relate the target image to latent variables. It is not very clear how these models work, nor how to control the latent variable to change the output. MUNIT's approach is conceptually a lot different, but also a lot simpler to understand. It assumes that the source and target images share the same content space, but with different styles.

The following diagram shows the principal idea behind MUNIT:

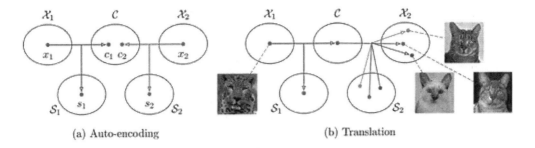

(a) Auto-encoding   (b) Translation

Figure 5.12 – Illustration of the MUNIT method.

(Redrawn from: X. Huang et al., 2018, "Multimodal Unsupervised Image-to-Image Translation" –
https://arxiv.org/abs/1804.04732)

Say we have two images, X_1 and X_2. Each of them can be represented as a content code and style code pair (C_1, S_1) and (C_2, S_2), respectively. It is assumed that both C_1 and C_2 are in a shared content space, C. In other words, the contents may not be exactly the same but are similar. The styles are in their respective domain-specific style spaces. Therefore, image translation from X_1 and X_2 can be formulated as generating image with content code from X_1 and style code from X_2, or, in other words, from code (C_1, S_2).

Previously in style transfer, we viewed styles as artistic styles with different brush strokes, colors, and textures. Now, we expand the meaning of style to beyond artistic painting. For example, tigers and lions are just cats with different styles of whiskers, skin, fur, and shapes. Next, let's look at the MUNIT model architecture.

Understanding the architecture

The MUNIT architecture is shown in the following diagram:

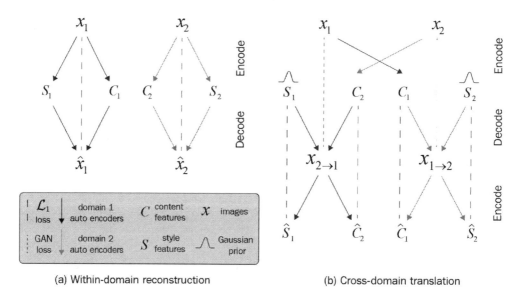

(a) Within-domain reconstruction   (b) Cross-domain translation

Figure 5.13 – MUNIT model overview
(Redrawn from: X. Huang et al., 2018, "Multimodal Unsupervised Image-to-Image Translation" –
https://arxiv.org/abs/1804.04732)

There are two autoencoders, one in each domain. The autoencoder encodes the image into its style and content codes, and then the decoder decodes them back into the original image. This is trained using adversarial loss, in other words, the model is made up of an autoencoder but is trained like a GAN.

In the preceding diagram, the image reconstruction process is shown on the left. On the right is the cross-domain translation. As mentioned earlier, to translate from X_1 to X_2, we first encode the images into their respective content and style codes, and then we do two things with it as follows:

1. We generate a fake image in style domain 2 with (C_1, S_2). This is also trained using GANs.

2. We encode the fake image into content and style code. If the translation works well, then it should be similar to (C_1, S_2).

Well, if this is sounding very familiar to you, that is because this is the *cycle consistency constraint* from CycleGAN. Except, here the cycle consistency is not applied to the image, but to the content and style codes.

Looking into autoencoder design

Finally, let's look at the detailed architecture of the autoencoder, as shown in the following diagram:

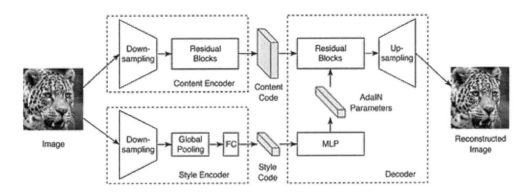

Figure 5.14 – MUNIT model overview

(Source: X. Huang et al., 2018, "Multimodal Unsupervised Image-to-Image Translation" – https://arxiv. org/abs/1804.04732)

Unlike other style transfer models, MUNIT doesn't use VGG as an encoder. It uses two separate encoders, one for content and another for style. The content encoder consists of several residual blocks with instance normalization and downsampling. This is quite similar to VGG's style feature.

The style encoder is different from the content encoder in two aspects:

- Firstly, there is no normalization. As we have learned, normalizing activations to zero means removing the style information.

- Secondly, the residual blocks are replaced with fully connected layers. This is because style is seen as spatially invariant and therefore we don't need convolutional layers to provide the spatial information.

This is to say that the style code only contains information about the eye color and doesn't need to know where the eyes are as it is the responsibility of the content code. The style code is a low-dimensional vector and usually has the size of 8, which is in contrast to high-dimensional latent variables in GAN and VAE, and styles features in style transfer. The reason for a small style code size is so that we have a fewer number of knobs to control the styles, which make things more manageable. The following diagram shows how the content and style code feed into the decoder:

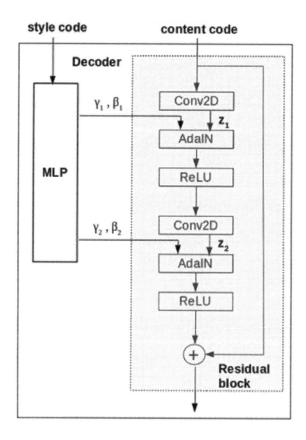

Figure 5.15 – AdaIN layers within the decoder

The generator within the decoder is made up of a group of residual blocks. Only residual blocks within the first group have AdaIN as the normalization layer. The equation for AdaIN, where z is the activation from the previous convolutional layer, is shown here:

$$AdaIN(z, \gamma, \beta) = \gamma \left(\frac{z - \mu(z)}{\sigma(z)} \right) + \beta$$

In the arbitrary feed-forward neural style transfer, we use the mean and standard deviation from a single style layer as gamma and beta in AdaIN. In MUNIT, the gamma and beta are generated from the style code with a **multilayer perceptron (MLP)**.

Translating animal images

The following screenshot shows samples of *1-to-many* image translations by MUNIT. We can generate a variety of output images by using different style codes:

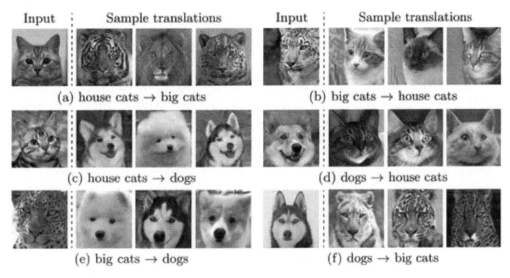

Figure 5.16 – Animal image translation by MUNIT

(Source: X. Huang et al., 2018, "Multimodal Unsupervised Image-to-Image Translation" – https://arxiv. org/abs/1804.04732)

At the time of writing, MUNIT is still the state-of-the-art model for multimodal image-to-image translation, according to `https://paperswithcode.com/task/ multimodal-unsupervised-image-to-image`.

If you are interested in the code implementation, you can refer to the official implementation by NVIDIA at `https://github.com/NVlabs/MUNIT`.

Summary

In this chapter, we covered the evolution of styled-based generative models. It all started with neural style transfer, where we learned that the image can be disentangled into content and style. The original algorithm was slowed and the iterative optimization process in inference time replaced with a feed-forward style transfer that could perform style transfer in real time.

We then learned that the Gram matrix is not the only method for representing style, and that we could use the layers' statistics instead. As a result, normalization layers have been explored to control the style of an image, which eventually led to the creation of AdaIN. By combing a feed-forward network and AdaIN, we implemented arbitrary style transfer in real time.

With the success in style transfer, AdaIN found its way into GANs. We went over the MUNIT architecture in detail in terms of how AdaIN was used for multimodal image generation. There is a style-based GAN that you should be familiar with, and it is called StyleGAN. It was made famous for its ability to generate ultra-realistic, high-fidelity face images. The implementation of StyleGAN requires pre-requisite knowledge of progressive GANs. Therefore, we will defer the detailed implementation to *Chapter 7, High Fidelity Face Generation.*

At this point, GANs are moving away from the black box method, which uses only random noise as input, and toward the disentangled representation approach, which better exploits data properties. In the next chapter, we will look at how to use specific GAN techniques in drawing paintings.

6
AI Painter

In this chapter, we are going to look at two **generative adversarial networks (GANs)** that could be used to generate and edit images interactively; they are iGAN and GauGAN . The **iGAN (interactive GAN)** was the first network to demonstrate how to use GANs for interactive image editing and transformation, back in 2016. As GANs were still in fancy at that time, the generated image quality was not impressive as that of today's networks, but the door was opened to the incorporation of GANs into mainstream image editing.

In this chapter, you will be introduced to the concepts behind iGANs and some websites that feature video demonstrations of them. There won't be any code in that section. Then, we will go over a more recent award-winning application called **GauGAN**, produced by Nvidia in 2019, that gives impressive results in converting semantic segmentation masks into real landscape photos.

We will implement GauGAN from scratch, starting with a new normalization technique known as **spatially adaptive normalization**. We will also learn about a new loss known as **hinge loss** and will go on to build a full-size GauGAN. The quality of the image generated by GauGAN is far superior to that of the general-purpose image-to-image translation networks that we covered in previous chapters.

We will cover the following topics in this chapter:

- Introduction to iGAN
- Segmentation map-to-image translation with GauGAN

Technical requirements

The relevant Jupyter notebooks and code can be found here:

```
https://github.com/PacktPublishing/Hands-On-Image-Generation-
with-TensorFlow-2.0/tree/master/Chapter06
```

The notebook used in this chapter is ch6_gaugan.ipynb.

Introduction to iGAN

We are now familiar with using generative models such as pix2pix (see *Chapter 4, Image-to-Image Translation*)to generate images from sketch or segmentation masks. However, as most of us are not skilled artists, we are only able to draw simple sketches, and as a result, our generated images also have simple shapes. What if we could use a real image as input and use sketches to change the appearance of the real image?

In the early days of GANs, a paper titled *Generative Visual Manipulation on the Natural Image Manifold* by J-Y. Zhu (inventor of CycleGAN) et al. was published that explored how to use a learned latent representation to perform image editing and morphing. The authors made a website, http://efrosgans.eecs.berkeley.edu/iGAN/, that contains videos that demonstrate a few of the following use cases:

- **Interactive image generation**: This involves generating images from sketches in real time, as shown here:

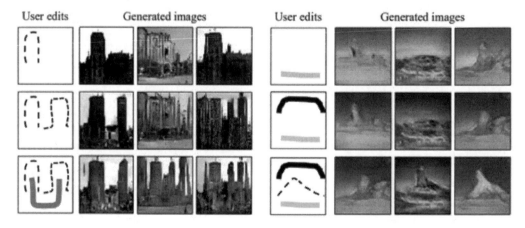

Figure 6.1 – Interactive image generation, where an image is generated only from simple brush strokes
(Source: J-Y. Zhu et al., 2016, "Generative Visual Manipulation on the Natural Image Manifold",
https://arxiv.org/abs/1609.03552)

- **Interactive image editing**: A picture is imported and we perform image editing using a GAN. Early GANs generated images uses only noise as input. Even BicycleGAN (which was invented a few years after the iGAN) could only change the appearance of generated images randomly without direct manipulation. iGANs allow us to specify changes in color and texture, which is impressive.

- **Interactive image transformation (morphing)**: Given two images, an iGAN can create sequences of images that show a morphing process from one image to the other, as follows:

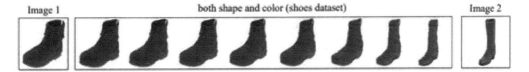

Figure 6.2 – Interactive image transformation (morphing). Given two images, sequences of intermediates images can be generated

(Source: J-Y. Zhu et al., 2016, "Generative Visual Manipulation on the Natural Image Manifold", https://arxiv.org/abs/1609.03552)

The term **manifold** appears in the paper a lot. It also appears in other machine learning literature, so let's spend some time understanding it.

Understanding manifold

We can understand manifold from the perspective of a natural image. A color pixel can be represented by 8-bit or 256-bit number; a single RGB pixel alone can have 256x256x256 = 1.6 million different possible combinations! Using the same logic, the total possibilities for all pixels in an image is astronomically high!

However, we know that the pixels are not independent of each other; for example, the pixels of grassland are confined to the green color range. Thus, the high dimensionality of an image is not as daunting as it seems. In other words, the dimension space is a lot smaller than we might think at first. Thus, we can say that a high-dimensional image space is supported by a low-dimensional manifold.

Manifold is a term in physics and mathematics that's used to describe smooth geometric surfaces. They can exist in any dimension. One-dimensional manifolds include lines and circles; two-dimensional manifolds are called **surfaces**. A *sphere* is a three-dimensional manifold that is smooth everywhere. In contrast, *cubes* are not manifolds as they are not smooth at the vertices. In fact, we saw in *Chapter 2, Variational Autoencoder*, that a latent space of an autoencoder with a latent dimension of 2 was a 2D manifold of the MNIST digits projected. The following diagram shows a 2D latent space of digits:

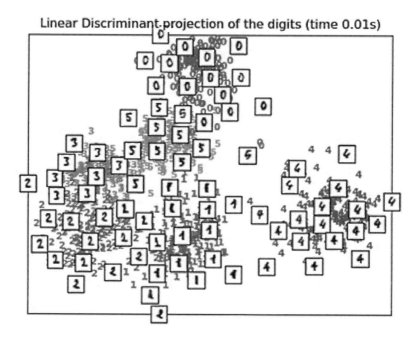

Figure 6.3 – Illustration of a 2D manifold of digits.
(Source: https://scikit-learn.org/stable/modules/manifold.html)

A good resource to visualize manifolds in GAN is the interactive tool at `https://poloclub.github.io/ganlab/`. In the following example, a GAN is trained to map uniformly distributed 2D samples into 2D samples that have a circular distribution:

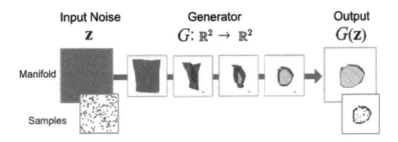

Figure 6.4 – The generator's data transformation is visualized as a manifold, which turns input noise (on the left) into fake samples (on the right).

(Source: M. Kahng, 2019, "GAN Lab: Understanding Complex Deep Generative Models using Interactive Visual Experimentation," IEEE Transactions on Visualization and Computer Graphics, 25(1) (VAST 2018) https://minsuk.com/research/papers/kahng-ganlab-vast2018.pdf)

We can visualize this mapping using a manifold, where the input is represented as a uniform square grid. The generator wraps the high-dimensional input grid into a warped version with fewer dimensions. The output shown at the top right of the figure is the manifold approximated by the generator. The generator output, or the fake image (bottom right in the figure), is the samples sampled from the manifold, where an area with smaller grid blocks means a higher sampling probability.

The assumption of the paper is that a GAN's output sampled from random noise z, $G(z)$, lies in on a smooth manifold. Therefore, given two images on the manifold, $G(z_0)$ and $G(z_N)$, we could get a sequence of $N + 1$ images $[G(z_0), G(z_0), ..., G(z_N)]$ with a smooth transition by interpolation in the latent space. This approximation of the manifold of natural images is used for performing *realistic image editing*.

Image editing

Now that we know what a manifold is, let's see how to use that knowledge to perform image editing. The first step in image editing is to project an image onto the manifold.

Projecting an image onto a manifold

What projecting an image onto a manifold means is using a pre-trained GAN to generate an image that is close to the given image. In this book, we will use a pre-trained DCGAN where the input to the generator is a 100-dimension latent vector. Therefore, we will need to find a latent vector that generates an image manifold that is as close as possible to the original image. One way to do this is to use optimization such as **style transfer**, a topic we covered in detail in *Chapter 5, Style Transfer*.

1. We first extract the features of the original image using a pretrained **convolutional neural network** (**CNN**), such as the output of the *block5_conv1* layer in VGG (see *Chapter 5, Style Transfer*), and use it as a target.

2. Then, we use the pre-trained DCGAN's generator with frozen weights and optimize on the input latent vector by minimizing the L2 loss between the features.

As we have learned regarding style transfer, optimization can be slow to run and hence not responsive when it comes to interactive drawing.

Another method is to train a feedforward network to predict the latent vector from the image, which is a lot faster. If the GAN is to translate a segmentation mask into an image, then we can use a network such as U-Net to predict the segmentation mask from the image.

Manifold projection using a feedforward network looks similar to using an autoencoder. The encoder encodes (predicts) the latent variable from the original image, then the decoder (the generator, in the case of a GAN) projects the latent variable onto the image manifold. However, this method is not always perfect. This is where the *hybrid* method comes in. We use the feedforward network to predict the latent variables, which we then fine-tune using optimization. The following figure shows the images generated using different techniques:

Figure 6.5 – Projecting real photos onto an image manifold using a GAN. (Source: J-Y. Zhu et al, 2016, "Generative Visual Manipulation on the Natural Image Manifold," https://arxiv.org/abs/1609.03552)

As we have now obtained the latent vector, we will use it to edit the manifold.

Editing the manifold using latent vector

Now that we have obtained the latent variable z_0 and the image manifold $x_0 = G(z_0)$, the next step is to manipulate z_0 to modify the image. Now, let's say the image is a red shoe and we want to change the color to black – how can we do that? The simplest and crudest method is to open an image editing software package to select all the red pixels in the picture and change them to black. The resulting picture is likely to not look very natural as some details may be lost. Traditional image editing tools' algorithms tend to not work that well on natural images with complex shapes and fine texture details.

On the other hand, we know we probably could change the latent vector and feed that to the generator and change the color. In practice, we do not know how to modify the latent variables to get the results we want.

Therefore, instead of changing the latent vector directly, we could attack the problem from a different direction. We can edit the manifold, for example, by drawing a black stripe on the shoes, then use that to optimize the latent variables, and then project that to generate another image on the manifold.

Essentially, we are performing optimization as previously described for manifold projection but with different loss functions. We want to find an image manifold x that minimizes the following equation:

$$x^* = \begin{array}{c} \arg min \\ x \in M \end{array} \{\sum_g \|f_g(x) - v_g\|^2 + \lambda_s S(x, x_0)\}$$

Let's start with the second loss term $S(x, x_0)$ for manifold smoothness. It is L2 loss, used to encourage the new manifold to not deviate too much from the original manifold. This loss term keeps the global appearance of the image in check. The first loss term is the data term, which sums up all the editing operation loss. This is best described using the following images:

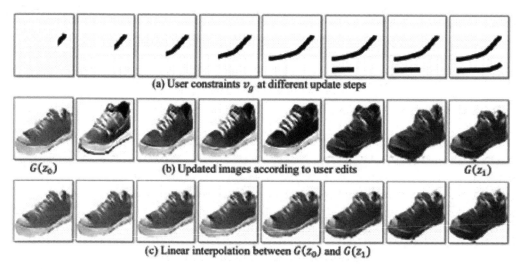

(a) User constraints v_g at different update steps

$G(z_0)$ (b) Updated images according to user edits $G(z_1)$

(c) Linear interpolation between $G(z_0)$ and $G(z_1)$

Figure 6.6 – Projecting real photos onto the image manifold using GAN. (Source: J-Y. Zhu et al, 2016, "Generative Visual Manipulation on the Natural Image Manifold," https://arxiv.org/abs/1609.03552)

This example uses a color brush to change the color of the shoe. The color change may not be obvious in the grayscale print of this book and you are encouraged to check out the color version of the paper, which you can download from https://arxiv.org/abs/1609.03552. The top row of the preceding figure shows the brush stroke as the constraint v_g and f_g as the editing operation. We want every manifold pixel in the brush stroke $f_g(x)$ to be as close to v_g as possible.

In other words, if we put a black stroke on the shoe, we want that part in the image manifold to be black. That is the intention, but to execute it, we will need to do the optimization of the latent variables. Thus, we reformulate the preceding equation from pixel space into latent space. The equation is as follows:

$$z^* = \begin{array}{c} \arg\min \\ z \in \mathbb{Z} \end{array} \{\sum_g \|f_g(G(z)) - v_g\|^2 + \lambda_s\|z - z_0\|^2 + E_D\}$$

The last term $E_D = \lambda_D \log(1 - D(G(z)))$ is the *GAN's adversarial loss*. This is used for making the manifold look real and improve the visual quality slightly. By default, this term is not used for increasing the frame rate. With all the loss terms defined, we can use a TensorFlow optimizer such as Adam to run the optimization.

Edit transfer

Edit transfer is the last step of image editing. Now we have two manifolds, $G(z_0)$ and $G(z_1)$, and we can generate sequences of intermediate images using linear interpolation in latent space between z_0 and z_1. Due to the capacity limitations of the DCGAN, the generated manifolds can appear blurry and may not look as realistic as we hoped them to be.

The way the authors of the previously mentioned paper address this problem is to not use the manifold as the final image but instead to estimate the color and geometric changes between the manifolds and apply the changes to the original image. The estimation of color and motion flow is performed using optical flow; this is a traditional computer vision technique that is beyond the scope of this book.

Using the preceding shoe example, if all we are interested in is the color change, we estimate the color change of the pixel between manifolds, then transfer the color changes on the pixels in the original image. Similarly, if the transformation involves warping, that is, a change in shape, we measure the motion of pixels and apply them to original image to perform morphing. The demonstration video on the website was created using both motion and color flow.

To recap, we have now learned that an iGAN is not a GAN but a method of using a GAN to perform image editing. This is done by first projecting a real image onto a manifold using either optimization or a feedforward network. Next, we use brush strokes as constraints to modify the manifold generated by the latent vector. Finally, we transfer the color and motion flow of the interpolated manifolds onto the real image to complete the image editing.

As there aren't any new GAN architectures, we will not be implementing an iGAN. Instead, we are going to implement GauGAN, which includes some new innovations that are exciting for code implementation.

Segmentation map-to-image translation with GauGAN

GauGAN (named after 19th-century painter Paul Gauguin) is a GAN from **Nvidia**. Speaking of Nvidia, it is one of the handful of companies that has invested heavily in GANs. They have achieved several breakthroughs in this space, including **ProgressiveGAN** (we'll cover that in *Chapter 7, High Fidelity Face Generation*), to generate high-resolution images, and **StyleGAN** for high-fidelity faces.

Their main business is in making graphics chips rather than AI software. Therefore, unlike some other companies, who keep their code and trained models as closely guarded secrets, Nvidia tends to open source their software code to the general public. They have built a web page (`http://nvidia-research-mingyuliu.com/gaugan/`) to showcase GauGAN, which can generate photorealistic landscape photos from segmentation maps. The following screenshot is taken from their web page.

Feel free to pause this chapter for a bit and have a play with the application to see how good it is:

Figure 6.7 –From brush stroke to photo with GauGAN

We will now learn about pix2pixHD.

Introduction to pix2pixHD

GauGAN uses **pix2pixHD** as a base and adds new features to it. pix2pixHD is an upgraded version of pix2pix that can generate **high-definition** (HD) images. As we haven't covered pix2pixHD in this book and we won't be using an HD dataset, we will build our GauGAN base on pix2pix's architecture and the code base that we are already familiar with. Nevertheless, it is good to know the high-level architecture of pix2pixHD, and I'll walk you through some of the high-level concepts. The following diagram shows the architecture of pix2pixHD's generators:

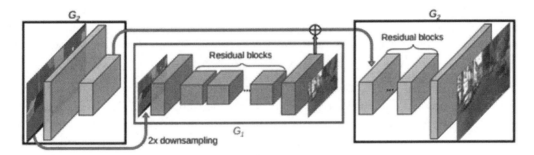

Figure 6.8 – The network architecture of the pix2pixHD generator.
(Source: T-C. W et al., 2018, "High-Resolution Image Synthesis and Semantic Manipulation with Conditional GANs," https://arxiv.org/abs/1711.11585)

In order to generate high-resolution images, pix2pixHD uses two generators at different image resolutions at coarse- and fine-scale. The coarse generator **G1** works at half the image resolution; that is, the input and target images are downsampled into half the resolution. When that is trained, we start training the coarse generator G_1 together with the fine generator **G2**, which works on the full-image scale. From the preceding architecture diagram, we can see that G_1's encoder output concatenates with G_1's features and feeds into the decoder part of G_2 to generate high-resolution images. This setting is also known as a **coarse-to-fine generator**.

pix2pixHD uses three PatchGAN discriminators that operate at different image scales. A new loss, known as feature matching loss, is used to match the layer features between the real and fake images. This is used in style transfer, where we use a pre-trained VGG for feature extraction and optimize on the style features.

Now that we've had a quick introduction to pix2pixHD, we can move on to GauGAN. But first, we will implement a normalization technique that demonstrates GauGAN.

Spatial Adaptive Normalization (SPADE)

The main innovation in GauGAN is a layer normalization method for segmentation map known as **Spatial-Adaptive Normalization (SPADE)**. That's right, another entry into the already-long list of normalization techniques in the GAN's toolbox. We will dive deep into SPADE, but before that, we should learn about the format of the network input – the **semantic segmentation map**.

One-hot encoded segmentation masks

We will use the `facades` dataset to train our GauGAN. In previous experiments, the segmentation map was encoded as different colors in an RGB image; for example, a wall was represented by a purple mask and a door was green. This representation is visually easy for us to understand but it is not that helpful for the neural network to learn. This is because the colors do not have semantic meaning.

Colors being closer in color space does not mean they are close in semantic meaning. We could use light green to represent grass and dark green to represent an airplane, and their semantic meanings would not be related even though the segmentation maps would be close in color shade.

For this reason, instead of labeling pixels using colors, we should use class labels. However, this still does not solve the problem as the class labels are numbers assigned randomly and they also do not have semantic meaning. Therefore, a better way is to use a **segmentation mask** with a label of 1 when an object is present in that pixel and a label of 0 otherwise. In other words, we one-hot encode the labels in a segmentation map into a segmentation mask with the shape (H, W, number of classes). The following figure shows an example of semantic segmentation masks for a building image:

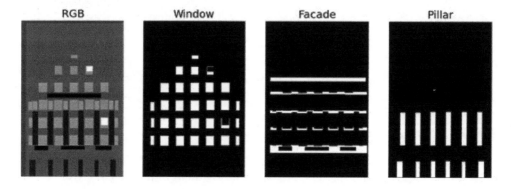

Figure 6.9 – On the left is a segmentation map encoded in RGB. On the right, the segmentation maps are separated into individual classes of window, façade, and pillar

The data in the `facades` dataset that we used in the previous chapters was encoded as JPEG, so we cannot use that to train GauGAN. In JPEG encoding, some visual information that is less important to the visuals is removed in the compression process. The resulting pixels may have different values even if they should belong to the same class and appear to be the same color. As a result, we cannot map the colors in a JPEG image to classes. To tackle this problem, I got the raw dataset from the original source and created a new dataset that includes three different image file types for each sample as follows:

- JPEG – real photo
- PNG – segmentation map using RGB color
- BMP – segmentation map using class labels

BMP is uncompressed. We can think of a BMP image as the image in RGB format in the preceding figure, except that the pixel values are 1-channel class labels rather than 3-channel RGB colors. In image loading and pre-processing, we will load all three files and convert them from BMP into one-hot encoded segmentation masks.

Sometimes, TensorFlow's basic image pre-processing APIs are not able to do some of the more complex tasks, so we need to resort to using other Python libraries. Luckily, `tf.py_function` allows us to run a generic Python function within a TensorFlow training pipeline.

In this file-loading function, as shown in the following code, we use `.numpy()` to convert TensorFlow tensors into Python objects. The function name is a bit misleading as it applies not only to numerical values but also string values:

```python
def load(image_file):
    def load_data(image_file):
        jpg_file = image_file.numpy().decode("utf-8")
        bmp_file = jpg_file.replace('.jpg','.bmp')
        png_file = jpg_file.replace('.jpg','.png')
        image = np.array(Image.open(jpg_file))/127.5 - 1
        map = np.array(Image.open(png_file))/127.5 - 1
        labels = np.array(Image.open(bmp_file),
                          dtype=np.uint8)
        h, w, _ = image.shape
        n_class = 12
        mask = np.zeros((h, w, n_class), dtype=np.float32)
        for i in range(n_class):
            one_hot[labels==i, i] = 1
```

```
                    return map, image, mask
[mask, image, label] = tf.py_function(
                              load_data, [image_file],
                              [tf.float32, tf.float32,
                              tf.float32])
```

Now that we understand the format of one-hot encoded semantic segmentation masks, we will look at how SPADE can help us generate better images from segmentation masks.

Implementing SPADE

Instance normalization has become popular in image generation, but it tends to wash away the semantic meaning of segmentation masks. What does that mean? Let's assume an input image consists of only one single segmentation label; for example, say the entire image is of the sky. As the input has uniform values, the output, after passing through the convolution layer, will also have uniform values.

Recall that instance normalization calculates the mean across dimensions (H, W) for each channel. Therefore, the mean for that channel will be the same uniform value, and the normalized activation after subtraction with mean will become zero. Obviously, the semantic meaning is lost and the sky has just vanished into thin air. This is an extreme example, but using the same logic, we can see that a segmentation mask loses its semantic meaning as its area grows larger.

To solve this problem, SPADE normalizes on local areas confined by the segmentation mask rather than on the entire mask. The following diagram shows the high-level architecture of SPADE:

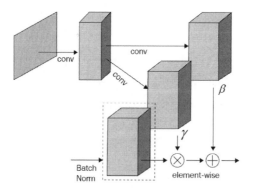

Figure 6.10 – High-level SPADE architecture.
(Redrawn from: T. Park et al., 2019, "Semantic Image Synthesis with Spatially-Adaptive Normalization," https://arxiv.org/abs/1903.07291)

In batch normalization, we calculate the means and standard deviations of channels across dimensions (N, H, W). This is the same for SPADE, as shown in the preceding figure. The difference is that gamma and beta for each channel are no longer scalar values (or vectors of C channels) but two-dimensional (H, W). In other words, there is a gamma and a beta for every activation that is learned from the semantic segmentation map. So, normalization is applied differently to different segmentation areas. These two parameters are learned by using two convolutional layers, as shown in the following diagram:

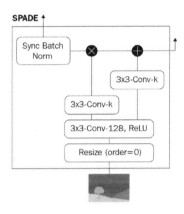

Figure 6.11 – SPADE design diagram, where k denotes the number of convolutional filters
(Redrawn from: T. Park et al., 2019, "Semantic Image Synthesis with Spatially-Adaptive Normalization,"
https://arxiv.org/abs/1903.07291)

SPADE is used not only at the network input stage but also in the internal layers. The resize layer is to resize the segmentation map to match the dimensions of the layer's activation. We can now implement a TensorFlow custom layer for SPADE.

We will first define the convolutional layers in the __init__ constructor as follows:

```
class SPADE(layers.Layer):
    def __init__(self, filters, epsilon=1e-5):
        super(SPADE, self).__init__()
        self.epsilon = epsilon
        self.conv = layers.Conv2D(128, 3, padding='same',
                                  activation='relu')
        self.conv_gamma = layers.Conv2D(filters, 3,
                                        padding='same')
        self.conv_beta = layers.Conv2D(filters, 3,
                                       padding='same')
```

Next, we will get the activation map dimensions to be used in resizing later:

```
def build(self, input_shape):
    self.resize_shape = input_shape[1:3]
```

Finally, we will connect the layers and operations together in `call()` as follows:

```
def call(self, input_tensor, raw_mask):
    mask = tf.image.resize(raw_mask, self.resize_shape,
                           method='nearest')
    x = self.conv(mask)
    gamma = self.conv_gamma(x)
    beta = self.conv_beta(x)
    mean, var = tf.nn.moments(input_tensor,
                              axes=(0,1,2), keepdims=True)
    std = tf.sqrt(var + self.epsilon)
    normalized = (input_tensor - mean)/std
    output = gamma * normalized + beta
    return output
```

This is a straightforward implementation based on the SPADE design diagram. Next, we will look at how to make use of SPADE.

Inserting SPADE into residual blocks

GauGAN uses **residual blocks** in the generator. We will now look at how to insert SPADE into residual blocks:

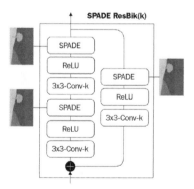

Figure 6.12 – SPADE residual blocks

(Redrawn from: T. Park et. al., 2019, "Semantic Image Synthesis with Spatially-Adaptive Normalization," https://arxiv.org/abs/1903.07291)

The basic building block within the SPADE residual block is the **SPADE-ReLU-Conv layer**. Each SPADE takes two inputs – the activation from the previous layer and the semantic segmentation map.

As with the standard residual block, there are two convolution-ReLU layers and a skip path. Whenever there is a change in the number of channels before and after the residual block, the skip connection is learned via the sub-block in the dashed-line box shown in the preceding diagram. When this happens, the activation maps at the inputs of the two SPADEs in forward path will have different dimensions. That is alright as we have built-in resizing within SPADE block. The following is the code for the SPADE residual block to build the needed layers:

```
class Resblock(layers.Layer):
    def __init__(self, filters):
        super(Resblock, self).__init__()
        self.filters = filters
    def build(self, input_shape):
        input_filter = input_shape[-1]
        self.spade_1 = SPADE(input_filter)
        self.spade_2 = SPADE(self.filters)
        self.conv_1 = layers.Conv2D(self.filters, 3,
                                    padding='same')
        self.conv_2 = layers.Conv2D(self.filters, 3,
                                    padding='same')
        self.learned_skip = False
        if self.filters != input_filter:
            self.learned_skip = True
            self.spade_3 = SPADE(input_filter)
            self.conv_3 = layers.Conv2D(self.filters,
                                        3, padding='same')
```

Then, we connect the layers up in `call()`:

```
    def call(self, input_tensor, mask):
        x = self.spade_1(input_tensor, mask)
        x = self.conv_1(tf.nn.leaky_relu(x, 0.2))
        x = self.spade_2(x, mask)
        x = self.conv_2(tf.nn.leaky_relu(x, 0.2))
        if self.learned_skip:
            skip = self.spade_3(input_tensor, mask)
```

```
            skip = self.conv_3(tf.nn.leaky_relu(skip, 0.2))
        else:
            skip = input_tensor
        output = skip + x
        return output
```

In the original GauGAN implementation, spectral normalization is applied after the convolutional layer. It is yet another normalization that we will cover in *Chapter 8, Self-Attention for Image Generation*, when we talk about self-attention GANs. Therefore, we will skip over that and put the residual blocks together to implement GauGAN.

Implementing GauGAN

We will first build the generator, followed by the discriminator. Finally, we will implement the loss functions and start training GauGAN.

Building the GauGAN generator

Before diving into the GauGAN generator, let's revise what we know about some of its predecessors. In pix2pix, the generator takes in only one input – the semantic segmentation map. As there is no randomness in the network, given the same input, it will always generate building facades with the same color and texture. The naive way of concatenating the input with random noise doesn't work.

One of the two methods used by **BicycleGAN** (*Chapter 4, Image-to-Image Translation*) to address this problem is using an encoder to encode the target image (the real photo) into latent vectors, which are then used to sample random noise for the generator input. This **cVAE-GAN** structure is used in the GauGAN generator. There are two inputs to the generator – the semantic segmentation mask and the real photo.

In the GauGAN web application, we can select a photo (the generated image will resemble the style of the photo). This is made possible by using the encoder to encode style information into latent variables. The code for the encoder is the same as that which we used in the previous chapters, so we will move on to look at the generator architecture. Feel free to revisit *Chapter 4, Image-to-Image Translation*, to refresh the encoder implementation. In the following diagram, we can see the GauGAN generator architecture:

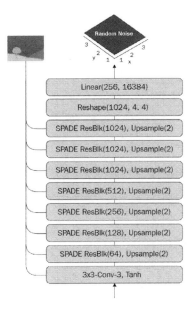

Figure 6.13 – GauGAN generator architecture

(Redrawn from: T. Park et al., 2019, "Semantic Image Synthesis with Spatially-Adaptive Normalization,"
https://arxiv.org/abs/1903.07291)

The generator is a decoder-like architecture. The main difference is that the segmentation mask goes into every residual block via SPADE. The latent variable dimension chosen for GauGAN is 256.

> **Note**
>
> The encoder is not an integral part of the generator; we can choose not to use any style image and sample from a standard multivariate Gaussian distribution.

The following is the code to build the generator using the residual block that we wrote previously:

```
def build_generator(self):
    DIM = 64
    z = Input(shape=(self.z_dim))
    mask = Input(shape=self.input_shape)
    x = Dense(16384)(z)
    x = Reshape((4, 4, 1024))(x)
    x = UpSampling2D((2,2))(Resblock(filters=1024)(x, mask))
    x = UpSampling2D((2,2))(Resblock(filters=1024)(x, mask))
```

```
x = UpSampling2D((2,2))(Resblock(filters=1024)(x, mask))
x = UpSampling2D((2,2))(Resblock(filters=512)(x, mask))
x = UpSampling2D((2,2))(Resblock(filters=256)(x, mask))
x = UpSampling2D((2,2))(Resblock(filters=128)(x, mask))
x = tf.nn.leaky_relu(x, 0.2)
output_image = tanh(Conv2D(3, 4, padding='same')(x))
return Model([z, mask], output_image, name='generator')
```

You now know about everything that makes GauGAN work – SPADE and the generator. The rest of the network architecture are ideas borrowed from other GANs that we have previously learned. Next, we will look at how to build the discriminator.

Building the discriminator

The discriminator is PatchGAN, where the input is a concatenation of the segmentation map and the generated image. The segmentation map has to have the same number of channels as the generated RGB image; therefore, we will use the RGB segmentation map instead of a one-hot encoded segmentation mask. The architecture of the GauGAN discriminator is as follows:

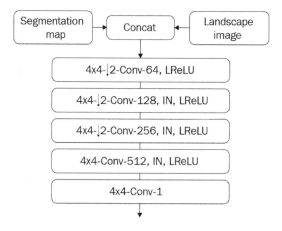

Figure 6.14 – GauGAN discriminator architecture
(Redrawn from: T. Park et al., 2019, "Semantic Image Synthesis with Spatially-Adaptive Normalization,"
https://arxiv.org/abs/1903.07291)

Except for the last layer, the discriminator layers consist of the following:

- A convolutional layer with a kernel size of 4x4 and a stride of 2 for downsampling
- Instance normalization (except for the first layer)
- Leaky ReLU

GauGAN uses multiple discriminators at different scales. Since our dataset image has a low resolution of 256x256, one discriminator is sufficient. If we were to use multiple discriminators, all we would need to do is downsample the input size by half for the next discriminator and calculate the average loss from all the discriminators.

The code implementation for a single PatchGAN is as follows:

```python
def build_discriminator(self):
    DIM = 64
    model = tf.keras.Sequential(name='discriminators')
    input_image_A = layers.Input(shape=self.image_shape,
                            name='discriminator_image_A')
    input_image_B = layers.Input(shape=self.image_shape,
                            name='discriminator_image_B')
    x = layers.Concatenate()([input_image_A, input_image_B])
    x1 = self.downsample(DIM, 4, norm=False)(x) # 128
    x2 = self.downsample(2*DIM, 4)(x1) # 64
    x3 = self.downsample(4*DIM, 4)(x2) # 32
    x4 = self.downsample(8*DIM, 4, strides=1)(x3) # 29
    x5 = layers.Conv2D(1, 4)(x4)
    outputs = [x1, x2, x3, x4, x5]
    return Model([input_image_A, input_image_B], outputs)
```

This is identical to pix2pix, except that the discriminator returns all downsampling blocks' output. Why do we need that? Well, this brings us to a discussion about loss functions.

Feature matching loss

Feature matching loss has been successfully used in style transfer. The content and style features are extracted using a pre-trained VGG and the losses are calculated between the target image and the generated image. The content features are simply the outputs from multiple convolutional blocks in VGG. GauGAN employs content loss to replace L1 reconstruction loss, which was common among GANs. The reason is that reconstruction loss makes comparisons pixel by pixel, and the loss can be large if the image shifts in location despite still looking the same to human eyes.

On the other hand, the content features of convolutional layers are spatially invariant. As a result, when using the content loss to train on the `facades` dataset, our generated buildings will look a lot less blurry and the lines will look straighter. The content loss in style transfer literature is sometimes known as **VGG loss** in code, as people love to use VGG for feature extraction.

> **Why do people still love using the old VGG?**
>
> Newer CNN architectures such as ResNet have long surpassed VGG's performance and achieve much higher accuracy in image classification. So, why do people still use VGG for feature extraction? Some have tried Inception and ResNet for neural style transfer but have found that the results generated using VGG were more visually pleasant. This is likely due to the hierarchy of VGG's architecture, with its monotonically increasing channel numbers across layers. This allows feature extraction to happen smoothly from low-level to high-level representation.
>
> In contrast, the residual blocks of ResNet have a bottleneck design that squeezes the input activation channels (say, 256) to a lower number (say, 64), before restoring it back to a higher number (256 again). Residual blocks also have a skip connection that could *smuggle* information for the classification task and bypass feature extraction in the convolutional layers.

The code to calculate the VGG feature loss is as follows:

```
def VGG_loss(self, real_image, fake_image):
    # RGB to BGR
    x = tf.reverse(real_image, axis=[-1])
    y = tf.reverse(fake_image, axis=[-1])
    # [-1, +1] to [0, 255]
    x = tf.keras.applications.vgg19.preprocess_input(
                                    127.5*(x+1))
    y = tf.keras.applications.vgg19.preprocess_input(
                                    127.5*(y+1))
```

```
# extract features
feat_real = self.vgg(x)
feat_fake = self.vgg(y)
weights = [1./32, 1./16, 1./8, 1./4, 1.]
loss = 0
mae = tf.keras.losses.MeanAbsoluteError()
for i in range(len(feat_real)):
    loss += weights[i] * mae(feat_real[i], feat_fake[i])
return loss
```

When calculating VGG loss, we first convert the images from [-1, +1] to [0, 255] and from RGB to BGR, which is the image format expected by Keras' VGG preprocess function. GauGAN gives more weights to higher layers to emphasize structural accuracy. This is to align the generated image with the segmentation mask. Anyway, this is not set in stone and you are welcome to try different weights.

Feature matching is also used on the discriminator, where we extract the discriminator layer outputs of real and fake images. The following code is used to calculate the L1 feature matching loss in the discriminator:

```
def feature_matching_loss(self, feat_real, feat_fake):
    loss = 0
    mae = tf.keras.losses.MeanAbsoluteError()
    for i in range(len(feat_real)-1):
        loss += mae(feat_real[i], feat_fake[i])
    return loss
```

Apart from this, we will also have **KL divergence loss** for the encoder. The last loss is **hinge loss** as the new adversarial loss.

Hinge loss

Hinge loss may be a newcomer in the GAN world, but it has long been used in **support vector machines** (**SVMs**) for classification. It maximizes the margin of the decision boundary. The following plots show the hinge loss for positive (real) and negative (fake) labels:

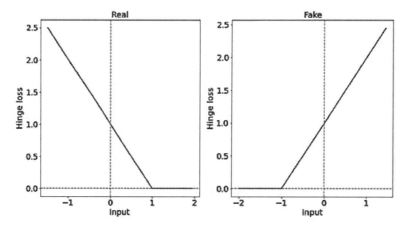

Figure 6.15 – Hinge loss for a discriminator

On the left is the hinge loss for the discriminator when the image is real. When we use hinge loss for the discriminator, the loss is bounded to 0 when prediction is over 1. If it is anything under 1, the loss increases to penalize for not predicting the image as real. It's similar for fake images but in the opposite direction: the hinge loss is 0 when the prediction of fake image is under -1 and it increases linearly once above that threshold.

We can implement the hinge loss using basic mathematic operations as follows:

```
def d_hinge_loss(y, is_real):
    if is_real:
        loss = tf.reduce_mean(tf.maximum(0., 1-y))
    else:
        loss = tf.reduce_mean (tf.maximum(0., 1+y))
    return loss
```

Another way of doing this is by using TensorFlow's hinge loss API:

```
def hinge_loss_d(self, y, is_real):
    label = 1. if is_real else -1.
    loss = tf.keras.losses.Hinge()(y, label)
    return loss
```

The loss for the generator isn't really hinge loss; it is simply a negative mean of prediction. This is unbounded, so the loss is lower when the prediction score is higher:

```
def g_hinge_loss(y):
    return -tf.reduce_mean(y)
```

We now have everything we need to train GauGAN using a training framework as we did in the previous chapter. The following figure shows the images generated using the segmentation mask:

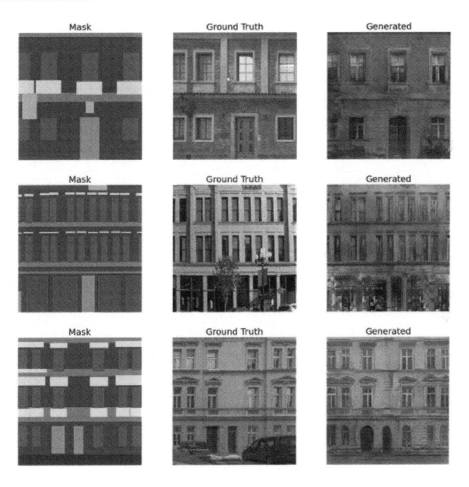

Figure 6.16 – Example of images generated by our GauGAN implementation

They look a lot better than the pix2pix and CycleGAN results! If we encode the ground truth image's style into random noise, the generated images will be almost indistinguishable from the ground truth. It is really impressive to look at on the computer!

Summary

Using AI in image editing is already prevalent now, and all this started at around the time that the iGAN was introduced. We learned about the key principle of the iGAN being to first project an image onto a manifold and then directly perform editing on the manifold. We then optimize this on the latent variables and generate an edited image that is natural-looking. This is in contrast with previous methods that could only change generated images indirectly by manipulating latent variables.

GauGAN incorporates many advanced techniques to generate crisp images from semantic segmentation masks. This includes the use of hinge loss and feature matching loss. However, the key ingredient is SPADE, which provides superior performance when using a segmentation mask as input. SPADE performs normalization on a local segmentation map to preserve its semantic meaning, which helps us to produce high-quality images. So far, we have been using images with up to 256x256 resolution to train our networks. We now have techniques that are mature enough to generate high-resolution images, as we briefly discussed when introducing pix2pixHD.

In the next chapter, we will move to the realm of high-resolution images with advanced models such as ProgressiveGAN and StyleGAN.

Section 3: Advanced Deep Generative Techniques

This section also covers the application of GANs, but there will be more advanced techniques, and each chapter will cover state-of-the-art models for given tasks. We will conclude this section by talking about future advancements in this area.

This section comprises the following chapters:

- *Chapter 7, High Fidelity Face Generation*
- *Chapter 8, Self-Attention for Image Generation*
- *Chapter 9, Video Synthesis*
- *Chapter 10, Road Ahead*

7
High Fidelity Face Generation

As GANs began to become more stable to train, thanks to improvements to loss functions and normalization techniques, people started to shift their focus to trying to generate higher-resolution images. Previously, most GANs were only capable of generating images up to a resolution of 256x256, and simply adding more upscaling layers to the generator did not help.

In this chapter, we will look at techniques that are capable of generating images of high resolutions of 1024x1024 and beyond. We will start by implementing a seminal GAN known as **Progressive GAN**, sometimes abbreviated to **ProGAN**. This was the first GAN that was successful at generating 1024x1024 high-fidelity face portraits. High-fidelity doesn't just mean high-resolution but also a high resemblance to a real face. We can have a high-resolution generated face image, but if it has four eyes, then it isn't high fidelity.

After ProGAN, we will implement **StyleGAN**, which builds on top of ProGAN. StyleGAN incorporates AdaIN from style transfer to allow finer style control and style mixing to generate a variety of images.

We will cover the following in this chapter:

- ProGAN overview
- Building a ProGAN
- Implementing StyleGAN

Technical requirements

The Jupyter notebooks and code can be found here:

`https://github.com/PacktPublishing/Hands-On-Image-Generation-with-TensorFlow-2.0/tree/master/Chapter07`

The notebooks used in this chapter are listed here:

- `ch7_progressive_gan.ipynb`
- `ch7_style_gan.ipynb`

ProGAN overview

In a typical GAN setting, the generator output shape is fixed. In other words, the training image size does not change. If we want to try to double the image resolution, we add an additional upsampling layer to the generator architecture and start the training from scratch. People have tried and failed to increase image resolution by this brute-force method. The enlarged image resolution and network size increases the dimension space, making it more difficult to learn.

CNNs faced the same problem and solved it by using a batch normalization layer, but this doesn't work well with GANs. The idea of ProGAN is to not train all the layers simultaneously but start by training the lowest layer in both the generator and the discriminator, so that the layer's weights are stabilized before adding new layers. We can see it as pre-training the network with lower resolutions. This idea is the core innovation brought by ProGAN, as detailed in the academic paper *Progressive Growing of GANs for Improved Quality, Stability, and Variation* by T. Karras et al. The following diagram illustrates the process of growing the network in ProGAN:

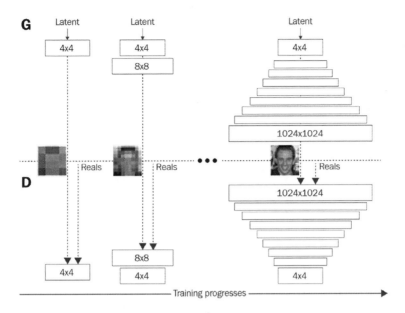

Figure 7.1 – Illustration of the progressive growing of layers.

(Redrawn from T. Karras et al. 2018, "Progressive Growing of GANs for Improved Quality, Stability, and Variation," https://arxiv.org/abs/1710.10196)

Like vanilla GANs, ProGAN's input is a latent vector sampled from random noise. As shown in the preceding diagram, we start with an image resolution of **4x4** and only have one block in both the generator and the discriminator. After training in the **4x4** resolution for a while, we add new layers for the **8x8** resolution. We then keep doing that until we reach the final image resolution of **1024x1024**. The following 256x256 images were generated using ProGAN and were released by NVIDIA. The image quality is breathtaking; they are literally indistinguishable from real faces:

Figure 7.2 – High-fidelity images generated by ProGAN

(Source: https://github.com/tkarras/progressive_growing_of_gans)

It is fair to say that the superior image generation is mostly down to growing the networks progressively. The network architecture is quite simple, consisting only of convolutional layers and dense layers, rather than more complex architectures such as residual blocks or VAE-like architectures that were more common among GANs.

It was not until two generations after the introduction of ProGAN, with StyleGAN 2, that the authors started exploring these network architectures. The loss function is also simple, just WGAN-GP loss, without any other losses such as content loss, reconstruction loss, or KL divergence loss. However, there are several minor innovations that we should go over before implementing the core part of growing layers progressively. These innovations are as follows:

- Pixel normalization

- Minibatch statistics

- Equalized learning rate

Pixel normalization

Batch normalization should reduce the covariate shift, but the ProGAN authors did not observe that in the network training. Therefore, they ditched batch normalization and used a custom normalization for the generator, known as **pixel normalization**. On a separate note, other researchers later found that batch normalization doesn't really solve the covariate problem despite stabilizing deep neural network training.

Anyway, the purpose of normalization in ProGAN is to limit the weight values to prevent them from growing exponentially. Large weights could escalate signal magnitudes and result in unhealthy competition between the generator and the discriminator. Pixel normalization normalizes the feature in each pixel location (H, W) across the channel dimension to unit length. If the tensor is a batched RGB image with dimension (N, H, W, C), the RGB vector of any pixel will have a magnitude of 1.

We can implement the equation using a custom layer as shown in the following code:

```python
class PixelNorm(Layer):
    def __init__(self, epsilon=1e-8):
        super(PixelNorm, self).__init__()
        self.epsilon = epsilon
    def call(self, input_tensor):
        return input_tensor / tf.math.sqrt(
                        tf.reduce_mean(input_tensor**2,
                        axis=-1, keepdims=True) +
                        self.epsilon)
```

Unlike other normalizations, pixel normalization doesn't have any learnable parameters; it only consists of simple arithmetic operations and hence is computationally efficient to run.

Increasing image variation with minibatch statistics

Mode collapse happens when a GAN generates similar-looking images as it captures only a subset of the variation found in the training data. One way to encourage more variation is to show the statistics of a minibatch to the discriminator. The statistics from a minibatch are more varied compared to only a single instance, and this encourages the generator to generate images that show similar statistics.

Batch normalization uses minibatch statistics to normalize the activation, which in some way serves this purpose, but ProGAN doesn't use batch normalization. Instead, it uses a **minibatch layer** that calculates the minibatch standard deviation and appends it to the activation without changing the activation itself.

The steps to calculate minibatch statistics are as follows:

1. Calculate the standard deviation for each feature in each spatial location over the minibatch – in other words, across dimension N.

2. Calculate the average of these standard deviations across the (H, W, C) dimensions to arrive at a single scale value.

3. Replicate this value across the feature map of (H, W) and append it to the activation. As a result, the output activation has a shape of $(N, H, W, C+1)$.

The following is the code for a minibatch standard deviation custom layer:

```
class MinibatchStd(Layer):
    def __init__(self, group_size=4, epsilon=1e-8):
        super(MinibatchStd, self).__init__()
        self.epsilon = epsilon
        self.group_size = group_size
    def call(self, input_tensor):
        n, h, w, c = input_tensor.shape
        x = tf.reshape(input_tensor, [self.group_size,
                       -1, h, w, c])
        group_mean, group_var = tf.nn.moments(x,
                                              axes=(0),
                                              keepdims=False)
        group_std = tf.sqrt(group_var + self.epsilon)
```

```
avg_std = tf.reduce_mean(group_std, axis=[1,2,3],
                         keepdims=True)
x = tf.tile(avg_std, [self.group_size, h, w, 1])
return tf.concat([input_tensor, x], axis=-1)
```

Before calculating the standard deviation, the activation is first split into groups of 4 or the batch size, whichever is lower. To simplify the code, we assume that the batch size is at least 4 during training. The minibatch layer can be inserted anywhere in the discriminator, but it was found to be more effective toward the end, which is the 4x4 layer.

Equalized learning rate

The name can be misleading, as the **equalized learning rate** does not modify the learning rate like **learning rate decay**. In fact, the learning rate of the optimizer stays constant throughout the training. To understand this, let's recap how backpropagation works. When using a simple **stochastic gradient descent (SGD)** optimizer, the negative gradients are multiplied by the learning rate before updating the weights. Therefore, the layers closer to the generator input will receive less gradient (remember the vanishing gradient?).

What if we want a layer to receive more gradient? Let's say we perform a simple matrix multiplication $y = w*x$, and now we add a constant 2 to make it $y = 2*w*x$. During backpropagation, the gradients will also be multiplied by 2, hence becoming larger. We could then set different multiplier constants for different layers to effectively have different learning rates.

In ProGAN, these multiplier constants are calculated from He's initializer. **He** or **Kaiming** initialization is named after Kaiming He, the inventor of ResNet. The **weight** initialization is designed specifically for networks that use the ReLU family of activation functions. Usually, weights are initialized using normal distribution with a specified standard deviation; for example, we used 0.02 in previous chapters. Instead of having to guess the standard deviation, He calculates it using the following equation:

$$std = \sqrt{\frac{2}{fan\ in}}$$

Fan in is the multiplication of the weights dimension except for the output channel. For a convolution weight with the shape (`kernel, kernel, channel_in, channel_out`), the *fan in* is the multiplication of `kernel x kernel x channel_in`. To use this in weight initialization, we can pass `tf.keras.initializers.he_normal` to the Keras layer. However, an equalized learning rate does this at runtime, so we will write custom layers to calculate the standard deviation.

The default gain factor for the initialization is 2, but ProGAN uses a lower gain for the dense layer for the input of the 4x4 generator. ProGAN uses standard normal distribution to initialize the layer weights and scale them with their normalization constant. This deviates from the trend of careful weight initializations that was common among GANs. We now write a custom Conv2D layer that uses pixel normalization:

```
class Conv2D(layers.Layer):
    def build(self, input_shape):
        self.in_channels = input_shape[-1]
        fan_in = self.kernel*self.kernel*self.in_channels
        self.scale = tf.sqrt(self.gain/fan_in)
    def call(self, inputs):
        x = tf.pad(inputs, [[0, 0], [1, 1], [1, 1],
                           [0, 0]], mode='REFLECT') \
                 if self.pad else inputs
        output = tf.nn.conv2d(x, self.scale*self.w,
                              strides=1,
                              padding="SAME") + self.b
        return output
```

The official ProGAN uses zero padding in the convolutional layer, and you can see the border artifacts, especially when viewing low-resolution images. Therefore, we added reflective padding except for the 1x1 kernel, where no padding is needed. Larger layers have smaller scale factors, which effectively reduces the gradient and hence the learning rate. This causes the learning rate to be adjusted based on the layer size so that weights in big layers do not grow too quickly, hence the name equalized learning rate.

The custom Dense layer can be written in a similar manner:

```
class Dense(layers.Layer):
    def __init__(self, units, gain=2, **kwargs):
        super(Dense, self).__init__(kwargs)
        self.units = units
        self.gain = gain
    def build(self, input_shape):
        self.in_channels = input_shape[-1]
        initializer = \
                tf.keras.initializers.RandomNormal(
                                mean=0., stddev=1.)
        self.w = self.add_weight(shape=[self.in_channels,
```

```
                                        self.units],
                            initializer=initializer,
                            trainable=True,
                            name='kernel')
        self.b = self.add_weight(shape=(self.units,),
                            initializer='zeros',
                            trainable=True,
                            name='bias')
        fan_in = self.in_channels
        self.scale = tf.sqrt(self.gain/fan_in)
    def call(self, inputs):
        output = tf.matmul(inputs,
                        self.scale*self.w) + self.b
        return output
```

Notice that the custom layer accepts `**kwargs` in the constructor, meaning we can pass in the usual Keras keyword arguments for the Dense layer. We now have all the ingredients required to start building a ProGAN in the next section.

Building a ProGAN

We have now learned about the three features of ProGANs – pixel normalization, minibatch standard deviation statistics, and the equalized learning rate. Now, we are going to delve into the network architecture and look at how to grow the network progressively. ProGAN grows an image by growing the layers, starting from a resolution of 4x4, then doubling it to 8x8, 16x16, and so on to 1024x1024. Thus, we will first write the code to build the layer block at each scale. The building blocks of the generator and discriminator are trivially simple, as we will see.

Building the generator blocks

We will start by building the 4x4 generator block, which forms the base of the generator and takes in the latent code as input. The input is normalized by `PixelNorm` before going to `Dense`. A lower gain is used for the equalized learning rate for that layer. Leaky ReLU and pixel normalization are used throughout all the generator blocks. We build the generator as follows:

```
def build_generator_base(self, input_shape):
    input_tensor = Input(shape=input_shape)
```

```
    x = PixelNorm()(input_tensor)
    x = Dense(8192, gain=1./8)(x)
    x = Reshape((4, 4, 512))(x)
    x = LeakyReLU(0.2)(x)
    x = PixelNorm()(x)
    x = Conv2D(512, 3, name='gen_4x4_conv1')(x)
    x = LeakyReLU(0.2)(x)
    x = PixelNorm()(x)
    return Model(input_tensor, x,
                name='generator_base')
```

After the 4x4 generator block, all subsequent blocks have the same architecture, which involves an upsampling layer followed by two convolutional layers. The only difference is the convolutional filter size. In the ProGAN's default setting, a filter size of 512 is used up to the 32x32 generator block, then it is halved at each stage to finally reach 16 at 1024x1024, as follows:

```
self.log2_res_to_filter_size = {
    0: 512,
    1: 512,
    2: 512, # 4x4
    3: 512, # 8x8
    4: 512, # 16x16
    5: 512, # 32x32
    6: 256, # 64x64
    7: 128, # 128x128
    8: 64,  # 256x256
    9: 32,  # 512x512
    10: 16} # 1024x1024
```

To make the coding easier, we can linearize the resolution by taking logarithm with base 2. Hence, *log2(4)* is *2*, *log2(8)* is *3*, ... to *log2(1024)* is *10*. Then, we can loop through the resolution linearly in `log2` from 2 to 10 as follows:

```
def build_generator_block(self, log2_res, input_shape):
    res = 2**log2_res
    res_name = f'{res}x{res}'
    filter_n = self.log2_res_to_filter_size[log2_res]
    input_tensor = Input(shape=input_shape)
```

```
    x = UpSampling2D((2,2))(input_tensor)
    x = Conv2D(filter_n, 3,
            name=f'gen_{res_name}_conv1')(x)
    x = PixelNorm()(LeakyReLU(0.2)(x))
    x = Conv2D(filter_n, 3,
            name=f'gen_{res_name}_conv2')(x)
    x = PixelNorm()(LeakyReLU(0.2)(x))
    return Model(input_tensor, x,
            name=f'genblock_{res}_x_{res}')
```

We can now use this code to build all the generator blocks from 4x4 all the way to the target resolution.

Building the discriminator blocks

We can now shift our attention to the discriminator. The basic discriminator is at a 4x4 resolution, where it takes 4x4x3 images and predicts whether the image is real or fake. It uses one convolutional layer, followed by two dense layers. Unlike the generator, the discriminator does not use pixel normalization; in fact, no normalization is used at all. We will insert the minibatch standard deviation layer as follows:

```
def build_discriminator_base(self, input_shape):
    input_tensor = Input(shape=input_shape)
    x = MinibatchStd()(input_tensor)
    x = Conv2D(512, 3, name='gen_4x4_conv1')(x)
    x = LeakyReLU(0.2)(x)
    x = Flatten()(x)
    x = Dense(512, name='gen_4x4_dense1')(x)
    x = LeakyReLU(0.2)(x)
    x = Dense(1, name='gen_4x4_dense2')(x)
    return Model(input_tensor, x,
            name='discriminator_base')
```

After that, the discriminator uses two convolutional layers followed by downsampling, using average pooling at every stage:

```
def build_discriminator_block(self, log2_res, input_shape):
    filter_n = self.log2_res_to_filter_size[log2_res]
    input_tensor = Input(shape=input_shape)
    x = Conv2D(filter_n, 3)(input_tensor)
```

```
x = LeakyReLU(0.2)(x)
filter_n = self.log2_res_to_filter_size[log2_res-1]
x = Conv2D(filter_n, 3)(x)
x = LeakyReLU(0.2)(x)
x = AveragePooling2D((2,2))(x)
res = 2**log2_res
return Model(input_tensor, x,
             name=f'disc_block_{res}_x_{res}')
```

We now have all the basic building blocks defined. Next, we will look at how to join them together to grow the network progressively.

Progressively growing the network

This is the most important part of ProGAN – growing the network. We can use the preceding functions to create generator and discriminator blocks at different resolutions. All we need to do now is to join them together as we grow the layers. The following diagram shows the process of growing the network. Let's start from the left-hand side:

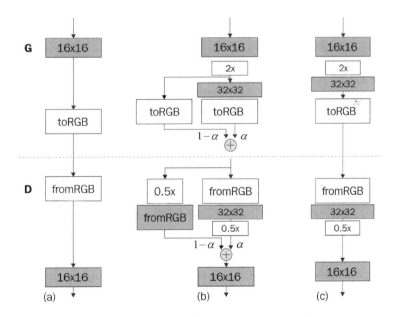

Figure 7.3 – Illustration of progressively growing layers.
Redrawn from T. Karras et al. 2018, "Progressive Growing of GANs for Improved Quality, Stability, and Variation," https://arxiv.org/abs/1710.10196)

In the generator and discriminator blocks that we have built, we assume both the input and output to be layer activations rather than RGB images. Thus, we will need to convert the activation from the generator block into an RGB image. Similarly, for the discriminator, we will need to convert the image into activation. This is shown by **(a)** in the preceding figure.

We will create two more functions that build the blocks to convert into and from RGB images. Both blocks use a 1x1 convolutional layer; the to_rgb block uses a filter size of 3 to match the RGB channels, while the from_rgb blocks use a filter size that matches the input activation of the discriminator block at that scale. The code of the two functions is as follows:

```
def build_to_rgb(self, res, filter_n):
    return Sequential([Input(shape=(res, res, filter_n)),
                       Conv2D(3, 1, gain=1,
                              activation='tanh')])
def build_from_rgb(self, res, filter_n):
    return Sequential([Input(shape=(res, res, 3)),
                       Conv2D(filter_n, 1),
                       LeakyReLU(0.2)])
```

Now, assume the network is at 16x16, meaning there are already layers at the lower resolutions of 8x8 and 4x4. Now we are about to grow the 32x32 layer. However, if we add a new untrained layer to the network, the newly generated images will look like noise and will result in a huge loss. This can in turn result in exploding gradients and destabilize the training.

To minimize this disruption, the 32x32 image generated by the new layer is not used immediately. Instead, we upsample the 16x16 image from the previous stage and fade in with the new 32x32 image. Fade is a technical term in image processing that refers to gradually increasing the opacity of an image. This is implemented by using a weighted sum with the following equation:

$$image = \alpha \times image_{log2\_res} + (1 - \alpha) \times image_{log2_{res}-1}$$

In this transition phase, alpha increases from 0 to 1. In other words, at the start of the phase, we discard the image from the new layer completely and use the one from the previous trained layer. We then increase alpha linearly to 1 when only the image generated by the new layer is used. The stable state is shown by *(c)* in the preceding diagram. We can implement a custom layer to perform the weighted sum as follows:

```
class FadeIn(Layer):
    @tf.function
    def call(self, input_alpha, a, b):
        alpha = tf.reduce_mean(input_alpha)
        y = alpha * a + (1. - alpha) * b
        return y
```

When using a subclass to define a layer, we can pass in a scalar alpha to the function. However, it is not possible when we use **Sequential** to define our Keras model. The variable within the model, for instance, `self.alpha = tf.Variable(1.0)`, will be converted to a constant when we compile the model and can no longer be changed in the training.

One way to pass in a scalar alpha is to write the entire model with subclassing, but I feel it is more convenient in this case to use the sequential or functional API to create the models. To address this problem, we define alpha as an input to the model. However, the model input is assumed to be a minibatch. To be concrete, if we define `Input(shape=(1))`, its actual shape will be *(None, 1)*, where the first dimension is the batch size. Therefore, `tf.reduce_mean()` in `FadeIN()` is meant to convert the batched value to a scalar value.

Now, we can look at the following steps to grow the generator to, say, 32x32:

1. Add a 4x4 generator, where the input is a latent vector.

2. In a loop, add subsequent generators of gradually increasing resolutions until the one before the target resolution (in our example, 16x16).

3. Add `to_rgb` from 16x16 and upsample it to 32x32.

4. Add the 32x32 generator block.

5. Fade in the two images to create one final RGB image.

The code is as follows:

```
def grow_generator(self, log2_res):
    res = 2**log2_res
    alpha = Input(shape=(1))
    x = self.generator_blocks[2].input
    for i in range(2, log2_res):
        x = self.generator_blocks[i](x)
    old_rgb = self.to_rgb[log2_res-1](x)
    old_rgb = UpSampling2D((2,2))(old_rgb)
    x = self.generator_blocks[log2_res](x)
    new_rgb = self.to_rgb[log2_res](x)
    rgb = FadeIn()(alpha, new_rgb, old_rgb)
    self.generator = Model([self.generator_blocks[2].input,
                           alpha], rgb,
                           name=f'generator_{res}_x_{res}')
```

The growing discriminator is done similarly but in the reverse direction, as follows:

1. At the resolution of the input image, say, 32x32, add `from_rgb` to the discriminator block of 32x32. The output is the activation with a 16x16 feature map.

2. Parallelly, downsample the input image to 16x16, and add `from_rgb` to the 16x16 discriminator block.

3. Fade in the two preceding features and feed that into the next discriminator block of 8x8.

4. Continue adding the discriminator blocks to the base of 4x4, where the output is a single prediction value.

The following is the code to grow the discriminator:

```
def grow_discriminator(self, log2_res):
    res = 2**log2_res
    input_image = Input(shape=(res, res, 3))
    alpha = Input(shape=(1))
    x = self.from_rgb[log2_res](input_image)
    x = self.discriminator_blocks[log2_res](x)
    downsized_image = AveragePooling2D((2,2))(input_image)
    y = self.from_rgb[log2_res-1](downsized_image)
```

```
    x = FadeIn()(alpha, x, y)
    for i in range (log2_res-1, 1, -1):
        x = self.discriminator_blocks[i](x)
    self.discriminator =  Model([input_image, alpha], x,
                name=f'discriminator_{res}_x_{res}')
```

Finally, we build a model from the grown generator and discriminator as follows:

```
def grow_model(self, log2_res):
    self.grow_generator(log2_res)
    self.grow_discriminator(log2_res)
    self.discriminator.trainable = False
    latent_input = Input(shape=(self.z_dim))
    alpha_input = Input(shape=(1))
    fake_image = self.generator([latent_input, alpha_input])
    pred = self.discriminator([fake_image, alpha_input])
    self.model = Model(inputs=[latent_input, alpha_input],
                outputs=pred)
    self.model.compile(loss=wasserstein_loss,
                    optimizer=Adam(**self.opt_init))
    self.optimizer_discriminator = Adam(**self.opt_init)
```

We reset the optimizer states after the new layer is added. This is because optimizers such as Adam have internal states that store the gradient history for each layer. The easiest way to do that is probably to instantiate a new optimizer using the same parameters.

Loss function

You may have noticed the **Wasserstein loss** in the preceding code snippet. That's right, the generator uses Wasserstein loss, where the loss function is a multiplication between predictions and the labels. The discriminator uses the WGAN-GP gradient penalty loss. We learned about WGAN-GP in *Chapter 3, Generative Adversarial Network*, but let's recap the loss function here.

WGAN-GP interpolates between fake and real images and feeds the interpolation to the discriminator. From there, gradients are calculated with respect to the input interpolation rather the usual optimization that calculate gradients against the weights. From there, we calculate the gradient penalty (loss) and add it to the discriminator loss for backpropagation. We will reuse the WGAN-GP that we developed in *Chapter 3, Generative Adversarial Network*. Unlike the original WGAN-GP, which trains the discriminator five times for every generator training step, ProGAN uses equal amounts of training for both the discriminator and the generator.

Apart from the WGAN-GP losses, there is an additional loss type known as **drift loss**. The discriminator output is unbounded and can be large positive or negative values. This drift loss aims to keep the discriminator output from drifting too far away from zero toward the infinity. The following code snippet shows how to calculate drift loss from the discriminator output:

```
# drift loss
all_pred = tf.concat([pred_fake, pred_real], axis=0)
drift_factor = 0.001
drift_loss = drift_factor * tf.reduce_mean(all_pred**2)
```

Now, we can start training our ProGAN!

Growing pains

ProGAN is extremely slow to train. It took the authors eight Tesla V100 GPUs and 4 days to train on the 1024x1024 `CelebA-HQ` dataset. If you have access to only one GPU, it would take you more than 1 month to train! Even for the relatively low resolution of 256x256, it would take a good 2 or 3 days to train with a single GPU. Take that into consideration before starting training. You might want to start with a lower target resolution, such as 64x64.

Having said that, for a start, we don't have to use a high-resolution dataset. Datasets with a 256x256 resolution are sufficient. The notebook left out the input part, so feel free to fill in the input to load your dataset. For your information, there are two popular 1024x1024 face datasets that are freely downloadable:

- CelebA-HQ on the official ProGAN TensorFlow 1 implementation: `https://github.com/tkarras/progressive_growing_of_gans`. It requires the download of the original `CelebA` dataset plus HQ-related files. The generation scripts also rely on some dated libraries. Therefore, I don't recommend you do it this way; you should try finding a dataset that is pre-converted.

- FFHQ: `https://github.com/NVlabs/ffhq-dataset`. This dataset was created for StyleGAN (a successor of ProGAN) and is more varied and diverse than the `CelebA-HQ` dataset. It can also be difficult to download due to the download limit set by the server.

When we download high-resolution images, we will need to downscale them to lower resolutions to be used for training. You can do that at runtime, but it can slow down the training slightly due to the additional computation to perform the downsampling, and it requires more memory bandwidth to transfer the images. Alternatively, you can create the multiscale images from the original image resolution first, which can save time in memory transfer and image resizing.

The other thing to note is the batch size. As the image resolution grows, so does the GPU memory required to store the images and the larger layer activations. We will run out of GPU memory if we set the batch size too high. Therefore, we use a batch size of 16 from 4x4 to 64x64, then halve the batch size as the resolution doubles. You should adjust the batch size accordingly to fit your GPU.

The following figure shows the generated images from 16x16 resolution to 64x64 resolution using our ProGAN:

Figure 7.4 – Images growing from 8x8 to 64x64 as generated by our ProGAN

ProGAN is a very delicate model. When reproducing the models in this book, I only implemented the key parts to match the details of the original implementation. I would leave out something that I thought was not that important and swap it for something that I hadn't covered. This applied to optimizers, learning rates, normalization techniques, and loss functions.

However, I found that I had to implement everything to almost the exact original specification for ProGAN in order to make it work. This includes using the same batch size, drift loss, and equalized learning rate gain. Nevertheless, when we get the network to work, it does generate high-fidelity faces that are unmatched by any models that came before it!

Now let's see how StyleGAN improves on ProGAN to allow for style mixing.

Implementing StyleGAN

ProGAN is great at generating high-resolution images by growing the network progressively, but the network architecture is quite primitive. The simple architecture resembles earlier GANs such as DCGAN that generate images from random noise but without fine control over the images to be generated.

As we have seen in previous chapters, many innovations happened in image-to-image translation to allow better manipulation of the generator outputs. One of them is the use of the AdaIN layer (*Chapter 5, Style Transfer*) to allow style transfer, mixing the content and style features from two different images. **StyleGAN** adopts this concept of style-mixing to come out with *a style-based generator architecture for generative adversarial networks* – this is the title of the paper written for **FaceBid**. The following figure shows that StyleGAN can mix the style features from two different images to generate a new one:

Figure 7.5 – Mixing styles to produce new images
(Source: T. Karras et al, 2019 "A Style-Based Generator Architecture for Generative Adversarial Networks," https://arxiv.org/abs/1812.04948)

We will now delve into the StyleGAN generator architecture.

Style-based generator

The following diagram compares the generator architectures of ProGAN and StyleGAN:

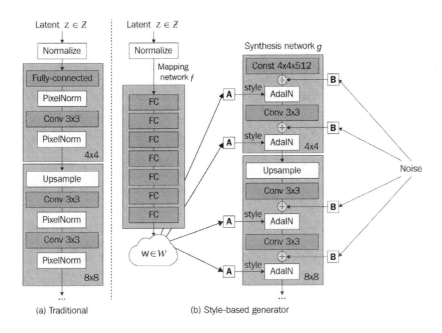

Figure 7.6 – Comparing generators between (a) ProGAN and (b) StyleGAN
Redrawn from T. Karras et al, 2019 "A Style-Based Generator Architecture for Generative Adversarial Networks," https://arxiv.org/abs/1812.04948)

The ProGAN architecture is a simple feedforward design, where the single input is the latent code. All the latent information, for example, content, style, and randomness, are included in the single latent code z. On the right in the preceding figure is the StyleGAN generator architecture, where the latent code no longer goes directly into the synthesis network. The latent code is mapped to style code that goes into a multi-scale synthesis network.

We will go through the generation pipeline now, which has the following the major building blocks:

- **Mapping network, f:** This is 8 dense layers with 512 dimensions. Its input is 512-dimensional latent code, and the output w is also a vector of 512. w is broadcast to every scale of the generator.

- **Affine transform, A**: In every scale, there is a block that maps *w* into styles $y = (y_s, y_b)$. In other words, the global latent vector is converted to localized style code at each image scale. The affine transform is implemented using dense layers.

- **AdaIN**: AdaIN modulates the style code and content code. The content code *x* is the convolutional layer's activation, while *y* is the style code:

$$AdaIN(x, y) = y_s \frac{x - \mu(x)}{\sigma(x)} + y_b$$

- **Synthesis network, g**: This is essentially made up of the ProGAN multiscale generator blocks. The notable difference with ProGAN is that the input to the synthesis network is just some constant values. This is because the latent code presents itself as style codes in every generator layer, including the first 4x4 block, so there is no need to have another random input to the synthesis network.

- **Multiscale noise**: There are many aspects of human portraits that can be seen as stochastic (random). For example, the exact placement of hairs and freckles can be random, but this does not change our perception of an image. This randomness comes from the noise that is injected into the generator. The Gaussian noise has a shape that matches the convolution layer activation map (H, W, 1). It is scaled per channel by *B* to (H, W, C) before being added to the convolutional activation.

In most GANs that came before StyleGAN, the latent code was injected only at input or into one of the internal layer. The brilliance of the StyleGAN generator is that we can now inject style code and noise at every layer, meaning we can tweak images at different levels. Styles at coarse spatial resolutions (from 4x4 to 8x8) correspond to high-level aspects such as poses and face shapes. Middle resolutions (from 16x16 to 32x32) are to do with smaller-scale facial features, hairstyles, and whether eyes are open or closed. Finally, higher resolutions (from 64x64 to 1024x1024) mainly change the color scheme and microstructure.

The StyleGAN generator may have looked complex at first, but hopefully it doesn't look that scary now. As with ProGAN, the individual blocks are simple. We will leverage code from ProGAN heavily; now let's start to build the StyleGAN generator!

Implementing the mapping network

The mapping network maps the 512-dimensional latent code into 512-dimensional features as follows:

```
def build_mapping(self):
    # Mapping Network
```

```
z = Input(shape=(self.z_dim))
w = PixelNorm()(z)
for i in range(8):
    w = Dense(512, lrmul=0.01)(w)
    w = LeakyReLU(0.2)(w)
w = tf.tile(tf.expand_dims(w, 0), (8,1,1))
self.mapping = Model(z, w, name='mapping')
```

It is a straightforward implementation of dense layers with leaky ReLU activation. One thing to note is that the learning rate is multiplied by 0.01 to make it more stable to train. Therefore, the custom `Dense` layer is modified to take in an additional `lrmul` argument. At the end of the network, we create eight copies of w, which will go into eight layers of generator blocks. We could skip the tiling if we don't intend to use style mixing.

Adding noise

We now create a custom layer to add noise to the convolution layer output, which includes the *B* block in the architectural diagram. The code is as follows:

```
class AddNoise(Layer):
    def build(self, input_shape):
        n, h, w, c = input_shape[0]
        initializer = \
            tf.keras.initializers.RandomNormal(
                                mean=0., stddev=1.)
        self.B = self.add_weight(shape=[1, 1, 1, c],
                                initializer=initializer,
                                trainable=True,
                                name='kernel')
    def call(self, inputs):
        x, noise = inputs
        output = x + self.B * noise
        return output
```

The noise is multiplied with the learnable B to scale it per channel, then it is added to the input activation.

Implementing AdaIN

The AdaIN that we will implement for StyleGAN is different from the one for style transfer for the following reasons:

- We will include affine transformation *A*. This is implemented with two dense layers to predict *ys* and *yb*, respectively.

- Original AdaIN involves the normalization of the input activation, but since the input activation to our AdaIN has undergone pixel normalization, we will not perform normalization within this custom layer. The code for the AdaIN layer is as follows:

```python
class AdaIN(Layer):
    def __init__(self, gain=1, **kwargs):
        super(AdaIN, self).__init__(kwargs)
        self.gain = gain
    def build(self, input_shapes):
        x_shape = input_shapes[0]
        w_shape = input_shapes[1]
        self.w_channels = w_shape[-1]
        self.x_channels = x_shape[-1]
        self.dense_1 = Dense(self.x_channels, gain=1)
        self.dense_2 = Dense(self.x_channels, gain=1)
    def call(self, inputs):
        x, w = inputs
        ys = tf.reshape(self.dense_1(w), (-1, 1, 1,
                              self.x_channels))
        yb = tf.reshape(self.dense_2(w), (-1, 1, 1,
                              self.x_channels))
        output = ys*x + yb
        return output
```

Comparing AdaIN with style transfer

The AdaIN in ProGAN is different from the original implementation for style transfer. In style transfer, the style feature is Gram matrix calculated from VGG features of an input image. In ProGAN, the 'style' is vector *w* generated from random noise.

Building the generator block

Now, we can put `AddNoise` and `AdaIN` into the generator block, which looks similar to ProGAN's code to build generator block, as follows:

```
def build_generator_block(self, log2_res, input_shape):
    res = int(2**log2_res)
    res_name = f'{res}x{res}'
    filter_n = self.log2_res_to_filter_size[log2_res]
    input_tensor = Input(shape=input_shape)
    x = input_tensor
    w = Input(shape=512)
    noise = Input(shape=(res, res, 1))
    if log2_res > 2:
        x = UpSampling2D((2,2))(x)
        x = Conv2D(filter_n, 3,
                    name=f'gen_{res_name}_conv1')(x)
    x = AddNoise()([x, noise])
    x = PixelNorm()(LeakyReLU(0.2)(x))
    x = AdaIN()([x, w])
    # ADD NOISE
    x = Conv2D(filter_n, 3,
                name=f'gen_{res_name}_conv2')(x)
    x = AddNoise()([x, noise])
    x = PixelNorm()(LeakyReLU(0.2)(x))
    x = AdaIN()([x, w])
    return Model([input_tensor, x, noise], x,
                name=f'genblock_{res}_x_{res}')
```

The generator block takes three inputs. For a 4x4 generator block, the input is a constant tensor of 1 and we bypass the upsampling and convolutional blocks. The other two inputs are the vector *w* and random noise.

Training StyleGAN

As mentioned at the beginning of the section, the main changes from ProGAN to StyleGAN are to the generator. There are some minor differences in the discriminator and training details, but they don't affect performance as much. Therefore, we will keep the rest of the pipeline the same as ProGAN.

The following figure shows 256x256 images generated by our StyleGAN. The same style *w* is used but with different randomly generated noise:

Figure 7.7 – Portraits generated using the same style but different noise

We can see that the faces belong to the same person but with varying details, such as length of hair and head pose. We can also mix styles by using *w* from different latent code as shown in the following figure:

Figure 7.8 – All images are generated by our StyleGAN. The face on the right was created by mixing styles from the first two faces

Knowing that StyleGAN can be difficult to train, therefore I have provided a pretrained 256x256 model that you can download. You can use the widget in the Jupyter notebook to experiment with the face generation and style mixing.

This concludes our journey with StyleGAN.

Summary

In this chapter, we entered the realm of high-definition image generation with ProGAN. ProGAN first trains on low-resolution images before moving on to higher-resolution images. The network training becomes more stable by growing the network progressively. This lays the foundation for high-fidelity image generation, as this coarse-to-fine training method is adopted by other GANs. For example, pix2pixHD has two generators at two different scales, where the coarse generator is pre-trained before both are trained together. We have also learned about equalized learning rates, minibatch statistics, and pixel normalization, which are also used in StyleGAN.

With the use of the AdaIN layer from style transfer in the generator, not only does StyleGAN produce better-quality images, but this also allows control of features when mixing styles. By injecting different style code and noise at different scales, we can control both the global and fine details of an image. StyleGAN achieved state-of-the-art results in high-definition image generation and remains the state of the art at the time of writing. The style-based model is now the mainstream architecture. We have seen the use of this model in style transfer, image-to-image translation, and StyleGAN.

In the next chapter, we will look at another popular family of GANs, which are known as attention-based models.

8
Self-Attention for Image Generation

You may have heard about some popular **Natural Language Processing** (**NLP**) models, such as the Transformer, BERT, or GPT-3. They all have one thing in common – they all use an architecture known as a transformer that is made up of self-attention modules.

Self-attention is gaining widespread adoption in computer vision, including classification tasks, which makes it an important topic to master. As we will learn in this chapter, self-attention helps us to capture important features in the image without using deep layers for large effective receptive fields. StyleGAN is great for generating faces, but it will struggle to generate images from ImageNet.

In a way, faces are easy to generate, as eyes, noses, and lips all have similar shapes and are in similar positions across various faces. In contrast, the 1,000 classes of ImageNet contain varied objects (dogs, trucks, fish, and pillows, for instance) and backgrounds. Therefore, the discriminator must be more effective at capturing the distinct features of various objects. This is where self-attention comes into play. Using that, with conditional batch normalization and spectral normalization, we will implement a **Self-Attention GAN** (**SAGAN**) to generate images based on given class labels.

After that, we will use the SAGAN as a base to create a BigGAN. We will add orthogonal regularization and change the method of doing class embedding. BigGANs can generate high-definition images without using ProGAN-like architecture, and they are considered to be state-of-the-art models in class labels conditioning image generation.

We will cover the following topics in this chapter:

- Spectral normalization

- Self-attention modules

- Building a SAGAN

- Implementing BigGAN

Technical requirements

The Jupyter notebooks can be found here (https://github.com/ PacktPublishing/Hands-On-Image-Generation-with-TensorFlow-2.0/ tree/master/Chapter08):

- ch8_sagan.ipynb

- ch8_big_gan.ipynb

Spectral normalization

Spectral normalization is an important method to stabilize GAN training and it has been used in a lot of recent state-of-the-art GANs. Unlike batch normalization or other normalization methods that normalize the activation, spectral normalization normalizes the weights instead. The aim of spectral normalization is to limit the growth of the weights, so the networks adhere to the 1-Lipschitz constraint. This has proved effective in stabilizing GAN training, as we learned in *Chapter 3, Generative Adversarial Network*.

We will revise WGANs to give us a better understanding of the idea behind spectral normalization. The WGAN discriminator (also known as the critic) needs to keep its prediction to small numbers to meet the 1-Lipschtiz constraint. WGANs do this by naively clipping the weights to the range of [-0.01, 0.01].

This is not a reliable method as we need to fine-tune the clipping range, which is a hyperparameter. It would be nice if there was a systematic way to enforce the 1-Lipschitz constraint without the use of hyperparameters, and spectral normalization is the tool we need for that. In essence, spectral normalization normalizes the weights by dividing by their spectral norms.

Understanding spectral norm

We will go over some linear algebra to roughly explain what spectral norm is. You may have learned about eigenvalues and eigenvectors in matrix theory with the following equation:

$$Av = \lambda v$$

Here A is a square matrix, v is the eigenvector, and the *lambda* is its eigenvalue.

We'll try to understand the terms using a simple example. Let's say that v is a vector of position (x, y) and A is a linear transformation as follows:

$$A = \begin{pmatrix} a & b \\ c & d \end{pmatrix}, \quad v = \begin{pmatrix} x \\ y \end{pmatrix}$$

If we multiply A with v, we'll get a new position with a change of direction as follows:

$$Av = \begin{pmatrix} a & b \\ c & d \end{pmatrix} \times \begin{pmatrix} x \\ y \end{pmatrix} = \begin{pmatrix} ax + by \\ cx + dy \end{pmatrix}$$

Eigenvectors are vectors that do not change their directions when A is applied to them. Instead, they are only scaled by the scalar eigenvalues denoted as lambda. There can be multiple eigenvector-eigenvalue pairs. The square root of the largest eigenvalue is the spectral norm of the matrix. For a non-square matrix, we will need to use a mathematical algorithm such as **singular value decomposition (SVD)** to calculate the eigenvalues, which can be computationally costly.

Therefore, a power iteration method is employed to speed up the calculation and make it feasible for neural network training. Let's jump in to implement spectral normalization as a weight constraint in TensorFlow.

Implementing spectral normalization

The mathematic algorithm of spectral normalization as given by T. Miyato et al., 2018, in the *Spectral Normalization For Generative Adversarial Networks* paper may appear complex. However, as usual, the software implementation is simpler than what the mathematics looks.

The following are the steps to perform spectral normalization:

1. The weights in the convolutional layer form a 4-dimensional-tensor, so the first step is to reshape it into a 2D matrix of W, where we keep the last dimension of the weight. Now the weight has the shape $(H \times W, C)$.

2. Initialize a vector u with N(0,1).

3. In a `for` loop, calculate the following:

    a) Calculate $V = (W^T) U$ with matrix transpose and matrix multiplication.

    b) Normalize V with its L2 norm, that is, $V = V/\|V\|_2$.

    c) Calculate $U = WV$.

    d) Normalize U with its L2 norm, that is, $U = U/\|U\|_2$.

4. Calculate the spectral norm as $U^T W V$.

5. Finally, divide the weights by the spectral norm.

The full code is as follows:

```python
class SpectralNorm(tf.keras.constraints.Constraint):
    def __init__(self, n_iter=5):
        self.n_iter = n_iter
    def call(self, input_weights):
        w = tf.reshape(input_weights, (-1,
                            input_weights.shape[-1]))
        u = tf.random.normal((w.shape[0], 1))
        for _ in range(self.n_iter):
            v = tf.matmul(w, u, transpose_a=True)
            v /= tf.norm(v)
            u = tf.matmul(w, v)
            u /= tf.norm(u)
        spec_norm = tf.matmul(u, tf.matmul(w, v),
                            transpose_a=True)
        return input_weights/spec_norm
```

The number of iterations is a hyperparameter, and I found 5 to be sufficient. Spectral normalization can also be implemented to have a variable to remember the vector u rather than starting from random values. This should reduce the number of iterations to 1. We can now apply spectral normalization by using it as a kernel constraint when defining layers, as in `Conv2D(3, 1, kernel_constraint=SpectralNorm())`.

Self-attention modules

Self-attention modules became popular with the introduction of an NLP model known as the Transformer. In NLP applications such as language translation, the model often needs to read sentences word by word to understand them before producing the output. The neural network used prior to the advent of the Transformer was some variant on the **recurrent neural network (RNN)**, such as **long short-term memory (LSTM)**. The RNN has internal states to remember words as it reads a sentence.

One drawback of that is that when the number of words increases, the gradients for the first words vanish. That is to say, the words at start of the sentence become less important gradually as the RNN reads more words.

The Transformer does things differently. It reads all the words at once and weights the importance of each individual word. Therefore, more attention is given to words that are more important, and hence the name **attention**. Self-attention is a cornerstone of state-of-the-art NLP models such as BERT and GPT-3. However, NLP is not in the scope of this book. We will now look at the details of how self-attention works in CNN.

Self-attention for computer vision

CNNs are mainly made up of convolutional layers. For a convolutional layer with a kernel size of 3×3, it will only look at 3×3=9 features in the input activation to compute each output feature. It will not look at pixels outside of this range. To capture the pixels outside of this range, we could increase the kernel size slightly to, say, 5×5 or 7×7, but that is still small compared to the feature map size.

We will have to move down one network layer for the convolutional kernel's receptive field to be large enough to capture what we want. As with RNNs, the relative importance of the input features fades as we move down through the network layers. Thus, we can use self-attention to look at every pixel in the feature map and work on what we should pay attention to.

We will now look at how the self-attention mechanism works. The first step of self-attention is to project each input feature into three vectors known as the **key**, **query**, and **value**. We don't see these terms a lot in computer vision literature, but I thought it would be good to teach you about them so that you can better understand general self-attention-, Transformer-, or NLP-related literature. The following figure illustrates how attention maps are generated from a query:

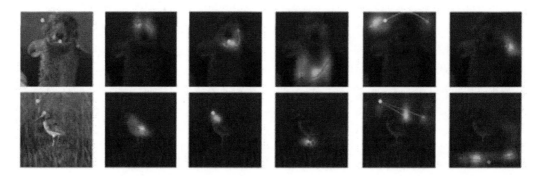

Figure 8.1 – Illustration of an attention map. (Source: H. Zhang et al., 2019, "Self-Attention Generative Adversarial Networks," https://arxiv.org/abs/1805.08318)

On the left is an image with queries marked with dots. The next five images show the attention maps given by the queries. The first attention map on the top queries one eye of the rabbit; the attention map has more white (indicating areas of high importance) around both the eyes and close to complete darkness (for low importance) in other areas.

Now, we'll now go over the technical terms of key, query, and value one by one:

- A **value** is a representation of the input features. We don't want the self-attention module to look at every single pixel as this will be too computationally expensive and unnecessary. Instead, we are more interested in the local regions of the input activation. Therefore, the value has reduced dimensions from the input features, both in terms of the activation map size (for example, it may be downsampled to have smaller height and width) and the number of channels. For convolutional layer activations, the channel number is reduced by using a 1x1 convolution, and the spatial size is reduced by max-pooling or average pooling.

- **Keys and queries** are used to compute the importance of the features of the self-attention map. To calculate an output feature at location x, we take query at location x and compare it with the key at all locations. To illustrate more on this, let's say we have an image of a portrait.

When the network is processing one eye of the portrait, it will take its query, which has a semantic meaning of *eye*, and check that with the keys of other areas of the portrait. If one of the other areas' keys is *eye*, then we know we have found the other eye, and it certainly is something we want to pay attention to so that we can match the eye color.

To put that into an equation, for feature *0*, we calculate a vector of *q0 × k0, q0 × k1, q0 × k2* and so on to *q0 × kN-1*. The vectors are then normalized using softmax so they all sum up to *1.0*, which is our attention score. This is used as a weight to perform element-wise multiplication of the value, to give the attention outputs.

The SAGAN self-attention module is based on the non-local block (X. Wang et al., 2018, *Non-local Neural Networks*, https://arxiv.org/abs/1711.07971), which was originally designed for video classification. The authors experimented with different ways of implementing self-attention before settling on the current architecture. The following diagram shows the attention module in SAGAN, where **theta θ**, **phi φ**, and **g** correspond to key, query, and value:

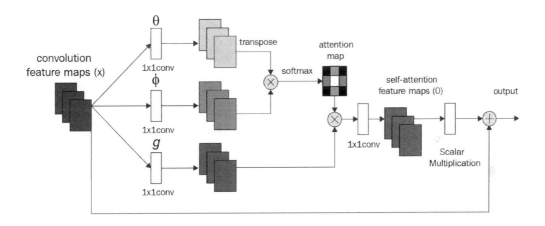

Figure 8.2 – Self-attention module architecture in SAGAN

Most computation in deep learning is vectorized for speed performance, and it is no different for self-attention. If we ignore the batch dimension for simplicity, the activations after 1×1 convolution will have a shape of (H, W, C). The first step is to reshape it into a 2D matrix with a shape of (H×W, C) and use the matrix multiplication between θ and φ to calculate the attention map. In the self-attention module used in SAGAN, there is another 1×1 convolution that is used to restore the channel number to the input channel, followed by scaling with learnable parameters. Furthermore, this is made into a residual block.

Implementing a self-attention module

We will first define all the 1×1 convolutional layers and weights in the custom layer's `build()`. Please note that we use a spectral normalization function as the kernel constraint for the convolutional layers as follows:

```python
class SelfAttention(Layer):
    def __init__(self):
        super(SelfAttention, self).__init__()
    def build(self, input_shape):
        n, h, w, c = input_shape
        self.n_feats = h * w
        self.conv_theta = Conv2D(c//8, 1, padding='same',
                        kernel_constraint=SpectralNorm(),
                        name='Conv_Theta')
        self.conv_phi = Conv2D(c//8, 1, padding='same',
                        kernel_constraint=SpectralNorm(),
                        name='Conv_Phi')
        self.conv_g = Conv2D(c//2, 1, padding='same',
                        kernel_constraint=SpectralNorm(),
                        name='Conv_G')
        self.conv_attn_g = Conv2D(c, 1, padding='same',
                        kernel_constraint=SpectralNorm(),
                        name='Conv_AttnG')
        self.sigma = self.add_weight(shape=[1],
                                initializer='zeros',
                                trainable=True,
                                name='sigma')
```

There are a few things to note here:

- The internal activation can have reduced dimensions to make the computation run faster. The reduced numbers were obtained by the SAGAN authors by experimentation.

- After every convolution layer, the activation (H, W, C) is reshaped into two-dimensional matrix with the shape (HW, C). We can then use matrix multiplication on the matrices.

The following is the `call()` function of the layer to perform the self-attention operations. We will first calculate `theta`, `phi`, and `g`:

```python
def call(self, x):
    n, h, w, c = x.shape
    theta = self.conv_theta(x)
    theta = tf.reshape(theta, (-1, self.n_feats,
                                theta.shape[-1]))
    phi = self.conv_phi(x)
    phi = tf.nn.max_pool2d(phi, ksize=2, strides=2,
                            padding='VALID')
    phi = tf.reshape(phi, (-1, self.n_feats//4,
                            phi.shape[-1]))
    g = self.conv_g(x)
    g = tf.nn.max_pool2d(g, ksize=2, strides=2,
                          padding='VALID')
    g = tf.reshape(g, (-1, self.n_feats//4,
                        g.shape[-1]))
```

We will then calculate the attention map as follows:

```python
    attn = tf.matmul(theta, phi, transpose_b=True)
    attn = tf.nn.softmax(attn)
```

Finally, we multiply attention map with the query `g` and proceed to produce the final output:

```python
    attn_g = tf.matmul(attn, g)
    attn_g = tf.reshape(attn_g, (-1, h, w,
                          attn_g.shape[-1]))
    attn_g = self.conv_attn_g(attn_g)
    output = x + self.sigma * attn_g
    return output
```

With the spectral normalization and self-attention layers written, we can now use them to build a SAGAN.

Building a SAGAN

The SAGAN has a simple architecture that looks like DCGAN's. However, it is a class-conditional GAN that uses class labels to both generate and discriminate between images. In the following figure, each image on each row is generated from different class labels:

Figure 8.3 – Images generated by a SAGAN by using different class labels. (Source: A. Brock et al., 2018, "Large Scale GAN Training for High Fidelity Natural Image Synthesis," https://arxiv.org/abs/1809.11096)

In this example, we will use the CIFAR10 dataset, which contains 10 classes of images with a resolution of 32x32. We will deal with the conditioning part later. Now, let's first complete the simplest part – the generator.

Building a SAGAN generator

At a high level, the SAGAN generator doesn't look very different from other GAN generators: it takes noise as input and goes through a dense layer, followed by multiple levels of upsampling and convolution blocks, to achieve the target image resolution. We start with 4×4 resolution and use three upsampling blocks to reach the final resolution of 32×32, as follows:

```
def build_generator(z_dim, n_class):
    DIM = 64
```

```
z = layers.Input(shape=(z_dim))
labels = layers.Input(shape=(1), dtype='int32')
x = Dense(4*4*4*DIM)(z)
x = layers.Reshape((4, 4, 4*DIM))(x)
x = layers.UpSampling2D((2,2))(x)
x = Resblock(4*DIM, n_class)(x, labels)
x = layers.UpSampling2D((2,2))(x)
x = Resblock(2*DIM, n_class)(x, labels)
x = SelfAttention()(x)
x = layers.UpSampling2D((2,2))(x)
x = Resblock(DIM, n_class)(x, labels)
output_image = tanh(Conv2D(3, 3, padding='same')(x))
return Model([z, labels], output_image,
             name='generator')
```

Despite using different activation dimensions within the self-attention module, its output has the same shape as the input. Thus, this can be inserted anywhere after a convolutional layer. However, it may be overkill to put it at 4×4 resolution when the kernel size is 3×3. So, the self-attention layer is inserted only once in the SAGAN generator at a higher spatial resolution stage to make the most out of the self-attention layer. The same goes for the discriminator, where the self-attention layer is placed at the lower layer when the spatial resolution is higher.

That's all for the generator, if we're doing unconditional image generation. We will need to feed the class labels into the generator so it can create images from the given classes. At the beginning of *Chapter 4, Image-to-Image Translation*, we learned about some common ways of conditioning on labels, but the SAGAN uses a more advanced way; that is, it encodes the class label into learnable parameters in batch normalization. We introduced **conditional batch normalization** in *Chapter 5, Style Transfer*, and we will now implement it for the SAGAN.

Conditional batch normalization

Throughout much of this book, we have been complaining about the drawback of using batch normalization in GANs. In CIFAR10, there are 10 classes: 6 of them are animals (bird, cat, deer, dog, frog, and horse) and 4 of them are vehicles (airplane, automobile, ship, and truck). Obviously, they look very different –the vehicles tend to have hard and straight edges, while the animals tend to have curvier edges and softer textures.

As we have learned regarding style transfer, the activation statistics dictate the image style. Therefore, mixing the batch statistics can create images that look a bit like an animal and a bit like a vehicle – for example, a car-shaped cat. This is because batch normalization uses only one gamma and one beta for an entire batch that's made up of different classes. The problem is resolved if we have a gamma and a beta for each of the styles (classes), and that is exactly what conditional batch normalization is about. It has one gamma and one beta for each class, so there are 10 betas and 10 gammas per layer for the 10 classes in CIFAR10.

We can now construct the variables required by the conditional batch normalization as follows:

- A gamma and a beta with a shape of *(10, C)*, where *C* is the activation channel number.

- A moving mean and variance with a shape of *(1, 1, 1, C)*. In training, the mean and variance are calculated from a minibatch. During inference, we use the moving averaged values accumulated in training. They are shaped so that the arithmetic operation is broadcast to the N, H, and W dimensions.

The following is the code for conditional batch normalization:

```python
class ConditionBatchNorm(Layer):
    def build(self, input_shape):
        self.input_size = input_shape
        n, h, w, c = input_shape
        self.gamma = self.add_weight(
                                shape=[self.n_class, c],
                                initializer='ones',
                                trainable=True,
                                name='gamma')
        self.beta = self.add_weight(
                                shape=[self.n_class, c],
                                initializer='zeros',
                                trainable=True,
                                name='beta')
        self.moving_mean = self.add_weight(shape=[1, 1,
                                1, c], initializer='zeros',
                                trainable=False,
                                name='moving_mean')
        self.moving_var = self.add_weight(shape=[1, 1,
                                1, c], initializer='ones',
```

```
                          trainable=False,
                          name='moving_var')
```

When we run the conditional batch normalization, we retrieve the correct `beta` and `gamma` for the labels. This is done using `tf.gather(self.beta, labels)`, which is conceptually equivalent to `beta = self.beta[labels]`, as follows:

```
def call(self, x, labels, training=False):
    beta = tf.gather(self.beta, labels)
    beta = tf.expand_dims(beta, 1)
    gamma = tf.gather(self.gamma, labels)
    gamma = tf.expand_dims(gamma, 1)
```

Apart from that, the rest of the code is identical to batch normalization. Now, we can place the conditional batch normalization in the residual block for the generator:

```
class Resblock(Layer):
    def build(self, input_shape):
        input_filter = input_shape[-1]
        self.conv_1 = Conv2D(self.filters, 3,
                                padding='same',
                                name='conv2d_1')
        self.conv_2 = Conv2D(self.filters, 3,
                                padding='same',
                                name='conv2d_2')
        self.cbn_1 = ConditionBatchNorm(self.n_class)
        self.cbn_2 = ConditionBatchNorm(self.n_class)
        self.learned_skip = False
        if self.filters != input_filter:
            self.learned_skip = True
            self.conv_3 = Conv2D(self.filters, 1,
                                    padding='same',
                                    name='conv2d_3')
            self.cbn_3 = ConditionBatchNorm(self.n_class)
```

The following is the runtime code for the forward pass of conditional batch normalization:

```
    def call(self, input_tensor, labels):
        x = self.conv_1(input_tensor)
        x = self.cbn_1(x, labels)
```

```
        x = tf.nn.leaky_relu(x, 0.2)
        x = self.conv_2(x)
        x = self.cbn_2(x, labels)
        x = tf.nn.leaky_relu(x, 0.2)
        if self.learned_skip:
            skip = self.conv_3(input_tensor)
            skip = self.cbn_3(skip, labels)
            skip = tf.nn.leaky_relu(skip, 0.2)
        else:
            skip = input_tensor
        output = skip + x
        return output
```

The residual block for the discriminator looks similar to the one for the generator but with a couple of differences, as listed here:

- There is no normalization.

- Downsampling happens inside the residual block with average pooling.

Therefore, we won't be showing the code for the discriminator's residual block. We can now proceed to the final building block – the discriminator.

Building the discriminator

The discriminator uses the self-attention layer as well, and it is placed near the input layers to capture the large activation map. As it is a conditional GAN, we will also use the label in the discriminator to make sure that the generator is producing the correct images matching the classes. The general approach to incorporating label information is to first project the label into the embedding space and then use the embedding at either the input layer or any internal layer.

There are two common methods of merging the embedding with the activation – **concatenation** and **element-wise multiplication**. The SAGAN uses architecture that's similar to the projection model by T. Miyato and M. Koyama's *cGANs with Projection Discriminator*, as shown at the bottom right of the following figure:

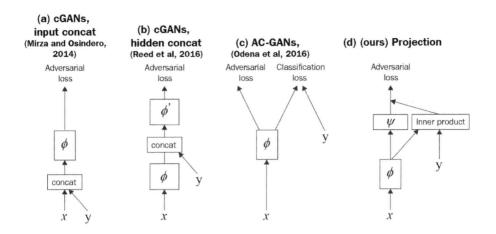

Figure 8.4 – Comparison of several common ways of incorporating labels as conditions in a discriminator. (d) is the one used in the SAGAN. (Redrawn from T. Miyato and M. Koyama's, 2018 "cGANs with Projection Discriminator," https://arxiv.org/abs/1802.05637)

The label is first projected into embedding space, and then we perform element-wise multiplication with activation just before the dense layer (ψ in the diagram). The result then adds to the dense layer output to give the final prediction as follows:

```
def build_discriminator(n_class):
    DIM = 64
    input_image = Input(shape=IMAGE_SHAPE)
    input_labels = Input(shape=(1))
    embedding = Embedding(n_class, 4*DIM)(input_labels)
    embedding = Flatten()(embedding)
    x = ResblockDown(DIM)(input_image) # 16
    x = SelfAttention()(x)
    x = ResblockDown(2*DIM)(x) # 8
    x = ResblockDown(4*DIM)(x) # 4
    x = ResblockDown(4*DIM, False)(x) # 4
    x = tf.reduce_sum(x, (1, 2))
    embedded_x = tf.reduce_sum(x * embedding,
                              axis=1, keepdims=True)
    output = Dense(1)(x)
    output += embedded_x
    return Model([input_image, input_labels],
                output, name='discriminator')
```

With the models defined, we can now train the SAGAN.

Training the SAGAN

We will use the standard GAN training pipeline. The loss function is **hinge loss** and we will use the **Adam optimizer**. Different initial learning rates are used for the generator *(1e-4)* and discriminator *(4e-4)*. As CIFAR10 has small images of size 32×32, the training is relatively stable and quick. The original SAGAN was designed for an image resolution of 128×128, but this resolution is still small compared to other training sets that we have used. In the next section, we will look at some improvements made to the SAGAN for training on bigger datasets with bigger image sizes.

Implementing BigGAN

The BigGAN is an improved version of the SAGAN. The BigGAN ups the image resolution significantly from 128×128 to 512×512, and it does it without progressive growth of layers! The following are some sample images generated by BigGAN:

Figure 8.5 – Class-conditioned samples generated by BigGAN at 512x512 (Source: A. Brock et al., 2018, "Large Scale GAN Training for High Fidelity Natural Image Synthesis," https://arxiv.org/abs/1809.11096)

BigGAN is considered the state-of-the-art class-conditional GAN. We'll now look into the changes and modify the SAGAN code to make ourselves a BigGAN.

Scaling GANs

Older GANs tend to use small batch sizes as that would produce better-quality images. Now we know that the quality problem was caused by the batch statistics used in batch normalization, and this is addressed by using other normalization techniques. Still, the batch size has remained small as it is physically limited by GPU memory constraints.

However, being part of Google has its perks: the DeepMind team, who created the BigGAN, had all the resources they needed. Through experimentation, they found that scaling up GANs helps in producing better results. In BigGAN training, the batch size used was eight times that of the SAGAN; the convolutional channel numbers are also 50% higher. This is where the name BigGAN came from: bigger proved to be better.

As a matter of fact, the bulking up of the SAGAN is the main contributor to BigGAN's superior performance, as summarized in the following table:

Configurations	Frechet Inception Distance	Inception Score
SAGAN baseline. Batch size = 256 Channel number = 64	18.65	52.52
Batch size=2048	12.39 (-6.26)	76.85 (+24.33)
Channel number=96	9.54 (-2.85)	92.98 (+16.13)
Shared class embedding	9.18 (-0.36)	94.94 (+1.96)
Skip-z	8.73 (-0.45)	98.76 (+3.82)
Orthogonal regularization	8.51 (-0.22)	99.31 (+0.55)

Figure 8.6 – Improvement in Frechet Inception Distance (FID) and Inception Score (IS) by adding features to the SAGAN baseline. The Configurations column shows the features added to the configuration in the previous row. The numbers in brackets show the improvement on the preceding row

The table shows the BigGAN's performance when trained on ImageNet. The **Frechet Inception Distance (FID)** measures the class variety (the lower the better), while the **Inception Score (IS)** indicates the image quality (the higher the better). On the left is the configuration of the network, starting with the SAGAN baseline and adding new features row by row. We can see that the biggest improvement came from increasing the batch size. This makes sense for improving the FID, as a batch size of 2,048 is larger than the class size of 1,000, making the GAN less likely to overfit to the small number of classes.

Increasing the channel size also resulted in significant improvement. The other three features add only a small improvement. Therefore, if you don't have multiple GPUs that can fit a large network and batch size, then you should stick to the SAGAN. If you do have such GPUs or just want to know about the feature upgrades, then let's crack on!

Skipping latent vectors

Traditionally, the latent vector z goes into the first dense layer of the generator, followed by a sequence of convolutional and upsampling layers. Although the StyleGAN also has a latent vector that goes only to the first layer of its generator, it has another source of random noise that goes into every resolution of the activation map. This allows the control of style at different resolution levels.

By merging the two ideas, the BigGAN split the latent vector into chunks, where each of them goes to different residual blocks in the generator. Later, we will see how that concatenates with the class label for conditional batch normalization. In addition to the default BigGAN, there is another configuration known as BigGAN-deep that is four times deeper. The following diagram shows their difference in concatenating labels and input noise. We will implement the BigGAN on the left:

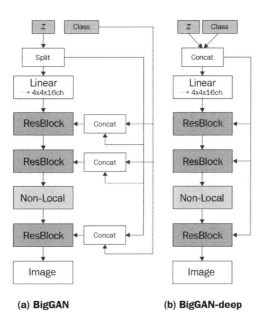

(a) BigGAN   (b) BigGAN-deep

Figure 8.7 – Two configurations of the generator (Redrawn from A. Brock et al., 2018, "Large Scale GAN Training for High Fidelity Natural Image Synthesis," https://arxiv.org/abs/1809.11096)

We will now look at how BigGAN reduces the size of the embedding in conditional batch normalization.

Shared class embedding

In the SAGAN's conditional batch normalization, there is a matrix of the shape [class number, channel number] for each beta and gamma in every layer. When the number of classes and channels increases, the weight size goes up rapidly too. When trained on the 1,000-class ImageNet with 1,024-channel convolutional layers, this will create over 1 million variables in one normalization layer alone!

Therefore, instead of having a weight matrix of 1,000×1,024, the BigGAN first projects the class into an embedding of smaller dimensions, for example, 128, that is shared across all layers. Within the conditional batch normalization, dense layers are used to map the class embedding and noise into betas and gammas.

The following code snippet shows the first two layers in the generator:

```
z_input = layers.Input(shape=(z_dim))
z = tf.split(z_input, 4, axis=1)
labels = layers.Input(shape=(1), dtype='int32')
```

```
y = Embedding(n_class, y_dim)(tf.squeeze(labels, [1]))
x = Dense(4*4*4*DIM, **g_kernel_cfg)(z[0])
x = layers.Reshape((4, 4, 4*DIM))(x)
x = layers.UpSampling2D((2,2))(x)
y_z = tf.concat((y, z[1]), axis=-1)
x = Resblock(4*DIM, n_class)(x, y_z)
```

The latent vector with dimensions of 128 is first split into four equal parts, for the dense layer and the residual blocks at three resolutions. The label is projected into a shared embedding that concatenates with the z chunk and goes into residual blocks. The residual blocks are unchanged from the SAGAN, but we'll make some small modifications to the conditional batch normalization in the following code. Instead of declaring variables for gamma and beta, we now generate from class labels via dense layers. As usual, we will first define the required layers in build() as shown here:

```
class ConditionBatchNorm(Layer):
    def build(self, input_shape):
        c = input_shape[-1]
        self.dense_beta = Dense(c, **g_kernel_cfg,)
        self.dense_gamma = Dense(c, **g_kernel_cfg,)
        self.moving_mean = self.add_weight(shape=[1, 1, 1, c],
                                          initializer='zeros',
                                          trainable=False,
                                          name='moving_mean')
        self.moving_var = self.add_weight(shape=[1, 1, 1, c],
                                         initializer='ones',
                                         trainable=False,
                                         name='moving_var')
```

At runtime, we will use dense layers to generate beta and gamma from the shared embedding. Then, they will be used like normal batch normalization. The code snippet for the dense layer parts are shown here:

```
    def call(self, x, z_y, training=False):
        beta = self.dense_beta(z_y)
        gamma = self.dense_gamma(z_y)
        for _ in range(2):
            beta = tf.expand_dims(beta, 1)
            gamma = tf.expand_dims(gamma, 1)
```

We added dense layers to predict `beta` and `gamma` from the latent vector and label embedding. That replaces the large weight variables.

Orthogonal regularization

Orthogonality is used extensively in the BigGAN to initialize weights and as a weight regularizer. A matrix is said to be orthogonal if multiplication with its transpose will produce an identity matrix. An **identity matrix** is a matrix with one in the diagonal elements and zero in all other places. Orthogonality is a good property because the norm of a matrix doesn't change if it is multiplied by an orthogonal matrix.

In a deep neural network, the repeated matrix multiplication can result in exploding or vanishing gradients. Therefore, maintaining orthogonality can improve training. The equation for original orthogonal regularization is as follows:

$$R_\beta = \beta \|W^T W - I\|^2$$

Here W is the weight reshaped as a matrix and beta is a hyperparameter. As this regularization was found to be limiting, the BigGAN uses a different variant:

$$R_\beta = \beta \|W^T W \odot (\mathbf{1} - I)\|^2$$

In this variant, *(1 – I)* removes the diagonal elements, which are dot products of the filters. This removes the constraint on the filter's norm and aims to minimize the pairwise cosine similarity between the filters.

Orthogonality is closely related to spectral normalization, and both can co-exist in a network. We implemented spectral normalization as a kernel constraint, where the weights are modified directly. Weight regularization calculates the loss from the weights and adds the loss to other losses for backpropagation, hence regularizing the weights in an indirect way. The following code shows how to write a custom regularizer in TensorFlow:

```
class OrthogonalReguralizer(
                tf.keras.regularizers.Regularizer):
    def __init__(self, beta=1e-4):
        self.beta = beta
    def __call__(self, input_tensor):
        c = input_tensor.shape[-1]
        w = tf.reshape(input_tensor, (-1, c))
        ortho_loss = tf.matmul(w, w, transpose_a=True) *\
                        (1 -tf.eye(c))
        return self.beta * tf.norm(ortho_loss)
    def get_config(self):
```

```
        return {'beta': self.beta}
```

We can then assign the *kernel initializer*, *kernel constraint*, and *kernel regularizer* to the convolution and dense layers. However, adding them to each of the layers can make the code look long and cluttered. To avoid this, we can put them into a dictionary and pass them as keyword arguments (kwargs) into the Keras layers as follows:

```
g_kernel_cfg={
    'kernel_initializer' : \
                    tf.keras.initializers.Orthogonal(),
    'kernel_constraint' : SpectralNorm(),
    'kernel_regularizer' : OrthogonalReguralizer()
}
Conv2D(1, 1, padding='same', **g_kernel_cfg)
```

As we mentioned earlier, orthogonal regularization has the smallest effect in improving image quality. The beta value of *1e-4* was obtained numerically, and you might need to tune it for your dataset.

Summary

In this chapter, we learned about an important network architecture known as self-attention. The effectiveness of the convolutional layer is limited by its receptive field, and self-attention helps to capture important features including activations that are spatially-distanced from conventional convolutional layers. We have learned how to write a custom layer to insert into a SAGAN. The SAGAN is a state-of-the-art class-conditional GAN. We also implemented conditional batch normalization to learn different learnable parameters specific to each class. Finally, we looked at the bulked-up version of the SAGAN known as the BigGAN, which trumps SAGAN's performance significantly in terms of both image resolution and class variation.

We have now learned about most, if not all, of the important GANs for image generation. In recent years, two major components have gained popularity in the GAN world – they are AdaIN for the StyleGAN as covered in *Chapter 7, High Fidelity Face Generation* and self-attention for the SAGAN. The Transformer is based on self-attention and has revolutionized NLP, and it's starting to make its way into computer vision. Therefore, it is now a good time to learn about attention-based generative models as this may be how future GANs look. In the next chapter, we will use what we learned about image generation at the end of this chapter to generate a deepfake video.

9
Video Synthesis

We have learned about and built many models for image generation, including state-of-the-art **StyleGAN** and **Self-Attention GAN** (**SAGAN**) models, in previous chapters. You have now learned about most if not all of the important techniques used to generate images, and we can now move on to video generation (synthesis). In essence, video is simply a series of still images. Therefore, the most basic video generation method is to generate images individually and put them together in a sequence to make a video. **Video synthesis** is a complex and broad topic in its own right, and we won't be able to cover everything in a single chapter.

In this chapter, we will get an overview of video synthesis. We will then implement what is probably the most well-known video generation technique, **deepfake**. We will use this to swap a person's face in a video with someone else's face. I'm sure you have seen such fake videos before. If you haven't, then just search for the word `deepfake` online and you'll be impressed by how real some of them seem.

We will cover the following in this chapter:

- Video synthesis overview
- Implementing face image processing
- Building a deepfake model
- Swapping faces
- Improving DeepFakes with GANs

Technical requirements

The code for this chapter can be accessed here:

`https://github.com/PacktPublishing/Hands-On-Image-Generation-with-TensorFlow-2.0/tree/master/Chapter09`

The notebook used in this chapter is this one:

- `ch9_deepfake.ipynb`

Video synthesis overview

Let's say your doorbell rings while you're watching a video, so you pause the video and go to answer the door. What would you see on your screen when you come back? A still picture where everything is frozen and not moving. If you press the play button and pause it again quickly, you will see another image that looks very similar to the previous one but with slight differences. Yes – when you play a series of images sequentially, you get a video.

We say that image data has three dimensions, or *(H, W, C)*; video data has four dimensions, *(T, H, W, C)*, where *T* is the temporal (time) dimension. It's also the case that video is just a big *batch* of images, except that we cannot shuffle the batch. There must be temporal consistency between the images; I'll explain this further.

Let's say we extract images from some video datasets and train an unconditional GAN to generate images from random noise input. As you can imagine, the images will look very different from each other. As a result, the video made from those images would be unwatchable. Like image generation, video generation can also be classified as unconditional or conditional.

In unconditional video synthesis, not only does the model need to generate good-quality content but it must also keep the temporal content or movement in check. As a result, the output video is generally quite short for some simple video content. Unconditional video synthesis is still not quite mature enough yet for practical application.

On the other hand, conditional video synthesis conditions on input content and therefore generates better-quality results. As we learned in *Chapter 4, Image-to-Image Translation*, there is very little randomness in images generated by pix2pix. The lack of randomness may be a drawback in some applications, but the consistency in generated images is a plus in video synthesis. Thus, many video synthesis models are conditioned on images or videos. In particular, conditional face video synthesis has achieved great results and has had a real impact in commercial applications. We will now look at some of the most common forms of face video synthesis.

Understanding face video synthesis

The most common forms of face video synthesis are **face re-enactment** and **face swapping**. It is best to explain the difference between them by using pictures as follows:

Figure 9.1 – Face re-enactment and face swapping
(Source: Y. Nirkin et al., 2019, "FSGAN: Subject Agnostic Face Swapping and Reenactment,"
`https://arxiv.org/pdf/1908.05932`)

The top row shows how face re-enactment works. In face re-enactment, we want to transfer the expression of the face in the target video (right) to the face of the source image (left) to produce the image in the middle. Digital puppetry is already used in computer animation and movie production, where the facial expression of an actor is used to control a digital avatar. Face re-enactment using AI has the potential to make this happen more easily. The bottom row shows face swapping. This time, we want to keep the facial expression of the target video but use the face from the source image.

Although technically different, face re-enactment and face swapping are similar. In terms of generated video, both could be used to create a *fake video*. As the name suggests, face swapping swaps just the face but not the head. Therefore, both the target and source faces should have a similar shape to increase the fidelity of the fake video. You can use this as a visual cue to differentiate between face swapping and face re-enactment videos. Face re-enactment is technically more challenging and it doesn't always require a driving video; it can use facial landmarks or sketches instead. We will introduce one such model in the next chapter. In the rest of this chapter, we will focus on implementing face swapping with the deepfake algorithm.

DeepFake overview

Many of you may have seen online videos where the face of an actor has been swapped with another celebrity's face. Quite often, that celebrity is the actor Nicolas Cage, and the resulting videos are quite hilarious to watch. This all started around the end of 2017, when an anonymous user named *deepfakes* posted the algorithm (which was later named after the username) on the social news website Reddit. This was quite unusual, considering that almost all of the breakthrough machine learning algorithms of the past decade had their origins in academia.

People have used the deepfake algorithm to create all sorts of videos, including some for TV advertisements and movies. However, as these fake videos can be very convincing, they have also raised some ethical issues. Researchers have demonstrated that it is possible to create fake videos to make the former US president Barack say things that he did not say. People have genuine reasons to be worried about deepfake and researchers have also been devising ways to detect these fake videos. You will want to understand how deepfake works, either to create funny videos or to combat fake news videos. So, let's crack on!

The deepfake algorithm can be roughly broken into two parts:

1. **A deep learning model** to perform face image translation. We will first collect datasets for two people, say, **A** and **B**, and use an autoencoder to train them separately to learn their latent code, as shown in the following figure. There is a shared encoder, but we use separate decoders for different people. The top diagram in the figure shows the training architecture. The bottom diagram shows the face swap.

    Firstly, **Face A** (the source) is encoded into a small latent face (the latent code). The latent code contains face representations such as the head pose (angle), facial expression, eyes open or shut, and more. We will then use decoder **B** to convert the latent code into **Face B**. The aim is to generate **Face B** using the pose and expression of **Face A**:

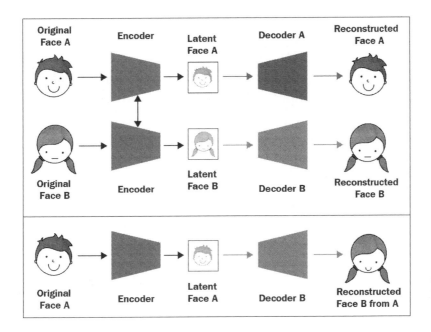

Figure 9.2 – deepfake using autoencoders. (Top) Training with one encoder and two decoders. (Bottom) Reconstructing Face B from A (Redrawn from: T.T. Nguyen et al, 2019, "Deep Learning for deepfakes Creation and Detection: A Survey," https://arxiv.org/abs/1909.11573)

In a normal image generation setting, a model is basically what we need for production. All we need to do is to send an input image to the model to produce an output image. But the production pipeline for deepfake is more involved, as will be described later.

2. We'll need a collection of traditional computer vision techniques to perform pre- and post-processing, including these:

    a) Face detection

    b) Face landmark detection

    c) Face alignment

    d) Face warping

    e) Face mask detection

The following figure shows the deepfake production pipeline:

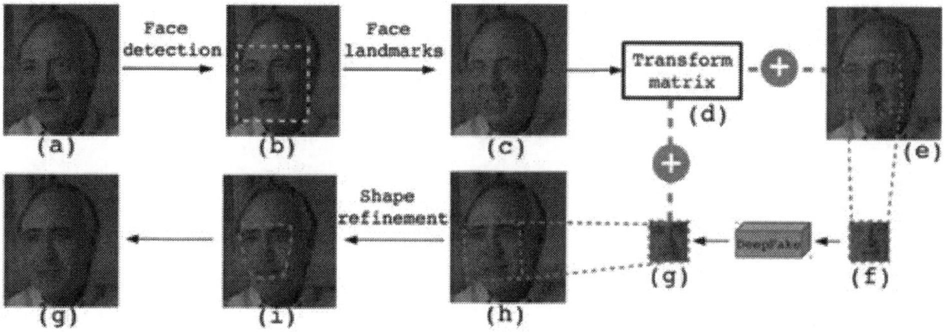

Figure 9.3 – DeepFake production pipeline (Source: Y. Li, S. Lyu, 2019, "Exposing deepfake Videos By Detecting Face Warping Artifacts," https://arxiv.org/abs/1811.00656)

The steps can be grouped into three stages:

1. Steps *(a)* to *(f)* are pre-processing steps to extract and align the source face from the image.

2. There is a face swap to produce target *face (g)*.

3. Steps *(h)* to *(j)* are post-processing steps to *paste* the target face into the image.

We learned about and built autoencoders in *Chapter 2, Variational Autoencoder,* and therefore it is relatively easy for us to build one for deepfake. On the other hand, many of the aforementioned computer vision techniques have not been introduced before in this book. Therefore, in the next section, we will implement the face processing steps one by one. Then, we will implement the autoencoder and finally implement all of the techniques together to produce a deepfake video.

Implementing face image processing

We will use mainly two Python libraries – **dlib** and **OpenCV** – to implement most of the face processing tasks. OpenCV is good for general-purpose computer vision tasks and includes low-level functions and algorithms. While dlib was originally a C++ toolkit for machine learning, it also has a Python interface, and it is the go-to machine learning Python library for facial landmark detection. Most of the image processing code used in this chapter is adapted from `https://github.com/deepfakes/faceswap`.

Extracting image from video

The first thing in the production pipeline is to extract images from video. A video is made up of a series of images separated by a fixed time interval. If you check a video file's properties, you may find something that says **frame rate = 25 fps**. **FPS** indicates the number of image **frames per second** in a video, and 25 fps is the standard video frame rate. That means 25 images are played within a 1-second duration, or every image is played for 1/25 = 0.04 seconds. There are many software packages and tools to split video into images, and **ffmpeg** is one such tool. The following command shows how to split a .mp4 video file into directory/images and name them using a number sequence – for example, image_0001.png, image_0002.png, and so on:

```
ffmpeg  -i video.mp4 /images/image_%04d.png
```

Alternatively, we can also use OpenCV to read the video frame by frame and save the frames into individual image files as shown in the following code:

```
import cv2
cap = cv2.VideoCapture('video.mp4')
count = 0
while cap.isOpened():
    ret,frame = cap.read()
    cv2.imwrite("images/image_%04d.png" % count, frame)
    count += 1
```

We will use the extracted images for all subsequent processing and not worry about the source video anymore.

Detecting and localizing a face

Traditional computer vision techniques detect faces by using the **Histogram of Oriented Gradients (HOG)**. The gradient of a pixel image can be calculated by taking the difference of the preceding and following pixels in the horizontal and vertical directions. The magnitude and direction of a gradient tells us about the lines and corners of a face. We can then use the HOG as a feature descriptor to detect the shape of a face. A modern approach is, of course, to use a CNN, which is more accurate but slower.

`face_recognition` is a library built on top of `dlib`. By default, it uses the HOG of `dlib` as a face detector, but it also has the option to use a CNN. Using it is simple, as shown here:

```
import face_recognition
coords = face_recognition.face_locations(image, model='cnn')[0]
```

This will return a list of coordinates for each of the faces detected in the image. In our code, we assume that there is only one face in the image. The coordinates returned are in css format, (top, right, bottom, left), so we'll need an additional step to convert them into `dlib.rectangle` objects for the `dlib` facial landmarks detector, as follows:

```
def _css_to_rect(css):
    return dlib.rectangle(css[3], css[0], css[1], css[2])
face_coords = _css_to_rect(coords)
```

We can read the bounding box coordinates from `dlib.rectangle` and crop the face from the image as follows:

```
def crop_face(image, coords, pad=0):
    x_min = coords.left() - pad
    x_max = coords.right() + pad
    y_min = coords.top() - pad
    y_max = coords.bottom() + pad
    return image[y_min:y_max, x_min:x_max]
```

If a face is detected in the image, we can then move on to the next step to detect facial landmarks.

Detecting facial landmarks

Facial landmarks are locations of interesting points (also known as **keypoints**) on an image of a human face. The points are around the edges of the chin, eyebrows, nose bridge, nose tip, eyes, and lips. The following figure shows an example of 68 points of facial landmarks produced by the `dlib` model:

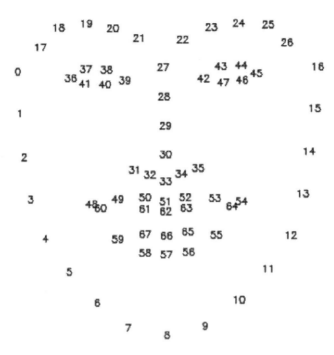

Figure 9.4 – The 68 points the dlib facial landmarks, for the chin, eyebrows, nose bridge, nose tip, eyes, and lips

dlib makes facial landmarks detection easy. We only need to download and load the model into dlib before using it as shown in the following code snippet:

```
predictor = dlib.shape_predictor(
            'shape_predictor_68_face_landmarks.dat')
face_shape = predictor(face_image, face_coords)
```

> **Note**
> We will also pass the face coordinates into the predictor to tell it where the face is. This means, we don't need to crop out the face before calling the function.

Facial landmarks are very useful features in machine learning problems. For example, if we want to know a person's facial expression, we could use the lips keypoints as input features to the machine learning algorithm to detect whether the mouth is open. This is more effective and efficient than looking at every single pixel in the image. We can also use facial landmarks to estimate the head pose.

In DeepFake, we use facial landmarks to perform face alignment, which I will explain shortly. Before that, we will need to convert the landmarks from `lib` format into a NumPy array:

```
def shape_to_np(shape):
    coords = []
    for i in range(0, shape.num_parts):
        coords.append((shape.part(i).x, shape.part(i).y))
    return np.array(coords)
face_shape = shape_to_np(face_shape)
```

Now we have everything we need for face alignment.

Aligning a face

Naturally, faces in video appear in various poses, such as looking to the left or open-mouthed. In order to make it easier for the autoencoder to learn, we will align the faces to the center of the cropped image, looking straight at the camera. This is known as **face alignment**. We can see it as a form of data normalization. The deepfake author defined a set of facial landmarks as a reference face and called this the *mean face*. The mean face includes all of the 68 `dlib` landmarks except for the first 18 points of the chin. This is because people have vastly different chin shapes, which could skew the alignment results, so they are not used as a reference.

> **Mean face**
>
> If you still remember, we looked at mean faces in *Chapter 1, Getting Started with Image Generation Using TensorFlow*. They were generated by directly sampling from the dataset, so not exactly the same way as used in `dlib`. Anyway, feel free to go to take a look if you have forgotten what mean faces look like.

We will need to perform the following operations on the face to align it with the mean face's position and angle:

- Rotation
- Scale
- Translation (shift in location)

These operations can be represented using a 2×3 affine transformation matrix. The affine matrix M is composed of matrices A and B as shown in the following equation:

$$M = [A \ B] = \begin{bmatrix} a_{00} & a_{01} & b_{00} \\ a_{10} & a_{11} & b_{10} \end{bmatrix}_{2 \times 3}$$

Matrix A contains the parameters for linear transformation (scale and rotation), while matrix B is used for translation. deepfake uses an algorithm from S. Umeyama to estimate the parameters. The source code of the algorithm is contained in a single file that I have included in our GitHub repository. We call the function by passing the detected facial landmarks and the mean face landmarks as shown in the following code. As explained earlier, we omit the chin landmarks as they are not included in the mean face:

```
from umeyama import umeyama
def get_align_mat(face_landmarks):
    return umeyama(face_landmarks[17:], \
                   mean_landmarks, False)[0:2]
affine_matrix = get_align_mat(face_image)
```

We can now pass the affine matrix into `cv2.warpAffine()` to perform affine transformation, as shown in the following code:

```
def align_face(face_image, affine_matrix, size, padding=50):
    affine_matrix = affine_matrix * \
                    (size[0] - 2 * padding)
    affine_matrix[:, 2] += padding
    aligned_face = cv2.warpAffine(face_image,
                                  affine_matrix,
                                  (size, size))
    return aligned_face
```

The following figure shows the faces before and after alignment:

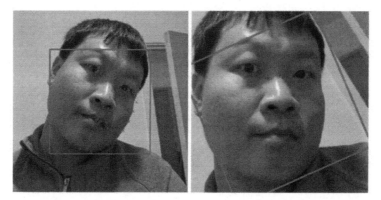

Figure 9.5 – (Left) Author's face with facial landmarks and face detection bounding box. (Right) Aligned face

The bounding boxes in the figure show the face detection at work. The picture on the left is also marked with facial landmarks. On the right is the face after alignment. We can see that the face has now been scaled larger to fit the mean face. In fact, the alignment output has the face more zoomed in, covering only the area between the eyebrows and the chin. I added padding to zoom out a little to include the bounding box in the final image. We can see from the bounding box that the face has been rotated so that it appears vertical. Next, we will learn about the last image pre-processing step: face warping.

Face warping

We'll need two images to train an autoencoder, the input image and the target image. In deepfake, the target image is the aligned face, while the input image is a warped version of the aligned face. A face in the image does not change its shape after the affine transformation that we implemented in the preceding section, but warping, for example, twisting one side of the face, can change the shape of a face. deepfake warps faces to imitate the variety of face poses in real video as data augmentation.

In image processing, transformation is the mapping of a pixel from one location in a source image to a different location in a target image. For example, translation and rotation is a one-to-one mapping that changes location and angle but retains size and shape. For warping, the mapping can be irregular, and the same point can be mapped to multiple points, which can give the effect of twisting and bending. The following diagram shows an example of mapping that warps an image from dimensions 256×256 to 64×64:

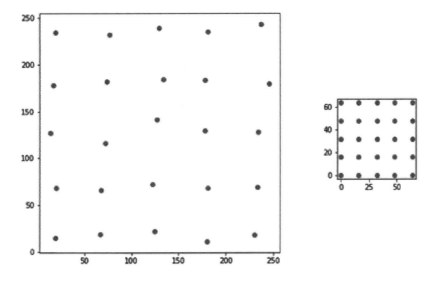

Figure 9.6 – Mapping to demonstrate warping

We will perform some random warping to twist a face slightly but not so much as to cause major distortion. The following code shows how to perform a face warp. You don't have to understand every line of the code; it is sufficient to know that it uses the mapping as previously described to warp a face into a smaller dimension:

```
coverage = 200
range_ = numpy.linspace(128 - coverage//2, 128 + coverage//2,
5)
mapx = numpy.broadcast_to(range_, (5, 5))
mapy = mapx.T
mapx = mapx + numpy.random.normal(size=(5, 5), scale=5)
mapy = mapy + numpy.random.normal(size=(5, 5), scale=5)
interp_mapx = cv2.resize(mapx, (80, 80))\
                     [8:72, 8:72].astype('float32')
interp_mapy = cv2.resize(mapy, (80, 80))[8:72,\
                     8:72].astype('float32')
warped_image = cv2.remap(image, interp_mapx,
                     interp_mapy, cv2.INTER_LINEAR)
```

I guess most people think that deepfake is just a deep neural network but do not realize there are so many image processing steps involved. Luckily, OpenCV and `dlib` make things easy for us. Now, we can move on to build the whole deep neural network model.

Building a DeepFake model

The deep learning model used in the original deepfake is an autoencoder-based one. There are a total of two autoencoders, one for each face domain. They share the same encoder, so there is a total of one encoder and two decoders in the model. The autoencoders expect an image size of 64×64 for both the input and the output. Now, let's build the encoder.

Building the encoder

As we learned in the previous chapter, the encoder is responsible for converting high-dimensional images into a low-dimensional representation. We'll first write a function to encapsulate the convolutional layer; leaky ReLU activation is used for downsampling:

```
def downsample(filters):
    return Sequential([
        Conv2D(filters, kernel_size=5, strides=2,
                padding='same'),
        LeakyReLU(0.1)])
```

In the usual autoencoder implementation, the output of the encoder is a 1D vector with a size of about 100 to 200, but deepfake uses larger dimensions of 1,024. In addition, it reshapes the 1D latent vector and upscales it back into 3D activation. Therefore, the output of the encoder is not a 1D vector of size (1,024) but a tensor of size (8, 8, 512), as shown in the following code:

```
def Encoder(z_dim=1024):
    inputs = Input(shape=IMAGE_SHAPE)
    x = inputs
    x = downsample(128)(x)
    x = downsample(256)(x)
    x = downsample(512)(x)
    x = downsample(1024)(x)
    x = Flatten()(x)
    x = Dense(z_dim)(x)
    x = Dense(4 * 4 * 1024)(x)
    x = Reshape((4, 4, 1024))(x)
    x = UpSampling2D((2,2))(x)
    out = Conv2D(512, kernel_size=3, strides=1,
                padding='same')(x)
    return Model(inputs=inputs, outputs=out, name='encoder')
```

We can see that the encoder can be grouped into three stages:

1. There are convolutional layers, which downscale a (64, 64, 3) image all the way to (4, 4, 1024).

2. There are two dense layers. The first one produces a latent vector of size 1024, then the second one projects it to a higher dimension, which gets reshaped to (4, 4, 1024).

3. The upsampling and convolution layers bring the output to size (8, 8, 512).

This can be understood better by looking at the following model summary:

```
Model: "encoder"

Layer (type)                        Output Shape
=================================================================
input_1 (InputLayer)                [(None, 64, 64, 3)]

Downsample_1 (Sequential)           (None, 32, 32, 128)

Downsample_2 (Sequential)           (None, 16, 16, 256)

Downsample_3 (Sequential)           (None, 8, 8, 512)

Downsample_4 (Sequential)           (None, 4, 4, 1024)

flatten (Flatten)                   (None, 16384)

dense (Dense)                       (None, 1024)

dense_1 (Dense)                     (None, 16384)

reshape (Reshape)                   (None, 4, 4, 1024)

up_sampling2d (UpSampling2D)        (None, 8, 8, 1024)

conv2d_4 (Conv2D)                   (None, 8, 8, 512)
=================================================================
```

Figure 9.7 – Model summary

The next step is to construct the decoder.

Building the decoder

The decoder's input comes from the encoder's output, so it expects a tensor of size (8, 8, 512). We use several layers of upsampling to upscale the activations gradually to the target image dimension of (64, 64, 3):

1. Similar to before, we will first write a function for the upsampling block that contains an upsampling function, a convolutional layer, and leaky ReLU, as shown in the following code:

```python
def upsample(filters, name=''):
    return Sequential([
        UpSampling2D((2,2)),
        Conv2D(filters, kernel_size=3, strides=1,
                padding='same'),
        LeakyReLU(0.1)
    ], name=name)
```

2. Then we stack the upsampling blocks together. The final layer is a convolutional layer that brings the channel number to 3 to match the RGB color channels:

```python
def Decoder(input_shape=(8, 8 ,512)):
    inputs = Input(shape=input_shape)
    x = inputs
    x = upsample(256,"Upsample_1")(x)
    x = upsample(128,"Upsample_2")(x)
    x = upsample(64,"Upsample_3")(x)
    out = Conv2D(filters=3, kernel_size=5,
                padding='same',
                activation='sigmoid')(x)

    return Model(inputs=inputs, outputs=out,
                name='decoder')
```

The decoder model summary is as follows:

```
Model: "decoder"

Layer (type)                    Output Shape
=================================================
input_1 (InputLayer)            [(None, 8, 8, 512)]

Upsample_1 (Sequential)         (None, 16, 16, 256)

Upsample_2 (Sequential)         (None, 32, 32, 128)

Upsample_3 (Sequential)         (None, 64, 64, 64)

conv2d_3 (Conv2D)               (None, 64, 64, 3)
=================================================
```

Figure 9.8 – Keras model summary of the decoder

Next, we will put the encoder and decoders together to construct the autoencoders.

Training the autoencoders

As mentioned earlier, the DeepFake model consists of two autoencoders that share the same encoder. To construct the autoencoders, the first step is to instantiate the encoder and decoders:

```python
class deepfake:
    def __init__(self, z_dim=1024):
        self.encoder = Encoder(z_dim)
        self.decoder_a = Decoder()
        self.decoder_b = Decoder()
```

Then, we build two separate autoencoders by joining the encoder with the respective decoders as follows:

```python
x = Input(shape=IMAGE_SHAPE)
self.ae_a = Model(x, self.decoder_a(self.encoder(x)),
                  name="Autoencoder_A")
self.ae_b = Model(x, self.decoder_b(self.encoder(x)),
                  name="Autoencoder_B")
optimizer = Adam(5e-5, beta_1=0.5, beta_2=0.999)
self.ae_a.compile(optimizer=optimizer, loss='mae')
self.ae_b.compile(optimizer=optimizer, loss='mae')
```

The next step is to prepare the training dataset. Although the autoencoder has an input image size of 64 × 64, the image preprocessing pipeline expects images of 256 × 256. We will need about 300 images for each face domain. There is a link in the GitHub repository to where you can download some prepared images.

Alternatively, you can also create datasets yourself by cropping the faces from collected images or video using the image processing techniques that we learned earlier. The faces in the dataset do not need to be aligned as the alignment will be performed in the image pre-processing pipeline. The image pre-processing generator will return two images – an aligned face and a warped version, both at a resolution of 64×64.

We can now pass the two generators into `train_step()` to train the autoencoder models as follows:

```
def train_step(self, gen_a, gen_b):
    warped_a, target_a = next(gen_a)
    warped_b, target_b = next(gen_b)
    loss_a = self.ae_a.train_on_batch(warped_a, target_a)
    loss_b = self.ae_b.train_on_batch(warped_b, target_b)
    return loss_a, loss_b
```

Writing and training the autoencoder is probably the easiest part of the deepfake pipeline. We don't need a lot of data; probably about 300 images per face domain is sufficient. Of course, more data should provide better results. As both the dataset and model aren't big, the training can happen relatively quickly even without the use of a GPU. Once we have a trained model, the final step is to perform the face swap.

Swapping faces

Here comes the last step of the deepfake pipeline, but let's first recap the pipeline. The deepfake production pipeline involves three main stages:

1. Extract a face from an image using `dlib` and OpenCV.

2. Translate the face using the trained encoder and decoders.

3. Swap the new face back into the original image.

The new face generated by the autoencoder is an aligned face of size 64×64, so we will need to warp it to the position, size, and angle of the face in the original image. We'll use the affine matrix obtained from *step 1* in the face extraction stage. We'll use `cv2.warpAffine` like before, but this time, the `cv2.WARP_INVERSE_MAP` flag is used to reverse the direction of image transformation as follows:

```
h, w, _ = image.shape
size = 64
new_image = np.zeros_like(image, dtype=np.uint8)
new_image = cv2.warpAffine(np.array(new_face,
                                    dtype=np.uint8)
                    mat*size, (w, h),
                    new_image,
                    flags=cv2.WARP_INVERSE_MAP,
                    borderMode=cv2.BORDER_TRANSPARENT)
```

However, directly pasting the new face onto the original image will create artifacts around the edges. This will be especially obvious if any part of the new face (which is a square 64×64) exceeds the original face boundary. To alleviate the artifacts, we will trim the new face with a face mask.

The first mask we will create is one that contours around the facial landmarks in the original image. The following code will first find the contours of given facial landmarks and then fill inside of the contour with ones (1) and return it as a hull mask:

```
def get_hull_mask(image, landmarks):
    hull = cv2.convexHull(face_shape)
    hull_mask = np.zeros_like(image, dtype=float)
    hull_mask = cv2.fillConvexPoly(hull_mask,
                                   hull, (1,1,1))
    return hull_mask
```

As the **hull mask** is bigger than the new face square, we will need to trim the hull mask to fit the new square. To do this, we can create a rectangle mask from the new face and multiply it with the hull mask. The following diagram shows an example of the mask for the image:

Figure 9.9 – (Left to right) (a) Original image (b) Rectangular mask of new face (c) Hull mask of original face (d) Combined mask

Then we use the mask to remove the face from the original image and fill it in with the new face using the following code:

```
def apply_face(image, new_image, mask):
    base_image = np.copy(image).astype(np.float32)
    foreground = cv2.multiply(mask, new_image)
    background = cv2.multiply(1 - mask, base_image)
    output_image = cv2.add(foreground, background)
    return output_image
```

The resulting face may still not look perfect. For instance, if the two faces have vastly different skin tone or shading, then we may need to use further and more sophisticated methods to iron out the artifacts.

This concludes the face swapping. We do this for each of the images extracted from a video, then we convert the images back into a video sequence. One way to do so is to use ffmpeg as follows:

```
ffmpeg -start_number 1 -i image_%04d.png -vcodec mpeg4 output.
mp4
```

The deepfake model and the computer vision techniques used in this chapter are fairly basic, as I wanted to make it easy to understand. Therefore, this code may not produce a realistic fake video. If you are keen on generating good fake videos, I would recommend you visit the https://github.com/deepfakes/faceswap GitHub repository, on which a big part of this chapter's code is based. Next, we will quickly look at how deepfake can be improved by using GANs.

Improving DeepFakes with GANs

The output image of deepfake's autoencoders can be a little blurry, so how can we improve that? To recap, the deepfake algorithm can be broken into two main techniques – face image processing and face generation. The latter can be thought of as an image-to-image translation problem, and we learned a lot about that in *Chapter 4, Image-to-Image Translation*. Therefore, the natural thing to do would be to use a GAN to improve the quality. One helpful model is **faceswap-GAN**, and we will now go over a high-level overview of it. The autoencoder from the original deepfake is enhanced with residual blocks and self-attention blocks (see *Chapter 8, Self-Attention for Image Generation*) and used as a generator in faceswap-GAN. The discriminator architecture is as follows:

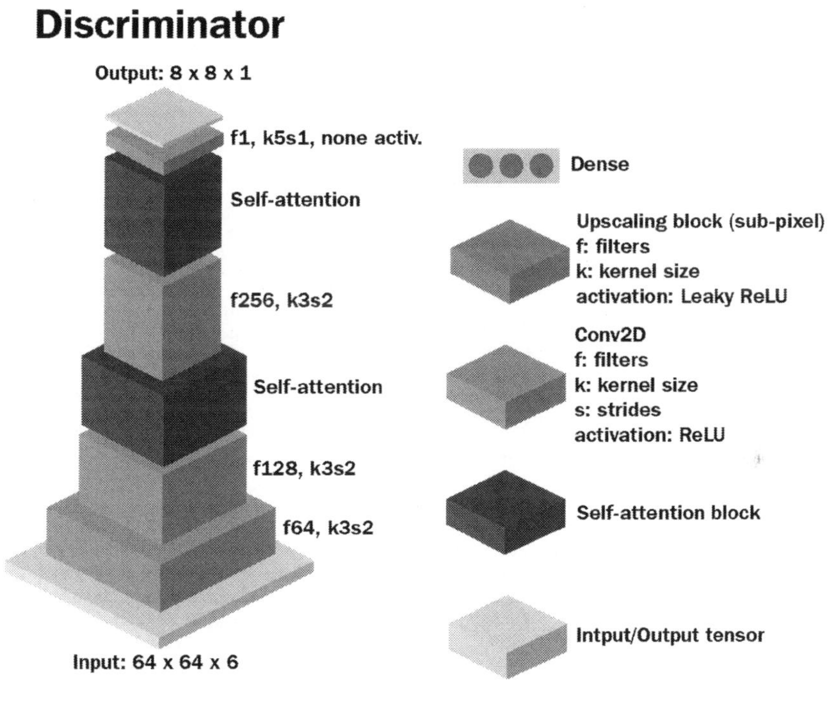

Figure 9.10 - faceswap-GAN's discriminator architecture (Redrawn from: https://github.com/shaoanlu/faceswap-GAN)

We can learn a lot about the discriminator by looking at the preceding diagram alone. First, the input tensor has a channel dimension of 6, which suggests it is a stack of two images – real and fake. Then there are two blocks of self-attention layers. The output has a shape of 8×8×1, so each of the output features looks at patches of the input image. In other words, the discriminator is PatchGAN with self-attention layers.

The following diagram shows the encoder and decoder architecture:

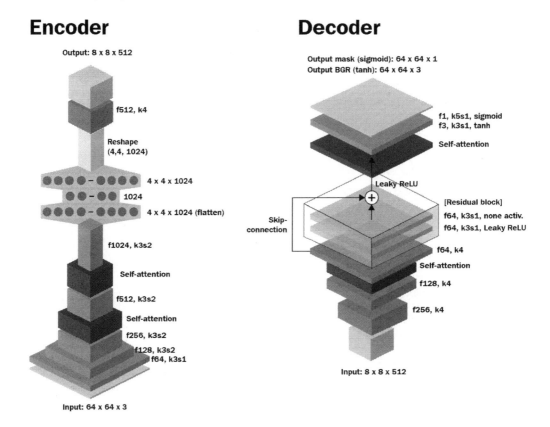

Figure 9.11 - faceswap-GAN's encoder and decoder architecture (Redrawn from: https://github.com/shaoanlu/faceswap-GAN)

There aren't a lot of changes to the encoder and decoder. Self-attention layers are added to both the encoder and decoder, and one residual block is added to the decoder.

The losses used in training are these:

- **Least-squares (LS) loss** is the adversarial loss.

- **Perception loss** is the VGG features an L2 loss between the real and fake faces.

- L1 reconstruction loss.

- **Edge loss** is the L2 loss of the gradients (in the x and y directions) around the eyes. This helps the model to generate realistic eyes.

One thing that I've been trying to achieve with this book is to instill you with the knowledge of most, if not all, of the fundamental building blocks of image generation. Once you know them, implementing a model is just like putting Lego bricks together. As we are already familiar with the losses (apart from edge loss), residual blocks, and self-attention blocks, I trust that you can now implement this model yourself, if you wish to. For interested readers, you can refer to the original implementation at `https://github.com/shaoanlu/faceswap-GAN`.

Summary

Congratulations! We have now finished all the coding in this book. We have learned how to use `dlib` to detect faces and facial landmarks and how to use OpenCV to warp and align a face. We also learned how to use warping and masking to do face swapping. As a matter of fact, we spent most of the chapter learning about face image processing and spent very little time on the deep learning side. We have implemented autoencoders by reusing and modifying the autoencoder code from the previous chapter.

Finally, we went over an example of improving deepfake by using GANs. faceswap-GAN improves deepfake by adding a residual block, a self-attention block, and a discriminator for adversarial training, all of which we have already learned about in previous chapters.

In the next chapter, which is also the final chapter, we will review the techniques we have learned in this book and look at some of the pitfalls in training GANs for real-world applications. Then, we will go over a few important GAN architectures, looking at image inpainting and text-to-image synthesis. Finally, we will look at up-and-coming applications such as video retargeting and 3D-to-2D rendering. There won't be any coding in the next chapter, so you can sit back and relax. Cheers!

10
Road Ahead

This is the final chapter of the book. We have learned about and implemented many generative models; and yet there are a lot more models and applications that we have not covered as they are beyond the scope of this book. In this chapter, we will start by summarizing some of the important techniques that we have learned, such as **optimizer and activation functions**, **adversarial loss**, **auxiliary loss**, **normalization**, and **regularization**.

Then, we will look at some of the common pitfalls when using generative models in real-world settings. After that, we will go over some interesting image/video generative models and applications. There is no coding in this chapter, but you will find that many of the new models that we introduce in this chapter are built using techniques we have learned previously. There are also a few links to resources where you can read papers and code to explore the technology.

We will cover the following topics in this chapter:

- Reviewing GANs
- Putting your skills into practice
- Image processing
- Text to image
- Video retargeting
- Neural rendering

Reviewing GANs

Apart from PixelCNN, which we covered in *Chapter 1, Getting Started with Image Generation Using TensorFlow*, which is a CNN, all the other generative models we have learned about are based on (variational) autoencoders or **generative adversarial networks** (**GANs**). Strictly speaking, a GAN is not a network but a training method that makes use of two networks – a generator and a discriminator. I tried to fit a lot of content into this book; so, the information can be overwhelming. We will now go over a summary of the important techniques we have learned, by grouping them into the following categories:

- Optimizer and activation functions
- Adversarial loss
- Auxiliary loss
- Normalization
- Regularization

Optimizer and activation functions

Adam is the most popular optimizer in training GANs, followed by RMSprop. Typically, the first moment in Adam is set to 0 and the second moment is set to 0.999. The learning rate for the generator is set to 0.0001, while the discriminator uses a learning rate that is two to four times larger than that. The discriminator is the key component in a GAN and it needs to learn well before the generator does. WGAN trains the discriminator more times than the generator in the training step, and an alternative to that is to use a higher learning rate for the discriminator.

On the other hand, the de facto activation function for internal layers is leaky ReLU with an alpha of 0.01 or 0.02. The choice of the generator's output activation functions depends on the image normalization, that is, sigmoid for a pixel range of [0, 1] or Tanh for [-1, 1]. On the other hand, the discriminator uses a linear output activation function for most adversarial losses, apart from sigmoid for the earlier non-saturated loss.

Adversarial loss

We have seen that an autoencoder can be used as a generator in a GAN setting. GANs are trained using adversarial loss (sometimes called GAN loss). The following table lists some of the popular adversarial losses:

Loss	Discriminator (real data)	Discriminator (fake data)	Generator
Non-saturated	log σ(x)	log σ(1-(x))	-log σ(x)
Wasserstein	x	-x	-x
Least-square	-(x-1)^2	-x^2	(x-1)^2
Hinge	min (0, x-1)	min (0, -x-1)	-x

Figure 10.1 – Important adversarial loss; σ refers to the sigmoid function

Non-saturated loss is used in vanilla GANs but it is unstable due to disjoining gradients. Wasserstein loss has theory underpinning it that proves it is more stable to train with. However, many GAN models choose to use least-square loss, which has shown to be stable too. In recent years, hinge loss has become the favorite choice of many state-of-the-art models. It is not clear which loss is the best. Nevertheless, we have used least-square and hinge loss in many models in this book and they seem to train well. So, I would suggest you try them first when designing your new GANs.

Auxiliary loss

Apart from adversarial loss, which acts as the main loss in GAN training, there are various auxiliary losses that help generate better images. Some of them are as follows:

- **Reconstruction loss** *(Chapter 2, Variational Autoencoder)* to encourage pixel-wise accuracy, this is usually L1 loss.

- **KL divergence loss** *(Chapter 2, Variational Autoencoder)* for the **variational autoencoder** (**VAE**) to bring the latent vector to a standard, multivariate normal distribution.

- **Cycle consistency loss** *(Chapter 4, Image-to-Image Translation)* for bi-direction image translation.

- **Perceptual loss** *(Chapter 5, Style Transfer)* measures high-level perceptual and semantic differences between images. It can be further divided into two losses:

  a) **Feature-matching loss**, which is normally the L2 loss of image features extracted from VGG layers. This is also called **perceptual loss**.

  b) **Style loss** features are normally derived from VGG features, such as the Gram matrix or activation statistics, and are calculated using L2 loss.

Normalization

Layer activations are normalized to stabilize network training. Normalization takes the following general form:

$$\hat{x} = \frac{x - \mu}{\sqrt{\sigma^2 + \varepsilon}}$$

$$y = \gamma \hat{x} + \beta$$

Here, x is the activation, μ is the mean of activations, σ is the standard deviation of the activations, and ε is the fudge factor for numerical stability. γ and β are learnable parameters; there is one pair for each activation channel. Many of the different normalizations differ only in how μ and σ are obtained:

- In **batch normalization** *(Chapter 3, Generative Adversarial Network)*, the mean and standard deviation are calculated across both batch (N) and spatial (H, W) locations, or in other words, (N, H, W).

- **Instance normalization** *(Chapter 4, Image-to-Image Translation)* which is the preferred method nowadays, only uses the spatial dimension (H, W).

- **Adaptive instance normalization** (**AdaIN**) *(Chapter 5, Style Transfer)* serves a different purpose to merge the content and style activation. It still uses the equation, except that now the parameters have different meanings. X is still the activation we consider from the content feature. γ and β are no longer learnable parameters but the mean and standard deviation from the style features. Like with instance normalization, the statistics are calculated across a spatial dimension of (H, W).

- **Spatially-adaptive normalization** (**SPADE**) *(Chapter 6, AI Painter)* has one γ and β value for each of the features (pixels), in other words, they have dimension of (H, W, C). They are produced by running convolutional layers across segmentation map to normalize pixels from different semantic objects separately.

Conditional batch normalization *(Chapter 8, Self-Attention for Image Generation)* is just like batch normalization except that γ and β are now multi-dimensional of (LABELS, C), so there is one set of them per class label.

Pixel normalization *(Chapter 7, High Fidelity Face Generation)* deviates from the preceding settings. It doesn't have μ, γ, or β, and σ is the L2 norm taken across the channel dimension for each spatial location. The normalized activations have a magnitude of 1.

Regularization

Apart from adversarial loss and normalization, the other important factor in stabilizing GAN training is regularization. Regularization aims to constrain the growth of the network weights in order to keep the competition between the generator and discriminator in check. This is normally done by adding a loss function that uses weights. The two common regularizations used in GANs aim to enforce the 1-Lipschitz constraint:

- **Gradient penalty** *(Chapter 3, Generative Adversarial Network)* penalizes the growth of gradients, hence the weights. However, it is not very commonly used due to the additional backpropagation required to calculate the gradients against the input. This slows down the computation considerably.

- **Orthogonal regularization** *(Chapter 8, Self-Attention for Image Generation)* aims to make the weights to be orthonormal matrices, this is because the matrix norm doesn't change if it multiplies with an orthogonal matrix. This can avoid the vanishing or exploding gradient problems.

- **Spectral normalization** *(Chapter 8, Self-Attention for Image Generation)* normalizes the layer weights by dividing it by its spectral norm. This is different from usual regularizations that use loss function to constrain the weights. Spectral normalization is computationally efficient, easy to implement, and independent of the training loss. You should use it when designing a new GAN.

This concludes the summary of GANs techniques. We will now look at new applications and models that we have not explored.

Putting your skills into practice

Now, you can apply the skills you have learned to implement your own image generation projects. Before you start, there are some pitfalls you should look out for and also some practical advice that you can follow.

Don't trust everything you read

A new academic paper is published and shows astonishing images generated by their model! Take it with a pinch of salt. Usually, these papers handpick the best result to showcase and hide the failed examples. Furthermore, the images are shrunk down to fit onto the paper, thus the image artifacts may not be visible from the paper. Before investing your time in using or re-implementing the information in the paper, try to find other resources of the claimed results. This can be the author's website or GitHub repository, which may contain the raw, high-definition images and videos.

How big is your GPU?

Deep learning models, especially GANs, are computationally expensive. Many of the state-of-the-art results are produced after training tons of data on multiple GPUs for weeks. You will almost certainly need that sort of computing power just to attempt to reproduce those results. Therefore, pay attention to the computation resources used in the papers to avoid disappointment.

If you don't mind waiting, you can use a single GPU and wait four times longer (assuming the original implementation used four GPUs). However, this will usually mean the batch size will also have to be reduced by four times, and this can have an effect on the results and convergence rate. You may have to reduce the learning rate to match the reduced batch size, which further slows down the training time.

Build your model using existing models

The renowned AI scientist Dr. Andrej Karpathy, in one of his talks in 2019, said *"don't be a hero."* When you want to create an AI project, do not invent your own model; always start from existing models. Researchers have spent huge amounts of time and resources on creating models. Along the way, they may have thrown in some tricks as well. Therefore, you should start from existing models, then tweak or build on top of them to suit your requirements.

As we have seen throughout this book, most often, state-of-the-art models do not come out of thin air but have been built on top of pre-existing models or techniques. There are usually implementations of the model available online, either officially by the authors or by re-implementation by enthusiasts in various different machine learning frameworks. One useful web resource to find them is the `http://paperswithcode.com/` website.

Understand the model's limitations

A lot of the AI companies I know do not create their own model architecture, for the reasons mentioned in the preceding sections. So, what is the point of learning to code TensorFlow to create image generation models? The first answer to that is that by writing from scratch, you now understand what the layers and models are, as well as their limitations. Say someone without knowledge of GANs was amazed by what AI could do, so they downloaded pix2pix to train on their own dataset to translate images of cats into trees. That did not work, and they had no clue why it failed; AI was a black box to them.

As an AI-educated person, we know that pix2pix requires a paired image dataset, and we will need to use CycleGAN for unpaired datasets. The knowledge that you have learned will help you choose the right model and the right data to use. Furthermore, you will now know how to tweak the model architecture for different image sizes, different conditioning, and so on.

We have now looked at some of the common pitfalls in using generative models. Now, we will look at some of the interesting applications and models that you could use generative models for.

Image processing

Out of all the things that image generative models can do, **image processing** is probably the one that produces the best results for commercial use. In our context, image processing refers to applying some transformation to existing images to produce new ones. We will look at the three applications of image processing in this section – **image inpainting**, **image compression**, and **image super-resolution** (ISR).

Image inpainting

Image inpainting is the process of filling in missing pixels of an image so that the result is visually realistic. It has practical applications in image editing, such as restoring a damaged image or removing obstructing objects. In the following example, you can see how image inpainting is used to remove people in the background. We first fill the people in with white pixels, then we use a generative model to fill in the pixels:

Figure 10.2 – Image inpainting using DeepFillv2 to remove people in the background (left) original image, (middle) people filled with white masks, (right) restored image
(source: J. Yu et al., 2018, "Free-Form Image Inpainting with Gated Convolution,"
https://arxiv.org/abs/1806.03589)

Traditional image inpainting works by finding a background patch with a similar texture and then pasting it into the missing regions. However, this usually only works for simple textures in a small area. One of the first GANs designed for image inpainting is the **context encoder**. Its architecture is similar to an autoencoder but trained with adversarial loss in addition to the usual L2 reconstruction loss. The result can appear blurry if there is a large area to be filled.

One approach to tackle this is to use two networks (course and fine) to train on different scales. Using this approach, **DeepFill** (J. Yu et al., 2018, *Generative Image Inpainting with Contextual Attention*, `https://arxiv.org/abs/1801.07892`) adds an attention layer to better capture the features from a distant spatial location.

In earlier GANs, a dataset for image inpainting was created by randomly cutting out square masks (holes), but the technique does not translate well to real-world applications. Yu et al. propose a partial convolution layer to create irregular masks. The layer contains a masked convolution like the one we implemented in PixelCNN in *Chapter 1, Getting Started with Image Generation Using TensorFlow*. The following image examples show the results of using a partial convolution-based network:

Figure 10.3 – Irregular masks and the inpainted results (source: G. Liu et al., 2018, "Image Inpainting for Irregular Holes Using Partial Convolutions," `https://arxiv.org/abs/1804.07723`)

DeepFillv2 uses gated convolution to improve and generalize masked convolutions. DeepFill uses only a standard discriminator that predicts real or fake images. However, this does not work well when there can be many holes in free-form inpainting. Therefore, it uses **spectral-normalized PatchGAN (SN-PatchGAN)** to encourage more realistic inpainting.

The following are some additional resources on this topic:

- The TensorFlow v1 source code for DeepFillv1 and v2: `https://github.com/JiahuiYu/generative_inpainting`

- Interactive inpainting demo where you can use your own photo to play with: `https://www.nvidia.com/research/inpainting/`

Image compression

Image compression is the process of transforming images from raw pixels into encoded data that is much smaller in size for storage or communication. For example, a JPEG file is a compressed image. When we open a JPEG file, the computer will reverse the compression process to restore the image pixels. The simplified image compression pipeline is as follows:

1. **Segmentation**: Divide the image into small blocks and each of them will be processed individually.

2. **Transformation**: Transform raw pixels into representations that are more compressible. At this stage, a higher compression rate is normally achieved by removing high-frequency content that makes the restored image blurrier. For example, consider a segment of a grayscale image containing [255, 250, 252, 251, ...] pixel values that are nearly white. The differences between them are so small that the human eye cannot pick up on them, so we can just transform all the pixels into 255. This will make the data easier to compress.

3. **Quantization**: Use a lower bit number to represent the data. An example is to convert a grayscale image with 256-pixel values between [0, 255] into two values of black and white of [0, 1].

4. **Symbol encoding** is used to encode data using some efficient coding. One of the common ones is known as **run-length coding**. Instead of saving every 8-bit pixel, we can save just the difference between the pixels. Therefore, instead of saving white pixels of [255, 255, 255, ...], we can just encode it into something such as [255] x 100, which says the white pixel repeats 100 times.

A higher compression rate is achieved by using more extreme quantization or removing more frequency contents. As a result, this information is lost (hence, this is known as lossy compression). The following diagram shows one such GAN for image compression:

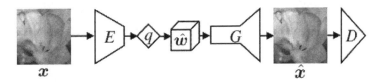

Figure 10.4 – Generative compression network. The encoder (E) maps the image into latent feature w. It is quantized by a finite quantizer, q, to obtain representation $\hat{w}$, which can be encoded into a bitstream. The decoder (G) reconstructs the image and D is the discriminator.
(Source: E. Agustsson et al., 2018, "Generative Adversarial Networks for Extreme Learned Image Compression," https://arxiv.org/abs/1804.02958)

In general, generative compression uses autoencoder architecture to compress an image into small, latent code and that is restored using the decoder.

Image super-resolution

We have used the upsampling layer a lot to increase the spatial resolution of the activation in the generator (GAN) or decoder (autoencoder). It works by spacing out the pixels and filling in the gaps by interpolation. As a result, the enlarged image is usually blurry.

In a lot of image applications, we want to enlarge the image while keeping its crispness, and this can be done via **image super resolution (ISR)**. ISR aims to increase the image from **low resolution (LR)** to **high resolution (HR)**. **Super-Resolution Generative Adversarial Network (SRGAN)** (C. Ledig et al., 2016, *Photo-Realistic Single Image Super-Resolution Using a Generative Adversarial Network*, `https://arxiv.org/abs/1609.04802`) was the first to use a GAN to do that.

SRGAN's architecture is similar to that of DCGAN but uses residual blocks instead of a plain convolutional layer. It borrows the perception loss from style transfer literature, that is, the content loss calculated from VGG features. In retrospect, we knew this was a better measure of visual perception quality rather than pixel-wise loss. We can now see how versatile the autoencoder is for various image processing tasks. Similar autoencoder architecture can be repurposed for other image processing tasks, such as image denoising or deblurring. Next, we will look at an application where the input to the model is not images but words.

Text to image

Text-to-image GANs are conditional GANs. However, instead of using class labels as conditions, they use words as the condition to generate images. In earlier practice, GANs used word embeddings as the conditions into the generator and discriminator. Their architectures are similar to conditional GANs, which we learned about in *Chapter 4, Image-to-Image Translation*. The difference is merely that the embedding of text is generated using a **natural language processing (NLP)** preprocessing pipeline. The following diagram shows the architecture of a text-conditional GAN:

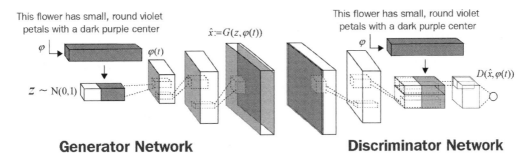

This flower has small, round violet petals with a dark purple center

$\hat{x} := G(z, \varphi(t))$

φ

$\varphi(t)$

$z \sim N(0,1)$

This flower has small, round violet petals with a dark purple center

φ

$D(\hat{x}, \varphi(t))$

Generator Network

Discriminator Network

Figure 10.5 – Text-conditional convolutional GAN architecture where text encoding
is used by both the generator and discriminator
(Redrawn from: S. Reed et al., 2016, "Generative Adversarial Text to Image Synthesis,"
`https://arxiv.org/abs/1605.05396`)

Like normal GANs, generated high-resolution images tend to be blurry. **StackGAN**
resolves this by stacking two networks together. The following diagram shows the text and
the generated images at different stages of StackGAN and a vanilla GAN:

Figure 10.6 – Images generated by StackGAN at different generator stages
(source: H. Zhang et al., 2017, "StackGAN: Text to Photo-realistic Image Synthesis with Stacked
Generative Adversarial Networks," `https://arxiv.org/abs/1612.03242`)

The first generator produces a low-resolution image from the word embedding. The second generator then takes the generated image and word embedding as input conditions to the second generator to produce refined images. The coarse-to-fine architecture has appeared in different forms in many high-resolution GANs, as we have learned in this book.

AttnGAN (T. Xu et al., 2017, *AttnGAN: Fine-Grained Text to Image Generation with Attentional Generative Adversarial Networks, at* `https://arxiv.org/abs/1711.10485`) further improves text-to-image synthesis by using an attention module. The attention module is different from the one used in SAGAN (*Chapter 8, Self-Attention for Image Generation*) but the principle is the same. There are two inputs into the attention module at the start of every stage of the generator – word features and image features. It learns to pay attention to different words and image regions when moving from coarse to fine generators. Most text-to-image models after that have some form of attention mechanism.

Text to image is still an unsolved problem; it still struggles to generate complex real-world images from text. As we can see in the following figure, the generated images are still far from perfect. Researchers are beginning to bring in recent advancement from NLP to improve text-to-image performance:

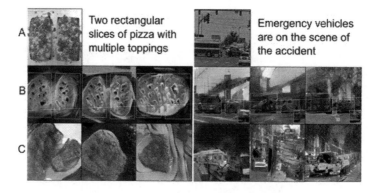

Figure 10.7 – Examples of images generated from the given caption from the MS-COCO dataset (A) original images and their image caption in the dataset (B) images generated by StackGAN + object pathway (C) images generated by StackGAN (source: T. Hinz et al., 2019, "Generating Multiple Objects at Spatially Distinct Locations," `https://arxiv.org/abs/1901.00686`)

Next, we will look at the exciting application of video retargeting.

Video retargeting

Video synthesis is a broad term used for describing all forms of video generation. This can include generating video from random noise or words, to colorize black-and-white video, and so on, much like image generation.

In this section, we will look at a subgroup of video synthesis known as **video retargeting**. We will first look at two applications – face reenactment and pose transfer – and then introduce a powerful model that uses motion to generalize video targeting.

Face reenactment

Face reenactment was introduced along with face swapping in *Chapter 9, Video Synthesis*. Face reenactment in video synthesis involves transferring the facial expression of the driving video to the face in the target video. This is useful in animation and movie making. Recently, Zakharov et al. proposed a generative model that requires only a few target 2D images. This is done by using facial landmarks as intermediate features, as shown in the following diagram:

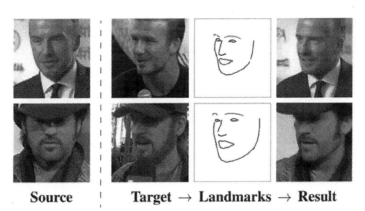

Figure 10.8 – Transferring the facial expression from the target image to the source image (source: E. Zakharov et al., 2019, "Few-Shot Adversarial Learning of Realistic Neural Talking Head Models," https://arxiv.org/abs/1905.08233)

Let's briefly look into the model architecture, as shown in the following diagram:

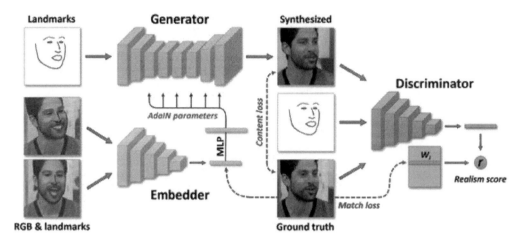

Figure 10.9 – Architecture of few-shot adversarial learning
(source: E. Zakharov et al., 2019, "Few-Shot Adversarial Learning of Realistic Neural Talking Head
Models," https://arxiv.org/abs/1905.08233)

The first thing that you should notice in the preceding diagram is **AdaIN**, which we immediately know is a style-based model. Therefore, we can see that the landmarks at the top are the content (the target's face shape and pose), while the style (the source's face attributes and expression) is extracted from the **embedder**. The generator then uses AdaIN to fuse the content and style to reconstruct the face.

Recently, a similar model has been deployed by NVIDIA to slash the bit rate of teleconferencing video transmission. You can view their blog at https://blogs. nvidia.com/blog/2020/10/05/gan-video-conferencing-maxine/ to learn how they use many of the AI techniques, such as ISR, face alignment, and face reenactment, in real-world deployment. Next, we will look at how to use AI to transfer the pose of a person.

Pose transfer

Pose transfer is similar to face reenactment except that now it will transfer the body (and head) pose. There are many ways to perform pose transfer but all of them involve the use of **body joints** (also known as **keypoints**) as features. The following diagram shows one example of images generated from a condition image and target pose:

Target poses

Condition image

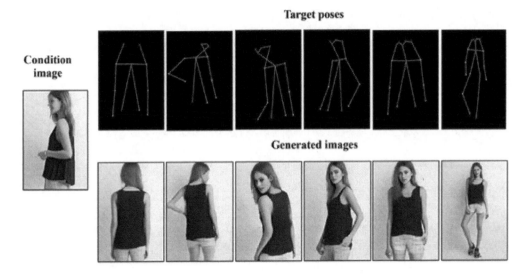

Generated images

Figure 10.10 – Transferring target poses onto the condition image
(source: Z. Zhu et al., 2019, "Progressive Pose Attention Transfer for Person Image
Generation," `https://arxiv.org/abs/1904.03349`)

Pose transfer has many potential applications, including generating a fashion modeling video from single 2D images. This task is more challenging than face reenactment due to the huge variety of human poses. Next, we will look at a motion model that could generalize both face reenactment and pose transfer.

Motion transfer

The face reenactment and pose transfer models introduced in the preceding section require object-specific priors, in other words, the facial landmark and human pose keypoints. Those features are normally extracted by separate models trained using a lot of data, which can be expensive to acquire and annotate.

Recently, an object-agnostic model known as a **first-order motion model** (A. Siarohin et al., 2019, *First Order Motion Model for Image Animation*, `https://arxiv.org/abs/2003.00196`) was introduced. It has rapidly gained popularity for its ease of use as it doesn't need a lot of annotated training data. The following screenshot shows the overall architecture of the model, which exploits the motion in video frames:

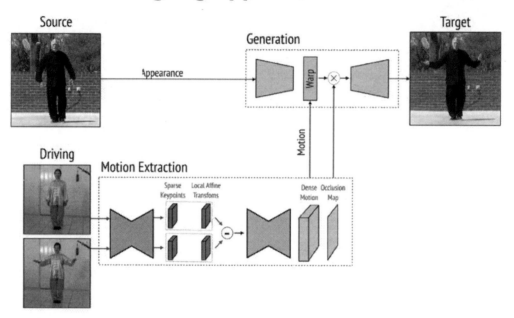

Figure 10.11 – First-order motion model that disentangles appearance and motion (source: `https://aliaksandrsiarohin.github.io/first-order-model-website/`)

In style transfer, an image is disentangled into content and style. Using the same terminology, **motion transfer** disentangles a video into appearance and motion. The motion module captures the motion of the object in the driving video. The generator network uses the appearance from the source image (similar to VGG content features) and motion information to create a new target video.

As a result, this model requires only a single source image and a driving video. It could do many of the video tasks we discussed, including face reenactment, pose transfer, and face swapping. You should definitely check out the website to see the demo video.

Although video retargeting GANs have improved dramatically in recent years, they are still not quite there yet to generate high-resolution images that are perfect for video production. An alternative is to combine 3D modeling with 2D GANs, which we will discuss in the next section.

Neural rendering

Rendering is the process of generating photo-realistic images from 2D or 3D computer models. The term **neural rendering** has recently emerged to describe rendering using a neural network. In traditional 3D rendering, we will need to first create a 3D model with a polygon mesh that describes the object's shape, color, and texture. Then, the lighting and camera position will be set and render the view into a 2D image.

There has been an ongoing research on 3D object generation, but it is still not able to generate satisfying results. We can take advantage of the advancement of GANs by projecting part of the 3D objects into 2D space. We then use GANs to enhance the image in 2D space, for example, to generate a realistic texture using style transfer before projecting that back into the 3D model. The top diagram in the following figure shows the general pipeline of this approach:

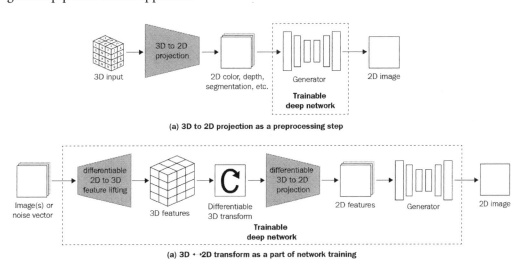

(a) 3D to 2D projection as a preprocessing step

(a) 3D → 2D transform as a part of network training

Figure 10.12 – Two common frameworks for neural rendering

(Redrawn from: M-Y. Liu et al., 2020, "Generative Adversarial Networks for Image and Video Synthesis: Algorithms and Applications," https://arxiv.org/abs/2008.02793)

Diagram *(b)* shows the framework that uses 3D data as input and 3D differentiable operations, such as 3D convolution. Apart from 3D polygons, 3D data can also exist in the form of a point cloud that can be obtained from lidar/radar or computer vision techniques such as structure from motion. A point cloud is made up of points in 3D space that depict the object's surface. One application of a 3D to 2D deep network framework is to render the point cloud into a 2D image, as shown in the following figure, where the input is the cloud points obtained from a room:

Figure 10.13 – (left) 3D point cloud to 2D rendering, (middle) point cloud synthesis image, (right) ground truth

(source: F. Pittaluga et al., 2019, "Revealing Scenes by Inverting Structure from Motion Reconstructions," https://arxiv.org/abs/1904.03303)

We can also perform rendering in the reverse direction, that is, from a 2D image to a 3D object. This is often known as **inverse rendering**. The following figure shows examples of 2D to 3D inverse rendering:

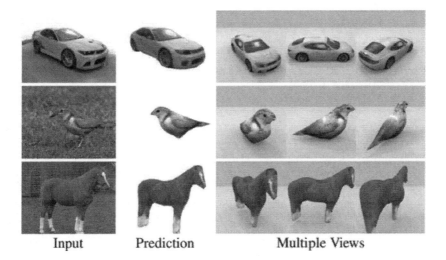

Input   Prediction   Multiple Views

Figure 10.14 – Given an input of 2D images (first column), the model predicts the 3D shape
and texture and renders them into the same viewpoint (second column). Images on
the right show the rendering in three different viewpoints.
(Source: Y. Zhang et al., 2020, "Image GANs Meet Differentiable Rendering for Inverse Graphics and
Interpretable 3D Neural Rendering," https://arxiv.org/abs/2010.09125)

The model by Y. Zhang et al., 2020, uses two *renderers*. One is a differentiable graphics
renderer to render 2D into 3D, which is outside the scope of this book. The other one is
a GAN to generate multi-view image data, or more specifically, StyleGAN. It is interesting
to know why they chose to use StyleGAN. The authors learned that StyleGAN could
generate faces of slightly different viewing angles by changing the latent code. Then, they
did an extensive study to find that styles in early layers control the camera viewpoint,
making it ideal for this task. This is also a good example that shows how we could leverage
2D generative models into the 3D world.

This concludes our introduction to neural rendering. It is an active area and there are
many more use cases that are yet to be explored.

Summary

Since the inception of GANs and VAEs in 2014, significant advancement has been made in 2D image generation. Generating high-fidelity images is still challenging in practice as it requires huge amounts of data, computing power, and hyperparameter tuning. However, as demonstrated by StyleGAN, it seems that we now have the technology to do this, especially in face generation.

In fact, at the time of writing this book, there haven't really been any major breakthroughs in this area since 2018. With this book, we have included all the important techniques leading to BigGAN. These techniques include the use of AdaIN and self-attention modules, which are now commonplace even in adjacent fields such as video synthesis. This gives us a solid foundation to explore other emerging generative technologies.

In this chapter, we looked back at the things we have learned and summarized them in different groups, such as losses and normalization techniques. We then looked at some practical advice in training generative models. Finally, we touched upon some of the upcoming technologies, especially in the area of video retargeting. I believe you now have the knowledge, skills, and confidence to explore the new and exciting AI world and I wish you all the best in your new adventure. I hope you have enjoyed reading this book. I welcome your feedback, which will help me improve my writing skills for my next book. Thanks!

Other Books You May Enjoy

If you enjoyed this book, you may be interested in these other books by Packt:

Generative Adversarial Networks Cookbook

Josh Kalin

ISBN: 978-1-78913-990-7

- Structure a GAN architecture in pseudocode
- Understand the common architecture for each of the GAN models you will build
- Implement different GAN architectures in TensorFlow and Keras
- Use different datasets to enable neural network functionality in GAN models
- Combine different GAN models and learn how to fine-tune them
- Produce a model that can take 2D images and produce 3D models
- Develop a GAN to do style transfer with Pix2Pix

Python Image Processing Cookbook

Sandipan Dey

ISBN: 978-1-78953-714-7

- Implement supervised and unsupervised machine learning algorithms for image processing

- Use deep neural network models for advanced image processing tasks

- Perform image classification, object detection, and face recognition

- Apply image segmentation and registration techniques on medical images to assist doctors

- Use classical image processing and deep learning methods for image restoration

- Implement text detection in images using Tesseract, the optical character recognition (OCR) engine

- Understand image enhancement techniques such as gradient blending

Leave a review - let other readers know what you think

Please share your thoughts on this book with others by leaving a review on the site that you bought it from. If you purchased the book from Amazon, please leave us an honest review on this book's Amazon page. This is vital so that other potential readers can see and use your unbiased opinion to make purchasing decisions, we can understand what our customers think about our products, and our authors can see your feedback on the title that they have worked with Packt to create. It will only take a few minutes of your time, but is valuable to other potential customers, our authors, and Packt. Thank you!

Index

V

W

Made in the USA
Las Vegas, NV
25 June 2021